A PA1

O! Gymru'r gweundir gwrm a'r garn,
Magwrfa annibyniaeth barn . . .

O! Wales of the brown heathland and cairn,
This nursery of independent thought . . .

Waldo Williams

A PARLIAMENT FOR WALES

Edited by John Osmond

First Impression—October 1994

ISBN 1 85902 173 5

© The contributors

All rights reserved. No part of this book may be reproduced, stored in a retrieval system, or transmitted in any form or by any means, electronic, electrostatic, magnetic tape, mechanical, photocopying, recording or otherwise without permission in writing from the publishers, Gomer Press, Llandysul, Dyfed.

Printed in Wales by
J. D. Lewis, and Sons Ltd., Gomer Press, Llandysul, Dyfed

CONTENTS

Acknowledgements

Preface   **THE THINGS WE SHARE**
Paul Flynn MP

Introduction   **RE-MAKING WALES**
John Osmond

PART I
THE POLITICAL SETTING

1) **WELSH POLITICS COME OF AGE**
   The transformation of Wales since 1979   P 39
   J. Barry Jones

2) **POLITICAL IDENTITY IN A STATELESS NATION**
   The Relationship Between Levels of Government in Wales
   Ioan Bowen Rees

3) **SOVEREIGNTY, SUBSIDIARITY AND SUSTAINABILITY**
   The Scottish Experience
   Canon Kenyon Wright

4) **A EUROPE OF THE PEOPLES**
   The European Union and a Welsh Parliament
   David Morris MEP and Martin Caton

PART II
CONSTITUTIONAL MATTERS

5) **CALLING THE TUNE**
   Funding a Welsh Parliament
   Stephen Hill and Jon Owen Jones MP

6) **PUTTING THE PEOPLE FIRST**
   Electing a Welsh Parliament
   Tom Ellis

7) **DEFENDING THE HIGH GROUND OF DEMOCRACY**
   Local Government and a Welsh Parliament
   Mari James

8) **INCLUDE US IN**
   Women and a Welsh Parliament
   Siân Edwards

PART III
ECONOMY AND THE ENVIRONMENT

9) **DEVELOPMENT FROM WITHIN**
   Economic Renewal and a Welsh Parliament
   Kevin Morgan

10) **SUSTAINING THE HEARTLAND**
    The Rural Economy and a Welsh Parliament
    Neil Caldwell

11) **LOOKING AFTER OUR LAND**
    Farming and a Welsh Parliament
    John Osmond

12) **THE WALES WE NEED**
    Sustainable Development and a Welsh Parliament
    Margaret Minhinnick

PART IV
SOCIAL POLICY

13) **BUILDING OUR NATIONAL IDENTITY**
    Education Policy and a Welsh Parliament
    David Reynolds

14) **CLOSING THE GAP BETWEEN RHETORIC AND PRACTICE**
    The Health Service and a Welsh Parliament
    Emrys Roberts

15) **A POLICY FOR WALES, NOT ENGLAND**
    Housing and a Welsh Parliament
    Gareth Hughes

PART V
CULTURAL QUESTIONS

16) **STRANGERS IN OUR OWN LAND?**
    Our languages and cultures and a Welsh Parliament
    Hywel Francis

17) **THE CULTURAL HEALTH OF THE NATION**
    The Arts and a Welsh Parliament
    Gilly Adams

18) **ARE WE BEING SERVED?**
    The Press, Broadcasting and a Welsh Parliament
    Kevin Williams

PART VI
THE POSITION OF THE PARTIES

19) **HARNESSING OUR LATENT ENTREPRENEURIALISM**
    A Liberal Democrat View
    Alex Carlile MP

20) **A WELSH GOVERNMENT THAT EVOLVES**
    A Plaid Cymru View
    Cynog Dafis MP

21) **A STEP ON THE ROAD TO INDEPENDENCE**
    A Conservative View
    Jonathan Evans MP

22) **EMPOWERING THE PEOPLE**
    A Labour View
    Peter Hain MP

APPENDICES

1) **Democracy Conference Declaration**
2) **A Note on the Contributors**

ACKNOWLEDGEMENTS

There are always numerous debts of gratitude to be paid by an editor when dealing with such a large collection of essays. In this case the acknowledgements are not just to the 25 authors but also the 250 people who participated in the Democracy Conference organised by the Parliament for Wales Campaign at Llandrindod Wells in March 1994. This book grew out of that Conference and the debates that took place in its workshops, round the dinner tables and in the bar of the Metropole Hotel. As such it is much more than the offerings of the individual authors. Rather, it is the product of an, at times, complex process of debate, discussion and negotiation, much of it in the wake of the Conference itself. I am grateful to all who helped in this process, and in particular to those who lead the Conference discussions or acted as workshop rapporteurs. As well as the authors they include David Barnes, Val Feld, Bob Roberts, Russell Davies, Jane Hutt, Ken Jones, Cllr Janet Davies, Robin Reeves, Alan Brown, Maldwyn Pate, Sian Meredudd, and Aled Davies.

The Conference was held together by the competent chairing skills of Joe England, Principal of Coleg Harlech. An inspirational address was delivered by Professor Hywel Teifi Edwards, of the University College of Wales, Swansea.

Many were responsible for the success of the Conference but in particular its organisation rested heavily on the Campaign's Administrative Secretary Merfyn Griffiths, the Campaign's Co-ordinator Mari James and the other members of the Executive Committee. Kieron Hill and the National Union of Civil and Public Servants provided vital logistical back-up. Tom Barrance dealt with graphic design and printing. Gwerfyl Hughes Jones gave untiring support, especially in handling the taped transcripts of the proceedings in both Welsh and English. Mari James and Robin Reeves provided valuable editorial assistance at key moments and Sue Gow handled the final proofs. The Conference itself could not have been held without the financial support of the Rowntree Trust, the Friedrich Ebert Foundation and also the European Parliament.

As ever, my family — Alphie, Elin and Tomos — provided encouragement and forbearance in equal measure.

Finally, the book could not have been produced without the help and encouragement of the staff at Gwasg Gomer and the Welsh

Books Council, in particular Mairwen Prys Jones, Dyfed Elis-Gruffydd and Ann Ffrancon.

The Parliament for Wales Campaign is a cross-party and non-party organisation. For information about the Campaign and to join (affiliations from organisations — such as local authorities, trade unions, churches and others — are welcome) write to: The Administrative Secretary, Parliament for Wales Campaign, 11 Gordon Road, Roath, Cardiff CF2 3AJ.

John Osmond
Penarth
September 1994

PREFACE

THE THINGS WE SHARE

Paul Flynn MP

Recently I visited two schools in my constituency, in Pillgwenlly and Pentrepoeth. Pillgwenlly in the Pill area of Newport contains a rainbow of all the races and religions of the world. At the school I was greeted with a song *Bore Da i Ti* sung enthusiastically and confidently by the whole assembly. At Pentrepoeth which is a prosperous, suburban area in Bassaleg, we listened to a concert in which the children sang *Mae Gen i Dipyn o Dy Bach Twt* and *Heno Heno Hen Blant Bach.*

This is in Newport where fifteen years ago, if *Hen Wlad fy Nhadau* was taught at all it was taught in English. To hear such songs would have been inconceivable. Wales is a very different place to what it was in 1979 when the Assembly proposals of that time were so heavily defeated in the referendum.

In 1979 we were divided; they ruled. The divisions were cleverly exploited. Different myths were propagated depending on which part of Wales you were in. In the north people were suspicious that they might be dominated by English-speakers in the south. Everyone was going to be dominated by someone else. As somebody in Pembrokeshire said, they were going to be dominated by the urban socialists of Cardiff, Newport and Swansea. That has a certain ring about it: urban socialists sounding like urban guerillas — very frightening! I heard someone from Wrexham say that the Valleys of south Wales would take all the jobs. The ultimate calumny was when the then MP for Torfaen took half a page in the *Herald of the Hills,* a paper which has a circulation in Cwmbran and Pontypool, saying that if this devolution thing comes about all our jobs will be taken by Welsh-speakers from Cardiff.

For more than a century there was a sad history of politicians who started out as great patriots, great democrats, great enthusiasts for a Welsh parliament, but whose enthusiasm withered when they were transplanted to London, and made their homes there. Now, however, we have a generation of MPs who by and large live in Wales and travel to London.

Even so we haven't done anything like enough, especially when we consider the achievements of the Irish MPs at Westminster in the last century. They managed to manipulate the parliamentary processes to great effect, and there has been very little change in those processes since. We could, for instance, look to an organisation that is called the Welsh parliamentary party. Yet its existence is hardly known. When it met for the first time in many years in 1993 we discovered that its last secretary was Leo Abse and that the chairman and vice-chairman had long since passed away. Yet it is a group that represents all Welsh MPs. If we are to achieve a Parliament for Wales we must reach out to every party in Wales including the Conservative party.

The Welsh Tory MPs, with one possible exception, are men of intelligence and integrity. They have a love of their constituencies and a love of Wales. I am grateful that we can see from some of them at least, a realisation of what has been happening in Wales and in the rest of Britain, too, since 1979. We've seen our democracy being battered, abused and degraded to an extent that none of us thought possible . An orgy of patronage has taken place. Now a plan has been suggested to have a group of five members on each police authority, members who are not representatives, not councillors, not even magistrates, but just ordinary card-carrying Conservatives. The idea is that they will be selected locally by a local person who happens to be the lord lieutenant.

I wanted to be a lord lieutenant once and wrote to the queen asking for a job description, and whether there was a vacancy in Gwent. Of course, there wasn't. I suppose it's essential for all lord lieutenants to be white, male, gentile, rich enough to do a full-time job without a salary, live in a large house in its own grounds, be a former major in the army and probably also a member of a certain organisation.

In campaigning for a Senedd, for a Parliament for Wales, we are not seeking supremacy or dominance for our own political parties, our own areas, our own councils, or even our own views whatever they might be. Rather, we are trying to achieve what generally we are not very good at in Wales. And that is, from across the parties to pool the convictions we all share.

We did it on the fourth television channel, and look what we managed to achieve: Sianel Pedwar Cymru. After more than a decade of acrimonious debate before it was established, and now, after more than a decade of its existence, S4C is applauded on all sides and generally recognised as an enormous cultural advance for our country, a unifying force in a community prone to division.

We have these great squabbles at election time and then every night when parliament is in session, all the non-Conservative Welsh members of parliament are in the same lobby time and again. There is very little difference between us on many issues, yet we allow the divisions to destroy and take away the impetus from many of our aspirations. It must not happen again. We must see the campaign for a Welsh Parliament as a celebration of those ideals that bind us together, and the things that we share - our joy at being Welsh, our delight in our literature and our culture.

Ga' i derfynu gyda darn bach o farddoniaeth sy'n rhoi ysbrydoliaeth i fi ac wedi gwneud hynny erioed, ac mae'n perthyn, mae'n addas, i'n pwrpas ni:

> Aros mae'r mynyddoedd mawr
> Rhuo trostynt mae y gwynt
> Clywir eto gyda'r wawr
> Gân bugeiliaid megis cynt.
> Eto tyf y llygad dydd
> O gylch traed y graig a'r bryn,
> Ond bugeiliaid newydd sydd
> Ar yr hen fynyddoedd hyn.
>
> Ar arferion Cymru gynt
> Newid ddaeth o rod i rod,
> Mae cenhedlaeth wedi mynd
> A chenhedlaeth wedi dod.
> Wedi oes dymhestlog hir
> Alun Mabon mwy nid yw,
> Ond mae'r heniaith yn y tir
> A'r alawon hen yn fyw.

I'd like to finish with a small piece of poetry that has always inspired me and which is appropriate for our cause:

> Still do the great mountains stay,
> And the winds above them roar;
> There is heard at break of day

Songs of shepherds as before.
Daisies as before yet grow
Round the foot of hill and rock;
Over these old mountains, though,
A new shepherd drives his flock.

To the customs of old Wales
Changes come from year to year;
Every generation fails;
One has gone, the next is here.
After a lifetime tempest-tossed
Alun Mabon is no more,
But the language is not lost
And the old songs yet endure.

Editor's note: The translation of this poem by John Ceiriog Hughes (1832-87) is by Tony Conran and taken from his *Welsh Verse* (Seren, 1986) p.255-6.

INTRODUCTION

RE-MAKING WALES

John Osmond

Wales in the 1990s is a very different place from the Wales of the 1970s. In less than twenty years there has been a dramatic transformation of Welsh society. A glance through the contents of this book reveals that no part of our economy, culture or politics has been left untouched. Unconsciously and without democratic debate — because as yet we have no effective democratic forum — we are re-making our country.

In the Spring of 1994 more than 250 people from a cross-section of Welsh civil society came together for two days in Llandrindod Wells to review these changes and promote the case for a democratic advance. They included representatives from three county councils, ten district councils, the Welsh Association of Town and Community Councils and more than 25 of their member councils, five trade unions, the Free Churches of Wales, the University of Wales Guild of Graduates, the National Union of Students in Wales, the National Eisteddfod Committee, the Welsh Association of Disabled Groups, Friends of the Earth Cymru, and CND Cymru, as well as representatives from the political parties in Wales: the Labour Party, Welsh Liberal Democrats, Plaid Cymru, the Welsh Conservative Party, the Wales Green Party, the Democratic Left, and the Welsh Committee of the Communist Party.

It was a formidable gathering. The people who came together were not mandated by their various organisations, but for a rare collective moment they did represent a sense of what Welsh civic society could become. In a spirit of tolerance and humour they debated and agreed the *Democracy Declaration* printed near the end of this book. During the European Parliament election campaign in June the *Declaration* was further supported by 900 people who sponsored full-page advertisements in the Western Mail and Daily Post. Later in the year the *Declaration* was presented as a petition to the European Parliament in Strasbourg.

The *Declaration* and the papers given at the Conference form the basis of this volume. They reflect the changes that are re-making

Wales as we approach the 21st Century. We are living through an acceleration of a new industrial revolution that began in the 1950s. In this period Wales is being transformed from a country dependent on agriculture, coal-mining and steel-making, into one with an increasingly sophisticated and diversified manufacturing base and with most of its people employed in the service sector of the economy.

AN ECONOMIC TRANSFORMATION

Wales is one of the few countries in the Western world where the proportion of manufacturing jobs is rising. Open-cast coal mining persists, but all our deep-mine collieries, apart from Point of Ayr in north Wales, have been closed. Some have been resurrected as tourist attractions. There is a much smaller, but technologically advanced steel industry at Port Talbot and Llanwern. In their place has arisen what one research report described as 'a Welsh manufacturing renaissance in the late 1980s and early 1990s'.[1]

During the 1980s manufacturing increased its share of Welsh gross domestic product (GDP) from 24.8 per cent to 27.3 per cent, while the manufacturing share declined from 24.8 per cent to 22.4 per cent in the UK as a whole. Indeed, manufacturing output growth outstripped that of all other UK regions in the 1980s, a trend which is largely explained by the strong inflow of foreign inward investment. These advances have involved real manufacturing jobs and not merely the assembly of parts made in other countries.

By 1991 25,000 people in Wales worked in electronics compared to 20,000 in mining and steel, whilst 70,000 worked in financial services. Between 1983 and 1992 Wales attracted more than 300 projects in the Welsh Development Agency's key target areas for diversification — financial services; vehicles and components; food processing; telecommunications, aerospace and information technology; and healthcare. With 25,000 component manufacturing jobs, Wales has joined the West Midlands as a leading automotive centre of Britain.[2]

By 1992 over 400 foreign-owned manufacturing companies in Wales employed around 70,000 people, almost 30 per cent of the Welsh manufacturing workforce. And despite increased competition, especially from Eastern Europe, high levels of inward investment into Wales continued through the mid-1990s. For instance, in the 1993-4 financial year 64 projects came in from overseas and 105 from other parts of the Britain. They brought capital expenditure of £765 million, creating 8,081 new jobs and safeguarding 5,800 existing ones.[3]

The typical foreign-owned company in Wales pays wages slightly in excess of the Welsh norm, and has high levels of investment per employee, reflected in advanced production facilities. Since the mid 1980s, therefore, manufacturing output in Wales has grown by more than 30 per cent, three times the average for the rest of the UK, Moreover, Wales has the second highest manufacturing productivity in Britain (10 per cent higher than the UK norm). More important still in terms of relative unit labour costs Wales has moved from being the highest UK region in 1979 to the lowest in 1988 and since. Manufacturing labour in Wales, though a bit more expensive than the UK average, has been much more productive.[4]

The overall result and benefits of the manufacturing renaissance described here has been not only employment creation and capital expenditure, but the complete re-structuring of the Welsh economy. As this book was going to press in July-August 1994 another inward investment announcement was made: for a £200m cathay ray tube glass television factory in the Cardiff Bay development. A joint venture by Nipon Electric Glass of Japan and Schott Glaswerke of Germany, the project was clinched for Wales ahead of Germany. The new factory will eventually employ around 750 people. One of its customers will be the Sony television plant in Bridgend which with other factories, such as Panasonic in Cardiff, makes Wales a world centre for television manufacturing.

It is noteworthy, too, that not all the new development is concentrated in the narrow south Wales coastal belt. There are hi-tech investments in west and mid Wales, along the A55 corridor in the north, and even in the Valleys despite the challenges of industrial location and access.

THE WELSH GOVERNMENT THAT EXISTS

This economic transformation has been overseen by a rapidly evolving Welsh government structure, albeit one that it is administrative and bureaucratic rather than democratic. The powers and budget of the Welsh Office have expanded. The Welsh Office is now responsible for overseeing the expenditure of some £7 billion a year, representing something like 70 per cent of public expenditure in Wales.

Much of this expenditure is channelled through 'Quasi Autonomous Non-Government Organisations', the Quangos, or as the Welsh Office prefers to call them, Non-Departmental Public Bodies (NDPBs). These are the appointed bodies such as the Welsh Development Agency, the Health Authorities, the Land Authority for Wales, the Countryside Council for Wales, the Higher Education Funding Council for Wales, Tai Cymru-Housing for Wales, the Arts Council of Wales and many others. Since 1979 the number of Quangos at the all-Wales level has doubled to over 80, while their total expenditure has increased three-fold, to around £2.5 billion a year.

The development in Welsh governmental institutions represents a more extensive decentralisation of bureaucratic functions from Whitehall to Wales than was envisaged in the ill-fated Wales Act of 1978. Since 1979, however, this brueaucracy has been in the hands of a political party and government not elected by a majority of the people of Wales. At the 1992 general election the Conservatives won 28.6 per cent of the vote and just six of the 38 Parliamentary constituencies. Labour polled 49.5 per cent (27 MPs), Liberal democrats 12.4 per cent (1 MP) and Plaid Cymru 9 per cent (4 MPs). An opinion poll conducted by Beaufort Research for BBC Wales in March 1994 gave the Tories only 16 per cent support. Labour scored 60 per cent, Plaid Cymru 11 per cent, and Liberal Democrats 9 per cent. The result of the 1994 Euro-election pushed the Conservatives into third place in Wales for the first time in electoral history. Labour polled 56 per cent of the vote, Plaid Cymru 17 per cent, Conservatives 15 per cent, and the Liberal Democrats 9 per cent.

In a foreword to the 1994 Welsh Conservative Manifesto for Europe, the Secretary of State for Wales, John Redwood, MP for Wokingham, wrote: 'Labour, Liberal Democrats and Plaid Cymru are indistinguishable. They all stand for a more federal Europe, with more regulation and intervention. They all want a Welsh Assembly which will tax people for the privilege of being Welsh . . . Starved of power through the front door, they are climbing in through windows at the back.'

These assertions were a breathtaking reversal of the facts. It is the

Conservatives who, from a minority electoral position, have climbed to power 'through windows at the back', by packing the Quangos with their political appointees. Because of their minority position the Conservatives have had to resort to running the Welsh Office with a succession of Secretaries of State who represent English seats. At the same time their appointees to the boards that run the Quangos are becoming increasingly partisan.

The one-time Welsh Office Minister Ian Grist, who lost his Cardiff North seat at the 1992 election, became chairman of South Glamorgan Health Authority not long afterwards. Beata Brookes, the former Conservative MEP for North Wales and chair of the Welsh Conservative Party, has been appointed chair of the Welsh Consumer Council. David Rowe-Beddoe, chairman of both the Welsh Development Agency and the Development Board for Rural Wales, has been a member of the Conservatives Abroad Strategy Committee and also chairman of its branch in Monaco where he has a home. The chairman of the Higher Education Funding Council, Sir Idris Pearce, stood for the Conservatives in Neath in the 1959 general election. Sir Geoffrey Inkin, Chairman of both the Cardiff Bay Development Corporation and the Land Authority for Wales, stood for the Conservatives in Ebbw Vale in the 1979 general election.

ONWARD MARCH OF THE QUANGOS

Just over 100 years ago, in 1888, the present system of county government was created, first of all in Wales. It brought an array of Boards of Poor Law Guardians, Justices of the Peace, Watch Committees, School Boards, and the self-perpetuating ascendancy of the squires and landowners on the magistrates bench under democratic control. In short, it democratised *the Quangos of that era*.

The first elections to the new councils created a social and political revolution in Wales. The Liberals won control of every county save Breconshire, most by a wide margin. In north Wales they won 175 out of 260 councillors, and in south Wales and Monmouthshire 215 out of 330. As Tom Ellis, the then Liberal MP for Meirionnydd, observed at the time: 'The Monmouthshire victory is of *immense* importance for it means it will cast its lot with Wales.'[6]

The elections resulted in a substantial transfer of power to the Welsh people on a local basis. This proved so successful that the wider objective of Welsh home rule, sought by the Liberal Cymru Fydd movement of the day, was blunted. As Kenneth O. Morgan has observed: 'In this sense the very success of the Welsh radicals in furthering social and political democracy heralded their own decline...'[7]

A little over a hundred years later we are witnessing the final removal of the county tier of government created in 1888. The 1974 reorganisation reduced the number of the counties from 13 to eight. The latest so-called Local Government Reform Act will merge the eight counties and the 37 districts into a single tier of 22 unitary authorities by 1996. However, just as the creation of the counties stymied the progress of the 1890s Home Rule Campaign, so their removal will provide part of the impetus in the 1990s for the final achievement of a Parliament for Wales.

The 19th century 'Quango' system has returned with a vengeance except that, generally speaking, they now function at the Welsh as much as at the local level. A few statistics drive the point home: in the 1993-4 financial year £2.4 billion — that is 34 per cent of Welsh Office spending — was dispensed by Quangos in Wales. The entire revenue expenditure budget for Welsh local authorities was only a shade higher, at £2.5 billion.[8] By the time the new unitary system of local authorities comes into being there is little doubt that the Quango budgets will add up to more than those of the local authorities. By 1996, too, there will be more Quango appointees running Wales than elected local councillors. At present there are 1,974 councillors on the eight counties and 37 districts. When the two tiers are merged the number of councillors will fall to 1,273. In contrast the number of Quango appointees presently totals around 1,400.

Delyn's Labour MP, David Hanson, has undertaken a penetrating analysis of the appointees to the Welsh Quangos. He found them to be 'stuffed with white, male businessmen, lawyers and accountants, with a sprinkling of establishment figures for good measure'. Those establishment figures included ten Deputy Lieutenants, eight High Sheriffs, 14 OBEs, nine MBEs, 15 CBEs, seven Knighthoods, five Honourables, two Peers, a Brigadier, a Major and a Lady in Waiting to the Princess Royal.[9]

It all sounds like a throwback to the nineteenth century. In reality it describes the present. And the onward march of the Quangos continues. In March 1994 a Welsh Economic Council was established with minimum publicity. The aim was to 'ensure greater cohesion and a more united effort on the part of the Principality's major employers' and employees' organisations,' according to the Welsh Conservatives 1992 Welsh election manifesto. It is, in fact, a return to the concept of a nominated all-Wales economic body, the Welsh Council, that was abolished by the incoming Conservative government in 1979 as part of a cut-back on Quangos. In a much quoted declaration, in 1980, Mrs Thatcher said, 'There will always be pressure for new bodies. We shall be robust in resisting them'.[10]

The revival of the advisory Economic Council only fifteen years after the Welsh Council was swept away was an acknowledgement that the all-Wales tier of government administration lacked direction and needed to be given strategic co-ordination. It was evidence, too, of an incremental dynamic in the growth of institutions at the all-Wales level that still proceeds, notwithstanding the ideological predilections of those at the helm.

It is worth emphasising that criticism of the all-Wales Quangos concentrates on the illegitimacy of the decision-makers on their Boards, rather than the existence of their functions at the Welsh rather than British or local level. Democracy at the Welsh level will result in the replacement of the appointed Boards with a legitimately elected administration directly accountable to appropriate committees of members of a Welsh Parliament. The expertise of the public servants staffing the new administrative structure will then be harnessed to an agenda set in Wales, for Wales, and directed by and accountable to elected members on the specialist committees of the Parliament.

The profound differences this could make in policy terms in all the key areas of Welsh administration are fully explored in the chapters in this book devoted to health, housing, education the arts, agriculture, the environment and the economy. The contrasting limitations of the current non-democratic arrangements is well made by simply listing of members of the new non-elected Welsh Economic Council. Many are leading Quango figures: David Rowe-Beddoe, chairman of the Welsh Development Agency and the Development Board for Rural Wales; Professor John Andrews, chief executive of both the Further and Higher Education Funding Councils; Tony Lewis, chairman of the Wales Tourist Board; and John Troth, chairman of the Training and Enterprise Councils in Wales. Glyn Davies was also a member until he resigned as chairman of the Development Board for Rural Wales in May 1994.

Business is also well represented: Carl Hadley, a Swansea businessman who is a member of the Wales CBI's council; Nigel Guy, a merchant banker; Richard Cuthbertson, a Gwynedd construction company chairman; and Professor Tim Congdon, of the Cardiff Business School and one of the Treasury's advisory panel of so-called 'wise men'. Local government is represented by Gwent county councillor John Pembridge, chairman of the Assembly of Welsh Counties Economic and Environment committee, and Tom Williams, former mayor of Islwyn, chairman of the Council of Welsh Districts. Other members of the Council are the Wales TUC general secretary David Jenkins, and Noreen Bray, the Equal Opportunities Commissioner for Wales, the only woman.

Undoubtedly these people have many talents. However, their role lacks democratic legitimacy. It is reflected in their relative powerlessness. They have no staff independent from Welsh Office civil servants, no direct powers and no statutory responsibility.They are chaired by the Secretary of State John Redwood, who can listen to them or not as he chooses. In the otherwise anodyne minutes of their first meeting, in March 1994, he is recorded as remarking on two criticisms he had heard about the new Economic Council: 'first, that it would be a mere talking shop; second, that it was to be a super quango.'[11]

THE ATTACK ON LOCAL GOVERNMENT

The growth in the number and influence of the Quangos has been to a large extent at the expense of elected local government. The 37 Welsh district councils have lost most of their housing responsibilities to Tai Cymru/Housing for Wales . The eight County Councils have lost control of further education to the Further Education Funding Council for Wales.

In 1996, as has been noted, the eight Counties will be abolished altogether. With the 37 districts they will be replaced with a single tier of 22 authorities (to be called counties) whose powers and influence will be much diminished. So, for example, it is plainly intended by the government that in the long run, and despite resistance from school governing bodies, the new counties will cede control of all schools to a new all-Wales Quango , a Schools Funding Council for Wales. As Professor David Reynolds points out in his chapter on education policy, the governing body of every school in Wales is now compelled to consider grant maintained status at least once a year and report the outcome to its parents. This Welsh Office move, in the form of an Order laid before the Westminster Parliament in July 1994 to amend the 1993 Education Act, was the result of frustration at the few Welsh schools choosing to 'opt out' of local authority control At that time only 11 out of 227 secondary schools had done so, and only five out of 1,704 primary schools.

To force its local Government (Wales) Bill through the House of Commons the Government suspended Standing Order No 86 which allows all Welsh MPs the right to participate in the committee stage of specifically Welsh legislation.[12] The Government then packed the Welsh Grand Committee with Conservative MPs representing English seats to give itself a voting majority.

Standing Order 86 was established in 1907, in the wake of the general election of the previous year in which the Conservatives lost all their seats in Wales. It was a gesture by the triumphant Liberals aimed at enshrining Wales's distinct political identity. This was pointed out by the Cardiff Labour MP Jon Owen Jones during the debate on its suspension. He quoted from Hansard 87 years earlier when, in the debate establishing the Standing Order, the Conservative Member for Gravesend, Sir Gilbert Parker, remarked, 'Behind the proposals of the Prime Minister is a process of devolution . . . intended to lead up to the larger policy.'

The Standing Order also ruled that the membership of a Commons Committee must not exceed 50. Given there are 32 Opposition MPs sitting for the 38 Welsh constituencies, the Standing Order meant that as it stood the Conservatives would lose their majority. So, the Government decided the Committee should be made up of 28 members, with 15 drawn from the Government's side, involving the drafting in of nine English Conservatives to buttress the voting strength of the six Welsh Conservative MPs.

As a result the Opposition parties in Wales, although representing a majority of seats, were only allowed 13 places. The 32 Labour, Plaid Cymru and Liberal Democrat MPs, anxious to have a say about legislation that affected each one of their localities, were outraged at this manipulation of representative democracy. In a unique display of cross-party unity, all 32 combined on a Labour amendment to oppose the Second Reading of the Bill because, amongst other defects, ' . . . it fails to establish a directly elected all-Wales tier of government.'

As both the Labour Shadow Secretary of State, Ron Davies, and Plaid Cymru President, Dafydd Wigley, pointed out, this was the first occasion on which such an amendment had united all Opposition members representing Welsh constituencies against the Second Reading of a Bill relating exclusively to Wales.

Labour's spokesman Rhodri Morgan, MP for Cardiff West, argued that the Conservatives steam-rollering of the Bill by suspending Standing Orders, had brought the whole character of the United Kingdom into question:

> The UK is not one homogeneous nation state comprising 651 Members of Parliament who all represent the same sort of constituency. As its name shows the United Kingdom is an amalgam of four different home countries . . . The UK works because there is protection for the smaller parts of the United Kingdom — Scotland and Wales — to prevent them from being abused and pushed around by the much larger majority, England, when legislation goes through the House . . . The Government are trying to turn the Standing Committee into another Quango and pack it with Tory placemen in exactly the same way as they have done with all Quangos.[13]

LEGISLATIVE POWERS

The steam-rollering of the Local Government (Wales) Act through the Westminster Parliament during 1993-4 is only the latest of a series of instances in which the wishes of a substantial majority of Welsh MPs have been overriden by their English counterparts. The passage of the Welsh Language Act during 1992 -3 was, if anything, an even more graphic instance. There was a cross-party consensus among Opposition parties, the advisory Welsh Language Board of the time and other civic society organisations, that the proposed Act should go much further.

Besides politicians and language activists, leading figures such as the Archbishop of Wales, and even the chair of the Conservative Party in Wales, Beata Brookes, in her position as chair of the Consumer Council, argued that the new Act should embody official status for the language and a clear framework of rights for the people of Wales. One example that was widely endorsed was that parents should have the right to have their children educated through the medium of Welsh in a school within reasonable reach of their home.

'People in Wales want rights not hand-outs,' said Labour's spokesman Rhodri Morgan. 'The advantages of a right is that it creates a corresponding duty,' said the leader of the Welsh Liberal Democrats, Alex Carlile.[14] In the event the Act eschewed such notions of rights, and corresponding obligations. Instead it created a statutory Welsh Language Board whose role and funding was dependent upon the determination of the Board itself and the goodwill of the government.

Such experiences make the case for a Welsh Assembly with legislative powers that would, as a result, be a Parliament. If the kind of Assembly envisaged in the 1978 Wales Act had been in existence it is impossible to imagine that it would not have been intimately involved in such issues as local government reorganisation and the future of the Welsh language. Indeed, this was conceded by policy-makers inside the Welsh Office in the 1970s . Though a Welsh Assembly might be denied legislative power it would, in practice, come to wield it through influence. A confidential paper prepared by the Welsh Office Devolution Unit in 1975 on 'The Role of the Welsh Assembly in Primary Legislation' noted that the Assembly's views would carry more weight than those of most other bodies:

> First, the Assembly will represent the people of Wales and will speak with a virtually unique political authority on matters affecting the Principality. Second, the Assembly will be responsible for implementation of legislation on devolved matters in Wales; it will know the situation 'on the ground' and will speak with knowledge on proposals relating to that situation. In reality, therefore, the Assembly's *influence* on legislation could be substantial.[15]

The contents of this book make it clear that legislative decision-making powers are a necessity. This is the case whether it be in the fields of health and housing, education, rural affairs or culture, all dealt with here in separate chapters. Legislative powers are most emphatically needed, however, to promote a sustainable economy, as Professor Kevin Morgan cogently argues in his chapter on economic renewal. Only a Parliament with legislative powers will be able to mobilise effectively the political will to create a modern society with a prosperous economy on a par with Wales's partner regions in the European Union.

The case was well made by the Shadow Secretary of State for

Wales, Ron Davies, in a wide-ranging speech on the regeneration of the Valleys to a Rhondda conference in November 1992:

> The Welsh Office makes much of our developing relations with the four 'motor regions' of Europe — Lombardy, Catalunya, Baden-Württemburg and Rhône-Alpes. I do not deny that the growth of co-operation between Welsh businesses and firms in these regions is an excellent initiative. It is significant, however, that all these Regions have in common a democratically-elected government which pursues an industrial strategy tailored to the needs of the region.

In particular, Ron Davies continued, the Valleys need a new vision based on partnership between the private and public sectors and extensive government intervention to renew their infrastructure:

> I do not believe, however, that all this can be done by us taking a begging bowl to Westminster. It is something that we can and must do ourselves, so we must have appropriate structures for local accountability and power. The present regime is thoroughly undemocratic and in the middle of it stands the Welsh Office. For a modern economy we need a modern democracy and this should be based on an elected Welsh Parliament and strengthened local councils. A more democratic and responsive Wales is not only right for democracy, it is also needed for the sake of industry, jobs and regeneration.[16]

A legislative Parliament rather than an executive Assembly is also needed to enable us to make a stronger case for an entrenched constitution, with powers that cannot simply be brushed aside by other authorities, whether at Westminster or Brussels. The experience of the Greater London Council should be remembered. It was an executive elected Assembly in all but name, with wide powers and an extensive budget. Yet when in the early 1980s it began to pursue policies, especially in the transport field, not to the liking of the Conservative government at Westminster, the GLC was simply abolished, along with the other metropolitan counties in England. Wales must have an institution that is national rather than local and therefore better able to withstand such pressures.

The demand for Welsh democratic representation now stretches back more than three generations. It is largely the result of our having a distinctive society and culture. We are not better nor worse than our neighbours, but different. It would have been impossible to conceive, for instance, that a Welsh Parliament, whatever its political complexion, would have introduced a poll tax in Wales. The mores of Welsh society would have ensured that the ability to pay was central to any system of local government finance. A Parliament with legislative powers is necessary to ensure that Wales will be able to make its own decisions in such matters.

THE ARGUMENTS AGAINST A PARLIAMENT

The arguments in favour of a legislative Parliament for Wales are so strong and coherent that they beg the question why they are not viewed as common sense across the political spectrum. The only party that remains implacably opposed is the Conservative Party. It is tempting to say this is simply because they judge they would have little chance of securing a majority in any all-Wales election. It is instructive, however, to examine the arguments commonly deployed against a Parliament for Wales. They fall into three main categories:

(i) A Parliament would be a costly exercise and would result in higher taxes being imposed on the people of Wales.
(ii) A Parliament would lead towards the break-up of Britain.
(iii) A Parliament would be a surrender to xenophobic forces of Welsh nationalism.

(i) <u>The Cost</u>

Cost is perhaps the favourite weapon of those opposed to a Parliament for Wales. They seem oblivious to the charge that by continually drawing attention to the usually exaggerated costs of democracy, they are attacking democracy itself. A typical statement was made by the then Welsh Office Minister of State, Sir Wyn Roberts, after the Parliament for Wales Democracy Conference in March 1994. 'A Welsh Assembly would send taxes soaring in order to meet its running costs and new policies on services like education,' he said.[17] John Redwood, the Secretary of Strate for Wales, was equally emphatic, in a statement he issued in August 1994. 'I stand ready to debate and reject any day of the week the idea that you should pay more tax for the privilege of being Welsh and that you should obey more laws in order to prove you're Welsh.'[18]
What such sweeping declarations deliberately ignore is the

overheads already incurred in maintaining the existing Welsh bureaucratic machine. The net running costs of the Welsh Office for 1994-5 were put at £70,235,000 in the Government's published expenditure plans.[19] This figure does not include the overheads incurred by the Quangos. Rarely are these revealed. However, the minutes of a meeting between the Economic Strategy Panel of the Council of Welsh Districts and the Secretary of State for Wales, John Redwood and his advisors, in June 1994, produced a startling insight:

> The Secretary of State expressed concern at what he considered to be the high overhead costs being incurred by the Development Board for Rural Wales. It required a £4.5 million overhead to distribute £20 million which was only 0.1 per cent of Welsh GDP.[20]

One can fairly speculate that if the Secretary of State is 'concerned' then a Welsh Parliament would be outraged at such an extraordinary waste of resources within the labyrinthine Welsh bureaucratic state.

It is a small but significant example of the way a Welsh Parliament could actually save money by properly supervising the operations of the Welsh Office and the Quangos. In 1993-4 the running costs of the Welsh Development Agency were £14.3 million (total expenditure £171.4 million); Tai Cymru/Housing for Wales £3m (total expenditure £135m), and the Wales Tourist Board £3.9 million (total expenditure £15.27 million).[21]

It should not be forgotten, too, that thousands of pounds are paid in salaries and expenses to the 1,400 appointed board members of the Quangos. For example, Sir Geoffrey Inkin, the chairman of the Cardiff Bay Development Corporation, is paid £31,105 a year for 2.5 days a week. He is also chairman of the Land Authority for Wales, salary £30,740 a year for 2.5 days a week. John Allen is chairman of Tai Cymru/Housing for Wales — salary £28,340 a year for 2.5 days per week. He is also deputy chairman of the Land Authority for Wales, with an honorarium of £8,730 a year. David Rowe-Beddoe receives £43,455 a year for chairing the Welsh Development Agency and £31,025 for chairing the Development Board for Rural Wales.[22]

The travails of the Welsh Development Agency during the early 1990s, when the House of Commons Public Accounts Committee exposed a litany of failures and dubious practices, are too well-known to need much elaboration here. In a lurid report in July 1993 the *Western Mail* dubbed them 'The WDA's seven deadly sins.'[23] Among the irregularities that were exposed were questionable redundancy payments costing more than £1m, an abortive £308,000 attempt to privatise the agency, known as 'Operation Wizard', free private motoring for board members, and the appointment of a discharged bankrupt as head of marketing.

It might be argued that the Public Accounts Committee, in exposing these irregularities, demonstrated the effectiveness of the House of Commons in holding Quangos to account. Yet such an examination of a particular organisation is a rare occurrence at Westminster and can only expose wrong-doing after the event. The wide-ranging network of Welsh administration needs much more constant and consistent monitoring. More fundamentally, however, the episode exposed a vacuum of responsibility at the core of Welsh administration.

In a House of Commons statement on the Public Accounts Committee report into the Welsh Development Agency, John Redwood distanced the Welsh Office from involvement. To gasps of incredulity from Opposition members he declared that it was clear that 'my predecessors were not to blame, and that the primary responsibility lay at executive level in the WDA.'[24] Yet there is no doubt that the motivation for 'Operation Wizard' came directly from Peter Walker when he was Secretary of State for Wales in the late 1980s.[25]

Answering questions following his Commons statement, John Redwood also absolved the chairman of the Agency at the time, Dr Gwyn Jones, from responsibility: 'the former chairman is not held primarily to blame for those events,' he said.[26] Yet this is contradicted in an internal inquiry into the affairs of the WDA, conducted by the former Permanent Secretary at the Department of Education and Science, Sir John Caines. His report was lodged in the library at the House of Commons by John Redwood the very day he made his Commons statement. It contains repeated references to Dr Jones's role in 'Operation Wizard': 'he was closely involved from mid-1988' it says, and more generally adds, 'accountability must start at the top with the board.'[27]

Dr Jones, who was appointed chairman of the WDA by Peter Walker after they met at a Tory fund-raising lunch at Langland Bay on the Gower, left his £40,610 a year, two-and-a-half days a week post just ahead of publication of the Public Accounts Committee report. However, he remains chairman of the Broadcasting Council for Wales (£15,140 a year) with a seat on the BBC Board of Governors.

Another Public Accounts Committe report was published in May 1994, this time directly criticising the Welsh Office for failure to account for more than £200m of its budget. This huge sum had been 'lost' over a period of years by the Welsh Office failing to keep track of activities like road spending and to adequately supervise bodies like the Training and Enterprise Councils.[28] The day the report appeared John Redwood was interviewed about it on television. Asked whether he took responsibility, he said: 'Politicians settle policy, debate policy, vote moneys. Officials are responsible for the proper conduct and expenditure of those moneys under the approved policies.' The interviewer was disbelieving: 'So politicians don't take responsibility if large sums of money are squandered?' he asked. 'Politicians take responsibility for the policy,' Mr Redwood replied. 'If they make mistakes then they will pay the price. Officials take the responsibility for keeping the paperwork straight. That's what we pay their salaries for.'[29]

The price John Redwood was referring to comes once every four or five years, at a British general election. Who can believe, however, that such a 'detailed' matter as an unaccounted £200m at the Welsh Office will be at the forefront of attention in the British general election in 1996 or 1997? Meanwhile, since it is not a matter of 'policy', nothing can be done. When was it that a Welsh Office official last resigned? John Redwood, in re-writing a convention of the unwritten British constitution — that Ministers are responsible for the activities of their departments — is making the case for a Parliament for Wales.

It might be, as Sir Wyn Roberts asserted, that a Welsh Parliament would decide to spend more money than now on matters like education or, perhaps, the health service. However, that would be a democratically agreed decision, reflecting the resources available and the wishes of the people of Wales, for which members of the Welsh Parliament would be answerable at the ballot box. Those who insist that a Parliament would result in greater tax burdens for the people of Wales are using this claim as a scare story in order to put people off greater democracy and responsibility for their own affairs.

Funding arrangements for a Welsh Parliament are explored by Jon Owen Jones MP and Stephen Hill in Chapter 5. There is no question that the central issue of decentralising power within a unitary state is finance. It is central because without a reasonable measure of control over the amount and source of its revenue, no institution can act responsibly. 'All experience shows that the man who pays the bill in the end collects the power,' was the way the British Civil Service itself put it, in evidence to the Layfield Committee on local government finance.[30]

And as the first chairman of the Commission on the Constitution, the late Lord Crowther, remarked to a Labour Party representative during an evidence session in Wales: 'Does not the whole history of administration show that he who pays the piper calls the tune?'[31]

(ii) Break-up of Britain

The suggestion that a Parliament for Wales would inevitably lead to separation from the rest of Britain and eventually a complete break-up of Britain is articulated in Chapter 21 by the Conservative MP for Brecon and Radnor, Jonathan Evans. It is the most principled stance of the opponents of a Parliament, by those who hold their first allegiance to the unitary British state and a conviction that within it sovereignty is indivisible and cannot be shared. 'I am a Unionist first and a Conservative second,' says Jonathan Evans. In his August 1994 statement John Redwood said, 'Some have misjudged the mood of Wales in thinking that people want our constitutional settlement ripped up and the union between England and Wales damaged by experiment.'[32]

The high priest of this outlook in the devolution debates of the 1970s was Enoch Powell . He declared that Britain was not a democracy but, rather, a Parliamentary nation and, because of that, could not be politically divided. As a general rule, allowing for his premises, Enoch Powell's logic was faultless. On this occasion, however, his premise contained an inherent contradiction. Not only that, subsequent history — most notably Britain's entry into the European Community, now the European Union — has further, and fatally, undermined his position. Speaking in France in February 1971 Enoch Powell gave one of the clearest utterances of his case:

> It is a fact that the British parliament in its paramount authority occupies a position in relation to the *British nation* which no other elective assembly in Europe possesses. Take Parliament out of the *history of*

England and that history itself becomes meaningless. Whole lifetimes of study cannot exhaust the reasons why this fact has come to be; but fact it is, so that the *British nation* could not imagine itself except with and through its parliament.[33] [my emphases]

The emphases noted in this quotation point to the contradiction: the seemingly unconscious confusion between the relationship of the Westminster Parliament with the 'British nation' on the one hand, and the reference to the 'history of England' on the other. Enoch Powell's general point might be valid if applied only to England. Undoubtedly there is a case for describing England as a 'parliamentary nation'. It goes to the heart of the English identity and why the English — especially those on the nationalist wing of the Conservative Party — find it so hard to come to terms with the European Union.

However, the attempt to conflate this central problem of the English identity with that of the other nations of the United Kingdom, swept up into a rubric 'British nation', only helps make the case that Enoch Powell is arguing against. For the English, sovereignty may be claimed to be one and indivisible, still contained inside the 1688 notion of 'Crown in Parliament' and all part of a mystical unwritten constitution stemming from that bloodless revolution. For the Welsh, the Scots and the Irish, however, sovereignty is more conventionally felt and understood to reside with the people. This is the democratic bedrock of *their* sense of nationhood.

But, in any event, the whole argument over sovereignty and where it resides in Britain has been overtaken by British membership of the European Union . The European Court of Justice has supremacy of jurisdiction over all member-state legal structures whose courts are subordinate. This applies retrospectively to pre-1973 legislation in the case of British law as well as a requirement that all subsequent legislation must harmonise with European Union law.

Moreover, the European legislative process provides for 'Directives' in which the British Parliament, like those of the other member-states, is obliged to legislate in detail to meet a general directive laid down by the Union. Remarking on the Westminster Parliament's subordinate role, as early as 1974, Lord Denning said, 'The Treaty (of Rome) is like an incoming tide. It flows into the estuaries and up the rivers. It cannot be held back.'[34]

There cannot any longer be any objection in principle, therefore, to the existence of more than one source of law-making within the British polity. There already is. This is just another way of saying that whatever constitutional arrangements we develop within the United Kingdom we will all remain part of the European Union. As David Morris and Martin Caton argue in Chapter 4, far from there being any threat of separation of Wales from the rest of Britain, we now urgently need a Parliament to enable us to take part in the affairs of the European Union more effectively.

The impact of this European dimension, the framework of the re-making of Wales, has been fully appreciated by such Conservative thinkers as Ferdinand Mount, head of Mrs Thatcher's policy unit from 1982-84. In Chapter 3, in an elegant essay on the relationship between levels of government in Wales Ioan Bowen Rees quotes Mount in the following terms: 'The encircling European girdle makes the UK *safe* for devolution. From the point of view of moderate Scots and Welshmen, the dangers of total separation are removed, since even their wilder compatriots no longer wish to float off into the blue yonder out of range of EC largesse.'[35]

(iii) <u>Nationalism</u>

More often than not, underlying fears about 'separatism' are related fears about 'nationalism'. Vexed questions about identity and choice of identities arise. During the devolution debate in the 1970s there was a widespread sense amongst Welsh people that they were being asked to choose whether they wanted to be Welsh or British. Forced to think about it some thought they were being asked whether Wales should be independent. Others immediately turned the question into one about language. Undoubtedly, many resented being confronted with a choice at all. To the extent that they thought it through, or thought about it at all, most Welsh people probably wanted to remain both Welsh and British. Certainly, that was one possible interpretation of the 1979 referendum result.

In the 1990s, as the forgoing section has made clear, the matter has become even more complex. The Welsh can be Welsh, they can be British, and they can be European as well. Whether we like it or not, the Maastricht Treaty has conferred European citizenship upon us. This is just one more way in which Wales is being re-made. In the process the heat is being taken out of the identity debate. People can choose to be what they like.

There are at least two senses in which nationalism can be understood. In mainstream experience nationalism and democracy have gone hand in hand. After all, from the end of the eighteenth century — from the American and French revolutions — nationalism has been about sovereignty residing with the people, and about the right of the people to rule themselves. This is the essence of citizenship and civic nationalism.

There is, however, another sense in which nationalism can express itself, in ethnic terms of exclusiveness. In Wales, because of the vivid presence of the Welsh language in determining peoples' sense of identity, the difference between civic and ethnic nationalism is often confused. The matter has not been helped by the over-identification of Plaid Cymru with the language. Although surveys have shown that only around a quarter of Welsh speakers support the party[36], it is an undeniable fact that Plaid Cymru's greatest strength electorally is in Welsh-speaking areas.

In Wales, therefore, nationalism is easily over-identified with the struggle for the Welsh language, and, moreover, with a particular geographically defined territory within Wales, the territory by and large represented by the four Plaid Cymru MPs. As a result it is very easy to describe Welsh nationalism in terms of 'the ethnic' rather than 'the civic' nation. Nevertheless, the easy identification of Plaid Cymru with 'ethnic nationalism' does not bear close examination. The point is made by reference to Scotland where such identification is more difficult, as the Scottish commentator, Neal Ascherson, remarked in November 1993:

> Up to now, the Scottish movement for self-government has been almost exclusively 'civic'. It has a classically nationalist interest in cultural identity and history. But it has no language grievance (all Scots speak English, although some also speak Gaelic or 'braid Scots'), and the overtly anti-English element has been marginal. The critic Joyce Macmillan wrote recently that 'anyone who lives in Scotland is a Scot.' The novelist William McIlvanney was cheered when he told the great nationalist rally in Edinburgh a year ago that 'Scottishness isn't some pedigree lineage, it's a mongrel condition!'[37]

The more substantive point Ascherson went on to make, however, was to say that gradually, almost imperceptibly, the position in

Scotland was changing. Anglophobia was on the increase, he argued. This was due to frustrations arising out of imposed English (Tory) government from Westminster, coupled with worries about in-migration of English people into Scotland, especially people who came to occupy key cultural jobs.

In Wales there is an analogous position, though rather different, due to the complications, often psychological, of a much more complex linguistic pattern. So it was interesting that the newly-appointed chairman of the Welsh Language Board, former Plaid Cymru President Lord Elis Thomas, in an early statement of policy in October 1993, pressed the case for taking the language out of the Welsh constitutional debate:

> Let's have more debates about the future political system of Wales and Europe through the medium of Welsh, but the future of the language itself must be above that debate. It should be the vehicle, not the cause of it. Too often in the past, political parties have played their version of the language card whenever it suited them. This reached its climax in the acrimonious devolution debate in the 1970s.[38]

The sense that the heat has gone out of the language debate in the 1990s is another indication that Wales is a very different place from what it was in the 1970s. One reason has been the success of Welsh-medium education and the growing demand from English-speaking parents that their children should have the opportunity of acquiring the language. Another has been the creation of the Welsh language television channel S4C and the association of the Welsh language with modernity and the future as much as being a badge of identity concerned with the past and survival. All this has made it easier to think of nationalism in Wales in civic rather than ethnic terms, as part of a democratic rather than exclusive mobilisation.

A NEW POLITICS

The forgoing list of the 'arguments against' a Parliament have omitted a further dimension, one that is less of an argument and more of a gut feeling. It is disaffection with the political process generally, and especially political parties and politicians. Typical responses to the call for a Parliament for Wales range from 'We've got one already and that's more than enough' and 'Another talking shop' to 'A Glamorgan County Council on stilts', 'Jobs for the Boys' and 'Another gravy train like that one in Brussels.'

Such cynicism could represent a healthy scepticism. More worrying is the likelihood that it indicates a dangerous lack of appreciation of the importance of democratic institutions to a civilised culture. It is not that people are unconcerned with the values and issues of politics. The growth of the many single issue campaigns and pressure groups that deliberately operate outside conventional politics testify to that. For instance, today's younger generation takes the green agenda more or less for granted. The politics of today's teenagers are dominated by animals, vegetarianism and the state of the planet to an extent that is sometimes incomprehensible to their parents. Underlying such convictions, however, is often to be found a widespread alienation from conventional politics, a feeling that the political process continually fails to have a positive outcome and that, anyway, the individual has no way of achieving a constructive influence. In some areas of Wales and especially at the local level, such feelings have been reinforced by many years of one-party rule in which stagnation rather than progress and empowerment are perceived as the order of the day.

It is hard to make the case for political reform and constitutional change in such an atmosphere of anti-politics. The challenge confronting those campaigning for a Parliament for Wales is to convey how it *is* relevant to the economy, the health service, education, housing, the environment, culture and the future of the Welsh language. The chapters in the book dealing with these concerns make an unequivocal case that until we get our politics and political institutions placed on a firm democratic footing we shall continually fail to produce the outcomes we desire in all these areas. A further point remains that a democratic system cannot function without political parties and politicians. If they deteriorate because too many people find them distasteful, democracy is the loser. Ultimately we depend on political parties to deliver.

At the same time we must ensure that, as Tom Ellis argues in Chapter 6, the political parties do not become too distant from the people. To prevent this happening we should put the people rather than the political parties at the centre of our consideration of constitutional change. This is the thrust of Tom Ellis's agenda for reforming the electoral system . Too often, as he says, the case for proportional representation has been argued in terms of fairness for parties rather than asking, first, how people can make the most meaningful positive contribution possible towards their country's governance: 'If we cannot work towards new and enhanced styles of democracy in Wales, then the many unfortunate features of Welsh political life we now experience will be perpetuated in the new arena, and support for a Welsh Parliament will be diluted.'

By itself, however, electoral reform, is not a sufficient answer. In that last quotation Tom Ellis was echoing Jane Hutt, director of *Chwarae Teg* (the organisation campaigning for greater opportunities for women in Wales). In her paper to the Llandrindod Democracy Conference she stressed that the case for electoral reform should not stand alone:

> It should be considered alongside a range of debates about ways in which we can engage the people of Wales in the political process and enable communities to become more actively involved in decisions which affect their well-being. This should include a debate about the ways in which we can engage and involve those who are often 'excluded' and 'disenfranchised' in a number of ways for reasons of age, gender, race, disability and other factors. There is need for debate and discussion about developing new styles of national and local government which enable people to have a 'voice' in civic and public affairs which will result in more active political interest and will make our elected representatives more accountable to the communities they serve.[39]

One of the most significant impacts a Welsh Parliament will have on such aspirations is through the greater opportunity it will offer women to become involved in the political process and the government of Wales. The second provision of the Llandrindod *Democracy Declaration* says that a, 'A Welsh Parliament will ensure, from the start, that there is a gender balance in its elected representatives . . . ' In light of this it is encouraging that both the Welsh Labour Party and Plaid Cymru are committed to equal representation for men and women. In Chapter 8 Siân Edwards explores the background and practical implications of this most radical of changes, especially so far as the traditionally male-oriented Welsh society is concerned. Carried through it will result in the single most important change in Welsh culture and politics that could be imagined. As much as the Parliament itself, it will signal a completely new era and new style in Welsh politics.

The need for a 'new politics' is part of the answer to another, underlying cynical reference point of those who find the call for a Parliament for Wales a distraction from dismal but concrete reality. This is the gloomy, but widely held view that the state of our economy and public services is not amenable to improvement by political intervention, from wherever it comes. Of course, by itself a Parliament for Wales is no panacea for all the ills of Wales. It is, however, a tool which we can use to begin to overcome them.

In this some encouragement is to be found in experience abroad and especially in the other larger member-states of the European Union, all of which have established Regional Governments in the second half of the Twentieth Century. One example is Italy. In 1970 the Italian State established twenty potentially powerful Regional governments. As institutions they were virtually identical in form, but the social, economic, political and cultural contexts in which they were implanted differed dramatically. They ranged from the pre-industrial societies of Sicily and the other Regions of the south to the post-industrial societies of Emilia Romagnia, Lombardy and the others of the north. Some were Catholic and feudal, others Communist and modern.

Their experiences over the past 25 years have varied greatly. Some have proved relative failures — inefficient, lethargic and corrupt. But others have been remarkably successful, promoting investment and economic development, pioneering environmental standards, creating innovative job-training centres for the young and day-care programmes for the elderly.

In his study of Italian regional government, *Making Democracy Work*, the American political scientist Robert D Putman asks the essential question: what is the explanation for these differences? He discounts government organisation, which is more or less the same from Region to Region in Italy, though of course the way government is *implemented* varies widely. Ruled out, too, are party politics and ideology, relative social stability and political harmony, population movements, and even differing levels of affluence and prosperity.

Putnam concludes the difference is due to what he calls *social capital*, by which he means social organisations such as co-operative networks, voluntary organisations and the depth of civic society generally. The Regional democratic governments of northern Italy have on the whole worked because they were dealing with societies that valued solidarity, civic participation, and integrity. They were communities traditionally organised in a horizontal way with a highly developed degree of individual citizenship expressed through strong civic, usually voluntary, institutions.

On the other hand Regions like Calabria and Sicily were traditionally less 'civic' in character. That is to say, they were organised more vertically, with hierarchic social structures, classically divided into peasants and bosses, in which obligations were imposed rather than mutually shared. Putnam traces the differences back more than a millennium, to when republics were established in places like Florence, Bologna and Genoa and developed traditions of civic engagement and successful government:

> For at least ten centuries, the North and South have followed contrasting approaches to the dilemmas of collective action that afflict all societies. In the North norms of reciprocity and networks of civic engagement have been embodied in guilds, mutual aid societies, co-operatives, unions, and even soccer clubs and literary societies. These horizontal civic bonds have undergirded levels of economic and institutional performance generally much higher than in the South, where social and political relations have been vertically structured. Although we are accustomed to thinking of the state and the market as alternative mechanisms for solving social problems, this history suggests that both states and markets operate more efficiently in civic settings. [40]

It might be objected that referring to the Italian experience is far from encouraging due to the record there of government corruption. In the recent scandals, however, it is precisely the northern, most civic Regions of Italy, for instance Emilia Romagna and Lombardy, that have come out best.

The point is not confined to Italy. The most advanced Regions of the other European Union countries all have sophisticated civic traditions. As Kevin Morgan points out in chapter 9, the Welsh Office has been encouraging us to look to best practice in other successful European Regions, but purely in terms of the economic dimension of their activities. Along with Ioan Bowen Rees in Chapter 2, he makes the point that the essential characteristic of the Regions the Welsh Office wants us to emulate — especially the 'Four Motors': Baden-Württemberg, Rhônes-Alpes, Catalunya and

Lombardy — is that they all have strong, democratic governments that have built on long traditions of civic co-operation.

The message for Wales from these varying European experiences is extremely positive. For, of course, we also have a long tradition of civic co-operation. It has occurred in a wide variety of settings, from the Eisteddfodau to rugby football, from the mining communities of the south Wales Valleys and the slate quarrying experience in Gwynedd to the various co-operative movements and the birth of socialism itself. This tradition has been vividly expressed in the personalities and commitment of people like Lloyd George, Jim Griffiths and Aneurin Bevan to social improvements such as pensions, national insurance and the health service.

It is a rich past. One that holds out hope for the future. But the future we have to make for ourselves. As Margaret Minhinnick says, in Chapter 12 where she discusses the need to develop a new ecological approach: 'There is little point in moving certain political powers to Cardiff just for the sake of it. If we do not seek to use those powers to create a culturally and environmentally sustainable Wales, then a Welsh Parliament could well prove a hollow achievement.'

RE-MAKING WALES

The title of this Introduction has been taken from our people's most celebrated remembrancer, Gwyn A. Williams. Writing during the year-long miners' strike, he reflected:

> The Welsh as a people have lived by making and remaking themselves in generation after generation, usually against the odds, usually within a British context. Wales is an artefact which the Welsh produce. If they want to. It requires an act of choice . . . [41]

If, as J. Barry Jones judges in his opening Chapter to this book, the 1979 referendum marked the end of an old Wales, then the miners' strike marked the beginning of a new one. Economically, it was the point at which a new manufacturing renaissance began in Wales. Culturally, and politically, it taught a hard lesson. It might have been an obvious one, but then those are always the hardest to learn. Kim Howells, now Labour's MP for Pontypridd, was Research

Officer with the South Wales Miners and a key strategist during the strike. At its end he wrote that, in their resistance the people of the coalfields rediscovered old collectivist truths:

> They realised that by uniting and sharing all that they had, they could survive and overcome the worst that the present state apparatus could throw at them. In South Wales we also discovered something else: that we are part of a real nation which extends northwards beyond the coalfield, into the mountains of Powys, Dyfed and Gwynedd. For the first time since the industrial revolution in Wales, the two halves of the nation came together in mutual support. Pickets from the south travelled to the nuclear and hydro-stations in the north. Support groups in the north brought food, money, clothes to the south. Friendships and alliances flourished; old differences of attitude and accent withered and out of it all grew the most important 'formal' political organisation to emerge during the course of the strike — the Wales Congress in Support of Mining Communities.
>
> Backed by MPs and elected officers of the Labour Party, Plaid Cymru and the Communist Party, it embraced organisations as diverse as the Welsh Language Society and the Wales TUC. It forced people out of their political trenches and provided a forum for debate and action of the kind sadly missing, not merely in Wales but throughout these islands. It has opened up the possibility of mutual action to defend and strengthen communities; whether their lifeblood is coal or farming or engineering or oil refining. Its existence has given certain politicians nightmares; it has perplexed others and given a new lease of life to still more. Its potential has hardly been realised . . .[42]

This short-lived and restricted 'Peoples' Parliament' was constructed in the midst of acute adversity. It did not long survive the return to more normal political infighting. Yet, as Professor Hywel Francis says in his contribution on the languages and cultures of Wales, it represented new possibilities, and signalled an intention. For what is the alternative? It is quite simply that we become atomised consumers in a more selfish society, rather than citizens in a more selfless society that rests more easily with the best of what the Welsh people have created for themselves down the centuries.

For us to be viewed as consumers, and treated as such, is the declared intention of those who espouse the free market and advocate the Quango system of administration in place of elected, democratic government. So, for example, in 1993 the Minister then responsible for the Citizen's Charter, William Waldegrave, made out the following robust case:

> The key point in this argument is not whether those who run our public services are elected, but whether they are producer-responsive or consumer-responsive. Services are not necessarily made to respond to the public simply by giving citizens a democratic voice in their make-up. They can be made responsive by giving the public choices . . . Far from presiding over a democratic deficit in the management of our public services, this government has launched a public service reform programme that has helped create a democratic gain.[43]

The claim here is that the traditional democratic mechanism of accountability — the ballot box — has been rendered redundant by new market-based mechanisms of accountability. In practice, what this philosophy extols is the superiority of the market over the ballot box. Worse still, it reduces the 'citizen' to being simply a consumer. In Wales we have a much stronger and traditional awareness that communities are more than the sum of their parts, more than a mere collections of individuals. Further, to be allowed full expression they need the focus that democratic institutions provide. The argument, so far as Wales is concerned, is that we are, as has so often been celebrated, a community of communities. It is the point at which the National and Labour movements come together and agree.

The vitality of communities, and specifically the Welsh national community, is dependent upon the way the various components connect. Where people live relates to where they work, how they travel, and where their children go to school. There needs to be an overview. Yet, by stripping any such capacity away from elected bodies — and in the Welsh case denying such an elected body, a Parliament — no such common view is allowed. Instead, there is delegation to agencies, trusts and associations whose primary concern is their own interest and an obligation to reduce costs.

In these circumstances, the only yardstick of the common good is efficiency as measured by an accountant. This constitutional revolution may be good for the placemen and women who fill the thousands of new offices in the scores of new Quangos. But it is a travesty of the community's wider needs. We may be consumers, but we are citizens too. In Wales we certainly need a constitutional revolution, but one that is democratic and not bureaucratic.

Living in Wales in the 1990s is like living in a very old house. The walls still stand, thick and made of stone. There is no damp course. The roof sometimes leaks but can be repaired. Inside, however, over the years the house has been completely transformed, a number of times. Now a new extension is being built on the back. Inside rooms have been knocked one into another and there are gadgets that would have been undreamt of a generation ago. It never stops changing. This year a new kitchen. Next year a new bathroom. Soon a cable will come creeping beneath the drive, linking the house to a worldwide satellite and computer network bringing new messages and new languages. Outwardly the house is still the same. Inside a revolution is going on. Wales is a bit like that. It is our responsibility, in our generation to ensure that this time the latest episode in the re-making of our country is also democratic.

NOTES

[1] Stephen Hill and Julie Keegan, *Made in Wales - An Analysis of Welsh Manufacturing Performance*, Welsh Economy and Research Unit, Cardiff Business School, May 1933 (A study commissioned by the Wales CBI).

[2] Coopers and Lybrand, *Inward Investment into the 1990s*, a background report commissioned as part of the Institute of Welsh Affairs study, 'Wales 2010: Creating Our Future', 1993.

[3] Welsh Office Press releases: W94222, 25 April 1994; W9 4344, 21 July 1994.

[4] Stephen Hill and Julie Keegan, op. cit. (note 1)

[5] *Quangos in Wales*, report to the Council of Welsh Districts Annual Meeting, 22 July 1994; see also K. Morgan and E. Roberts 'The Democratic Deficit, A Guide to Quangoland' (1993), Papers in Planning Research No 144, Department of City and Regional Planning, University of Wales College of Cardiff.

[6] Quoted in Kenneth O. Morgan: *Wales in British Politics, 1868-1922*, second edition, University of Wales Press (1970), p. 107.

[7] Ibid., p. 107.

[8] Kevin Morgan and Ellis Roberts, *The Democratic Deficit: A Guide to Quangoland*, Department of City and Regional Planning, University of Wales, Cardiff, 1993.

[9] David Hanson MP, *Unelected, Unaccountable and Untenable: A Study of appointments to public bodies in Wales* (December 1993)

[10] Quoted in the *Guardian*, 19 November 1993.

[11] 'Notes of Meeting of the Welsh Economic Council: 30 March 1994',

published with the agenda of the Assembly of Welsh Counties' Economic and Environment Committee, 20 May 1994.

[12] Standing Order 86 provides that 'for the consideration of any public bill relating exclusively to Wales, the committee shall be so constituted as to include all Members sitting for constituencies in Wales.'

[13] *Hansard*, 16 March 1994

[14] *Western Mail*, 19 July 1993

[15] Quoted in John Osmond, *Creative Conflict: The Politics of Welsh Devolution* (Routledge/Gomer, 1978) p. 153.

[16] Ron Davies: 'Regenerating the Valleys: The Partnership Approach', speech at Treorchy, Rhondda, 20 November 1992

[17] Quoted in the *Western Mail*, 31 March 1994.

[18] 'The Prime Minister's European Policy Forum Speech — the Welsh Dimension, by John Redwood', Welsh Office Press release, 5 August 1994

[19] *The Government's Expenditure Plans 1993-4 - 1995-6, a Report By the Welsh Office* (Cmnd 2215) p. 108.

[20] 'Minutes of Economic Strategy Panel Meeting with the Secretary of State for Wales on 14 June 1994', distributed by the Council of Welsh Districts ahead of its Annual meeting 22 July 1994.

[21] Op. cit. Cmnd. 2215 (note 19).

[22] Denis Balsom (ed.), *The Wales Year Book 1994* (HTV)

[23] *Western Mail*, 9 July 1993

[24] *Hansard*, 19 October 1993, p. 148.

[25] John Osmond, 'Who takes the blame for the failures of the WDA?', *Western Mail*, 25 October 1993.

[26] *Hansard*, op. cit., p. 154.

[27] 'Public Appointments in Wales - The Best and the Brightest?', *Economist*, 19 February 1994, p. 29-30.

[28] *Western Mail*, 19 May 1994.

[29] 'Wales Tonight', HTV Wales, 18 May 1994.

[30] Quoted in, *Local Government Finance — Report of the Committee of Inquiry* (Cmnd 6453, May 1976) Ch. 5, para. 7.

[31] Commission on the Constitution, 'Minutes of Evidence', vol. 7, *Wales* (HMSO, January 1970), para. 107. The Labour representative was Gwyn Morgan, then Assistant General Secretary to the British Labour Party.

[32] John Redwood, op. cit. (note 18).

[33] Enoch Powell, Speech to the Association of Chefs d'Enterprises Libres, Lyons, 12 February 1971, in *Still to Decide* (Paperfront, 1971), p. 221.

[34] Quoted in Ferdinand Mount, *The British Constitution Now* (Heineman, 1992), p. 219.

[35] Ibid., p. 255.

[36] See, for example, Denis Balsom and J. Barry Jones, 'The Faces of

Wales' in Ian McAllister and Richard Rose (eds.), *The Nationwide Competition for Votes: The 1983 British Election* (Francis Pinter, London, 1984), p. 116. This shows a break-down of support for the parties amongst Welsh-speakers as follows: Labour 28 per cent; Conservative 25 per cent; Alliance (Liberals and SDP) 23 per cent; and Plaid Cymru 24 per cent.

[37] *Independent on Sunday*, 21 November 1993.

[38] *Western Mail*, 26 October 1993.

[39] Jane Hutt, 'Electoral Reform and A Welsh Parliament', paper presented to the March 1994 Democracy Conference at Llandrindod.

[40] Robert. D. Putnam, *Making Democracy Work — Civic Traditions in Modern Italy* (Princeton University Press, 1993) p. 181.

[41] Gwyn A Williams, *When Was Wales?* (Penguin, 1985), p. 304.

[42] Kim Howells, 'Stopping Out' in Huw Beynon (ed.) *Digging Deeper* (Verso, 1985), p. 147.

[43] William Waldegrave: Speech to the Public Finance Foundation, 5 July 1993.

PART I

THE POLITICAL SETTING

CHAPTER 1

WELSH POLITICS COME OF AGE
The Tranformation of Wales Since 1979

J. Barry Jones

We have to begin by recognising the dimensions of the failure to achieve an Assembly in 1979. It was not just a marginal failure, but a rout. For many people it was the end of a dream they had had since their youth in the 1930s and it marked the end of an era in Welsh politics. Afterwards things could never be the same again. There was even a suspicion that 1979 marked the end of a process that could lead towards political democracy at the Welsh level.

But that did not happen. Instead, the archetypal Wales of myth and legend came to an end. The referendum in 1979 dealt a mortal blow to the twin myths of penillion singers in the north working their sheep by day and singing by night, and miners in the south working the coal face by day and singing in male voice choirs at night. That kind of illusion and mythology came to an end. The strategy employed in the 1955 Parliament for Wales Campaign and with some modifications in the 1979 devolution campaign had failed. A new approach is needed.

Things have certainly changed since 1979 but not in the way most people suspected when the referendum defeat overtook us.

First of all, the political establishment so hostile to devolution in the 1970s is now in disarray. In the 1970s the majority of the Labour Party still wanted to maintain a centrally-planned economy. Any concessions towards decentralisation was regarded by the mainstream as detrimental to that objective. The Conservatives were intent on keeping the constitutional unity of a sovereign parliament and the crown. And while the Liberal leadership was radical on constitutional change, the membership remained committed nervously to the status quo.

Today, however, the Labour party has shed much if not all of its socialism. It no longer believes in a centrally planned economy, a central tenet of its economic thinking in 1979. The Conservatives have slowly come round to realising that membership of the

European Union has undermined the sovereignty of the British parliament and they are divided on the issue. Meanwhile the Liberals, revived by the SDP which reached parts that the other parties could not reach, have restructured themselves into a serious party and pose a real threat to the Conservatives in the south-east of England. The Liberal Democrats are now dramatically committed to constitutional reform in a thorough-going way which was not the case in 1979.

These changes, affecting all the British parties, have happened so incrementally year-by-year that we haven't appreciated their enormity. However, there has not only been a change in politics since 1979, there have been fundamental changes in public administration as well.

First of all there has been privatisation at a speed and on a scale that none of us could have imagined back in 1979. We have witnessed the privatisation of the main public utilities: gas, electricity, telephones. Many utilities organised on a regional basis are now being dragged into a more centralised organisational structure. There's been the privatisation of nationalised industries, also in the past organised on a regional basis and now swept along into a kind of capitalist-organised centralised system. In Wales coal and steel are no longer the basic nationalised industries of the country.

Alongside this process of national privatisation there has been a continuous erosion of local authorities and their functions. As a result of the 1988 Education Reform Act any local education authority schools can opt out and become grant-aided trusts, run from the centre. Higher and further education colleges which used to be under the aegis of local authorities have now been swept into a centralist system of administration. Council housing owned and built by local authorities has virtually come to an end with the housing associations taking over the role. On a wide front local government has been reduced, undermined and demeaned.

Now there is talk of a move towards fewer and larger police authorities in which the role of local government will be reduced further.

Then there is what can be described as a quasi privatisation process — the creation of hospital trusts, the establishment of training and enterprise councils where you get a mixture of public and private so that no-one knows exactly where the line is to be drawn between the two. All of this has resulted in a weaker sense of local responsibility and local accountability. The government's move towards creating a unitary system of local authorities in order to clarify the lines of responsibility is widely regarded by many of those involved as almost doomed to failure.

There is a confusion about who is responsible for what and in which categories. This is not just a question of levels of local government and their relationship with Westminster and Whitehall. There is a plethora of public bodies, private bodies and public-private bodies all of which have some input. The result is a lack of focus, and especially a lack of democratic focus, which people can turn to for the redress of grievances. At the most basic level there is confusion as to who is responsible for what.

In all this there has been a growth of the central powers of the state, and simultaneously an erosion of what was already a weak sense of regionalism. At the same time, however, there is a serious paradox at the heart of the process because in Wales and Scotland the reverse has happened. While the government in Westminster and Whitehall has been taking power to the centre in England, at the Welsh and Scottish levels it has established increasingly significant 'regional' administrative entities.

In 1979 Mrs Thatcher came to the British electorate with essentially two propositions. The first was to reduce taxes, and the second to roll back the frontiers of the state. Though there is an argument over whether the total tax burden has been reduced, Mrs Thatcher certainly altered the taxation structure by substituting large amounts of direct with indirect taxes, for example by increasing the level and widening the range of VAT.

Rolling back the frontiers of the state, however, has proved harder to achieve. One of Mrs Thatcher's declared objectives was to 'cull the Quangos', to substantially reduce their number. While there was initially some reduction in England, in Wales the Quangos remained unscathed. The Welsh Development Agency was not only left untouched but its role was elaborated and increased. The Land Authority for Wales and the Development Board for Rural Wales were allowed to continue while new Quangos were actually created in important new fields. In 1993, for instance, the Higher and Further Education Funding Councils for Wales were established alongside similar institutions for England and Scotland. This is likely to prove highly significant. A traditionally centralised British system of administration of the universities has been replaced with a regionalised system, at least so far as Wales and Scotland are concerned. And this is from a party which in power has undermined and seriously weakened regional administration.

Quite unexpectedly given the government's credentials, since 1979 there has been a significant expansion of administration of government in Wales. The arts, sports, health, countryside, tourism, inward investment, land, housing, aspects of economic development, higher and further education are all areas where there is a substantial, and in some cases exclusive, Welsh input of administration. Of course the fundamental financial issues are dealt with elsewhere. Nevertheless, this is really quite a dramatic change from a government which came to power in 1979 totally opposed to any form of devolution.

Should we welcome this? Is this something that we should applaud? There is a problem, for when we are about with this regional level of Welsh administration, we are talking about Quangos. That is where the most dramatic expansion has taken place. There are approximately eighty Welsh Quangos on which there are about 1,400 people nominated to oversee and authorise expenditure of around £2,000 million a year. By any standards this is big business, it is a substantial function. The Welsh Office itself has also grown dramatically. When it came into being in 1965, it had just over 200 civil servants. Now it has 2,500 and whereas it spent hundreds of millions it now spends or authorises the expenditure of £7,000 million a year. So, despite everything, the administrative machine in Wales has grown in importance and responsibility. However, it has not grown in democratic accountability.

There are arguments about Quangos, about the value of Quangos, about the kind of skills that you can get in Quangos and not elsewhere. Such arguments apply to the whole of Britain. In Wales, however, there are additional problems . First of all, there is a special concentration of Quangos. In no other part of the UK is such a high proportion of public expenditure authorised by non-elected bodies. Secondly, we in Wales have a political complexion which is not the same as the political complexion of the party in power. To put it at its mildest, Wales is not a naturally Conservative country. Indeed, there is a lot of evidence to suggest that the Conservatives are the natural minority party in Wales. This is the role they have occupied for most of this century and it is a role they seem destined to occupy possibly for most of the next. At the moment, the Welsh Conservatives have six seats in the House of Commons which means that there are not enough Conservative MPs to fill the ministerial posts in the Welsh Office and occupy all the places on the Welsh Affairs Committee.

In 1979 the Welsh Affairs Committee was presented to the people of Wales not as the second best option to an elected Assembly, but as the most desirable option. Conservative party spokesmen said the way in which the Quangos and public expenditure could be made accountable in Wales was through a dynamic Welsh Affairs Committee responsible to the people of Wales through elected Welsh representatives. However, the scarcity of Welsh Conservative MPs means that non-Welsh representatives now have to serve.

Thus we have a Parliamentary system which is not able to work satisfactorily in Wales. It works even less well in the case of Scotland. So we have a situation in which the weakness of the Conservatives in Wales makes it very difficult, in some cases almost impossible, to realise proper public accountability of the government's activities. That is a basic constitutional fault which cannot be redressed without fundamental change either of parliamentary procedure or of the structure of government in this country.

Further down the line, the endemic weakness of the Conservatives in Wales is even more apparent. They have 32 county councillors out of a total of 494, and that is a measure of substantial weakness. The question that arises is how can a party which is so weak at the grass roots be able to push through policies with any conviction. How can a party which has such a low level of public support really be able to test the mood of the electorate? How can it be sensitive to shifts? How can its personnel and party organisers be able to go to head office and say this is what is happening in Wales? They have virtually no political antenna to test the mood. That weakness has severely flawed the system of government of Wales during the last fifteen years. It is a problem which is even more acute in Scotland, and of course is endemic in Northern Ireland.

So there are flaws in the system, not because one party is intrinsically evil, but because the inequality of electoral support renders the normal parliamentary processes increasingly difficult to operate.

We have in Wales a democratic deficit. There is a political vacuum which needs to be filled. How can we resolve that problem?

Alongside this domestic situation there is the European dimension which is having an important additional impact, providing another context within which the Welsh identity — in European terms the Welsh Regional identity — is becoming established.

Over the last fifteen years, and indeed before, Wales has informally constructed a consultative network within the European Community, now the European Union. It is a network that operates at two levels, one institutional and one informal. At the institutional level it includes the Welsh Office, the European Commission Office in Wales, the new Welsh bureau in Brussels, the Welsh Development Agency, local government and other organisations, the four Welsh representatives of European Commission's Committee of the Regions, the Welsh MEPs and those key directorates in the European Commission which have inputs of various kinds to regional policy. That is a significant network but it is limited.

Equally significant is the informal network that is being constructed alongside — a network concerned with consultation and identifying Welsh territorial interests. Various Welsh organisations are involved in such Europe-wide structures as the Conference of Maritime Regions, the Assembly of European Regions, the Arc Atlantique and others. Where previously the Welsh presence in Europe was only manifested on the rugby field, now other Europeans know about Wales in matters other than rugby.

As a result Welsh interests have been focused in a way that would have been inconceivable before 1979. Wales now lobbies politically in Brussels. Sometimes the lobbies are functionally oriented as with delegations from the farmers unions. More often you will find local government delegations filing into the offices and conference rooms of the Brussels administration. Sometimes these lobbies produce strange bedfellows such as the Wales TUC and the Wales CBI working together on the need for a second Severn crossing or speeding an electrified rail link to the Channel Tunnel.

During this period the Welsh Office has had responsibility for European directives as they apply to Wales. In 1973 its European Affairs division was established and since then it has gone through various organisational changes. A major impact has been to bring home to all divisions in the Welsh Office an awareness of what the Welsh interest is in European terms, whether it be rural or industrial, north or south. There is constant liaison, and constant contact. As a result the Welsh Office has become a much more clearly articulated

Welsh body than it was simply in order to respond to the opportunities provided by membership of the European Union.

In the last few years this European context has brought about three significant developments. In March 1990 the Welsh Office signed an agreement with Baden-Württemberg, one of most wealthy of the German Länder, to promote technological collaboration, cultural exchange and interaction at all levels. This has already happened. Subsequently similar arrangements have been set in train with Catalunya in Spain, Rhône-Alpes in France and with Lombardy in Italy. They are variously referred to as the technological tigers of Europe, the four regional engines, the 'Four Motors'. And Wales, through the initiative of the Welsh Office and successive Secretaries of State, has identified with them and their technological success.

A second significant development came in 1991 when it was decided after much prompting by local authorities to set up a Welsh bureau in Brussels whose job it would be to co-ordinate all the lobbying activities. It is funded by various organisations and acts as a conduit for transmitting information, providing help, expertise and advice to various lobbies from Wales when they want to promote their case in Brussels. We therefore have an example of the Welsh identity being clarified, and to some extent even institutionalised in Brussels.

The third development arises from the Maastricht treaty, and in particular its article 198a which established a Committee of the Regions. There are many problems with this new Committee, its composition and balance. The United Kingdom, in particular, has had difficulties in appointing members from the English regions to balance those from Scotland, Wales and Northern Ireland. As a result England is beginning to realise the problems of regionalism as it affects them. However, the importance of the Committee of the Regions is not what it is today but what it is likely to become. In continental Europe Regionalism has a capital R. It is not something to be admitted in the quietness of the corner. For European Union member states like Germany, Spain and Belgium in particular, but also Italy and France, Regionalism is a dimension of democratic government that works and is growing stronger. Ultimately the United Kingdom will have to decide whether it is going to participate in the process or just let the opportunities slide away.

Finally, in addition to all these outside factors that have brought about these developments since 1979, Wales itself has changed. In

1979, 43 per cent of the people still worked in the public sector and Wales had an economy close to an East European model. Since then there has been enormously rapid change. Where there were 70,000 steelworkers, there are now fewer than 18,000; where there were 43,000 miners there are now fewer than 1,000.

So we've seen a dramatic change in the Welsh industrial landscape. Alongside has been another a change in terms of inward investment. Since 1979 three hundred overseas firms have come to Wales, 130 of them from other parts of the European Union. We have the largest concentration of Japanese firms in Europe. The Welsh economy is changing and with it the Welsh political culture. People no longer recognise London as the sole focus for political decision-making. We live in a more pluralistic environment in which Europe has created a vast additional array of opportunities with significant political implications.

In 1992 the Labour party lost the fourth general election in a row. It was historic. It brought home to many Welsh Labour MPs the doubtful legitimacy of the Westminster government governing the whole of the United Kingdom while relying overwhelmingly on votes garnered in the south-east of England. Meanwhile the Liberal Democrats have become even stronger European federalists. Taken together these two perspectives raise fundamental questions about the notion of the sovereignty of parliament. That sovereignty was always more theoretical than practical, but new political factors which have come to the fore in Labour and Liberal Democrat thinking, are resulting in the ideas British sovereignty and parliamentary supremacy being called more seriously into question than ever before.

Furthermore the Welsh political culture is changing rapidly. Today Wales has a higher proportion of manufacturing businesses than the UK as a whole. There are more foreign businesses in Wales run by businessmen who have learnt the rules of the game in other countries and who do not share the steeped values and prejudices of British society. Instead they look to Europe and a wider world. If we take a combination of outward-looking industrialists, many of them not Welsh or English, a new and growing manufacturing base which is locked into a global economy, plus politicians of all parties increasingly aware of the regional dimension and calling into question the traditional notion of parliamentary supremacy, then you have the conditions for a move forward in the political life of Wales.

Moreover, such a move forward would not be into a novel area. What is surprising is how a concept such as democracy which is so complex and in many ways so confusing can be understood so clearly by people. In part that is what the changes that have taken place in Wales over the last fifteen years are all about. The call for a Parliament for Wales is not about changing the essential, existing framework of Welsh government. Rather, it is about democratising the framework of government that already exists. It is about further extending the principle of democracy to the new levels of government that have come into being as the result of the forces and circumstances of the 20th century.

There is no doubt that the battle to finally establish a Parliament for Wales will be difficult. The motives of the campaigners will be impugned. However, my feeling very powerfully is that in the 1990s, unlike in the 1970s, there is a sense that this policy of regional devolution is one whose time has come.

CHAPTER 2

POLITICAL IDENTITY IN A STATELESS NATION
The Relationship Between Levels of Government in Wales

Ioan Bowen Rees

The relationship between a Welsh Parliament and the other tiers of government is a difficult topic for a movement whose primary aim is to reform government in Wales alone. Ideally, every level of government should be reformed at the same time. In practice, creating the broadest possible front in favour of a Parliament for Wales inhibits proposals for radical change at other levels: one has to seek, in Macaulay's words, 'to remove a vast amount of evil without shocking a vast amount of prejudice.'[1]

Yet, if the proposed Welsh Parliament is merely the same old scenario in a different geographical setting, or the substitution of a majority party leader for a minority party minister, and little else, to many it may not seem worth the effort. My own instinct is to ally the Parliament for Wales Campaign with the Charter 88 movement which promotes a full blown written constitution for the United Kingdom, thoroughly decentralised, and transforming the people from subjects of the Crown into citizens with rights.

Like most observers of Swiss government, I was greatly impressed by the way in which the Jura, which broke away from Bern in 1979 to form a new canton with its own parliament, took the opportunity to enrich Swiss constitutional law by including in its first constitution a number of new rights in the fields of employment, housing, social welfare, nursery education, training, the status of women, the handicapped and foreigners, and freedom of information and public demonstration.[2] There may be philosophical and practical objections to basing political representation upon gender but I also applaud the policy of both the Labour Party and Plaid Cymru that each Welsh Parliament or Assembly constituency would elect one man and one woman. In rugby terms, this is letting the ball out, instead of trying to push over the line in a blind rolling maul which bores all but the most biased spectators.

Uniting Wales, and getting the whole project quickly off the ground, must be amongst the priorities of the Parliament for Wales Campaign, but where do you draw the line between inserting the kind of detail that promotes disagreement, and using such a broad brush that too many questions are left unanswered, or no interest is aroused? In the last resort, one can always argue that the creation of a democratically elected Welsh forum is the only vital necessity, and that it is up to the forum to define its ambitions and negotiate a formal relationship with other levels of government. Some will dismiss such an assembly as a talking shop but if the members are elected on the basis of detailed objectives, talk should lead to action.

To sum up, the Parliament for Wales campaign should be able to unite Wales on the negative basis that, in Western Europe at the end of the twentieth century, a substantial tier of territorial government unsupported by a democratically elected parliament defies logic, fails to meet the minimum civic standards of Western Europe, and tarnishes the self-respect of those who accept the situation. In order to destroy apathy, weariness and apprehension, however, the campaign has also to wake people up, and go some way towards defining the relations of a Welsh Parliament with the local, British and European institutions to which people are already accustomed.

LOCAL GOVERNMENT

At a time when the democratic reform of central government is so much more urgent than reforming the geographical structure of local government, it is exasperating that during 1993-4 the Westminster Parliament had as a priority a Welsh Office Bill on the latter, and completely ignored the former. As Section 12 of the aborted 1978 Wales Act anticipated, only a Welsh Parliament can legitimately reform the structure of local government in Wales. Even within fields such as Further Education, where there is a case for not allowing too great a dispersal of scarce human and financial resources, the Welsh Parliament should also beware the temptation of accepting the Welsh Office inheritance as a whole. If the basis of the case for a Welsh Parliament is democracy, that Parliament should be prepared to emancipate local democracy, to return the many assets which have been stripped from it, and to prepare a number of services for transfer from Quangos to a tier of local government.

How many tiers? The consensus in favour of a single tier of multi-purpose authorities, which I myself have only recently begun to doubt, has been blunted by the work of George Boyne of the University of Glamorgan.[3] Neither do the present single tier proposals for 22 unitary authorities, enacted at Westminster in July 1994, make it any easier to advocate the restoration of municipal control in fields such as hospitals, water and police. It is in any case difficult to envisage a revival of grass roots democracy, and an end to calls for vigilantes, without community councils with an executive as well as a consultative role, and their existence in every part of Wales, including the largest cities. By the standards of most Western European democracies, significant community councils are essential.

It would be fatal for the Campaign to become embroiled in the District/County squabble which has enabled the Welsh Office to divide and rule at the expense of any meaningful local democracy as regards most services. It may be that the single tier of local authorities, which will probably precede the Welsh Parliament, should initially be empowered to make their own arrangements in their own right, internally at the community level, and jointly at the level now occupied by, for example, health authorities. What the Campaign must advocate is *democratic* decentralisation within Wales, so that local authorities are again respected as autonomous bodies and allocated substantial resources in their own right.

At the very least, Wales must adopt the European Charter on Local Self-government, a moderate document, watered down considerably for the sake of the United Kingdom, but still too strong for our present rulers. This is not just a matter of retaining the support of the Welsh local authority associations, all of which do want a Welsh Assembly. It is a recognition of the fact that Wales contains, in spite of her modest size, a variety of diverse regions. Paradoxically, it is the defence of that internal diversity — as well as of the democratic ethos common to the whole of Wales — which must be used to cement us together. Most Welsh people would be happy to settle for a Minister of Education accountable to a Welsh Parliament and unlikely to have much in common with John Redwood. There is, however, another option. The Swiss Federation has no Minister of Education at all, not even — outside the university sector — a part-time one preoccupied with other important functions.[4] As soon as it takes over, the Welsh Parliament should initiate a thoroughgoing review of government within Wales, with the emphasis on function and finance rather than boundaries, and a substantial continental input.

Above all, we must prevent the accelerating process whereby the Welsh state is as disproportionately located in Cardiff as the English state is located in London, and the Irish state in Dublin: let us take heed of the warning in Joe Lee's brilliant *Ireland 1912-1985,* that the intense centralisation of Irish government — originally a British legacy — has helped to foster a dependency syndrome throughout Irish society.[5]

CENTRAL GOVERNMENT

The debate about whether a Welsh Parliament should have legislative as well as executive powers, power to tax as well as entitlement to grant, is essentially insular. It could only take place in one of the few Western democracies in which local as well as regional authorities are bereft of general powers within the basic laws, and of substantial powers of taxation in their own right.

There is nothing special about regional (and local) legislation, or regional (and local) taxation. Neither poses a threat to the efficiency of central government within fields proper to it alone. One has only to turn to Volume 4 (Local Government Administration Abroad) of the Maud Report on the Management of Local Government (1967) to see how the lack of an *ultra vires* principle promotes local initiative in several well administered states. *Of course* a Welsh Parliament should have power to legislate in any field from which it is not specifically excluded; *of course* it should have the right to tax in any way not repugnant to United Kingdom law. Additionally, and especially if it is considered convenient to let the Inland Revenue as now constituted do most of the assessment and collection, both the Welsh Parliament and, in due course, the Welsh local authorities could, like the German *Länder* and *Gemeinden,* have a *right* to a share of central taxation, based on a formula amended from time to time by negotiation. Fortunately, as between the Treasury and the Welsh Office, we already have a formula to work on, though — as the Kilbrandon Report recommended — the final arbiter should be an independent board.[6]

Neither, judging even by the extreme example of Switzerland, should we be apprehensive about any negative effect of differences in the level of taxation between regions and localities: often it is the boom towns which have the highest taxes. In spite of the fact that the bulk of the bureaucracy is already in place and can only cost less if subjected to the scrutiny of elected members, the Government is attempting to identify a Welsh Parliament or Assembly with higher taxation. To emphasise the cost of democratisation is not an edifying stance: what central government is really nervous about is any loss of control over funds now within their remit.

It should be stressed that, in every context, the relations between tiers of government depend more on finance than on fine words. The main reason why these relations appear to be fairly amicable in Switzerland is that the cantons and the communes levy 60 per cent of total taxation — and 80 per cent of taxation upon income and wealth — in their own right. A Welsh Parliament must have substantial funding in its own right, and at least some freedom to add to, or subtract from, the United Kingdom level in the light of Welsh circumstances, priorities and judgement.

At this stage, it is probably unrealistic to think in terms of reserving the powers of the United Kingdom government in a few obvious fields like foreign policy, defence, monetary policy and social security, and leaving the rest to Wales in the manner in which the Northern Ireland Government was empowered in 1920. It is enough to suggest that the Welsh Parliament should take over the powers of the Welsh Office and its Quangos, and of the Home Office as they apply to Wales, and that the act establishing it should also devolve general legislative power over the fields in question.

Until the United Kingdom has a written constitution which limits parliamentary sovereignty, we are also likely to have to accept a requirement that — quite apart from the kind of informal consultation which should always occur between friendly institutions with a common interest in stability — draft Welsh legislation should be submitted to, say, the Attorney General as a law officer, for an opinion on repugnancy, so that the Welsh Parliament cannot slip into an act on, say, the police service, some novel principle in a more general field like the right to a fair trial.

A more difficult question is the extent to which the United Kingdom Government should have power of veto on more general grounds, as in the Scotland Act 1978, which would have allowed the Secretary of State to lay before the Westminster Parliament any Scottish Parliament Bill with a provision which might affect 'directly or indirectly' a matter upon which only Westminster could legislate. A similar clause applying to executive action also reflects a timid obsession with apron strings apparent throughout the Kilbrandon Report.

Up to a point, we should perhaps be prepared to humour our English nannies and steady the nerves of Welsh doubters by accepting such strings for a running-in period. The crux to be overcome is the link between Westminster supremacy in general financial and economic policy and Thatcherite requirements in the schools and hospitals of Wales. The funding of the Welsh Parliament must allow for differences in costing standards arising from possible differences in philosophy. There is a grey area around counter-inflation policy and capital expenditure limits which requires much thought and within which Wales should be prepared to compromise rather than delay progress.

One doubts whether, for the time being, many of us would object to some authority outside Wales — and preferably outside the United Kingdom too — being able to call the Welsh government to account over breaches of human rights or anti-pollution standards. If there is a consensus in Wales over anything, it concerns those fields of government which have been of particular concern to the Welsh people during the last hundred years or so, fields in which one might claim that there is such a thing as a Welsh ethos, and notably education and training, health, the social services, employment and agriculture. But for the existence of the House of Lords, we would have had our own elected assembly for education as long ago as 1907, when Lloyd George had to accept a Welsh Board of Education instead. The Welsh Board of Health was established in 1919: relatively, its work suffered from the indifference of the Ministry of Health in London.

We cannot fob off the long suffering people of Wales with anything less than full legislative powers in education, culture, health and the social services, as well as local government, physical and economic planning, most aspects of transport, and the environment, including National Parks. This is, after all, the norm in most western democracies with Regional government, while all are now included in the Treasury Block Grant to the Welsh Office. Industry, employment, agriculture, fisheries and food are inside the Welsh Office but outside the block and will probably require more thought and negotiation. So will energy, water, broadcasting and the legal system.

As to Quangos, some — in fields such as broadcasting — may need to be retained as corporate bodies on the arms length principle, in an attempt to protect them from party politics in a way in which they are not protected now: if so, appointments to them should be made by a broad-based commission. Enough has already been published about the weakness of Quangos to excuse any elaboration on the need to return most of them to all-Wales or local democracy, tempered perhaps, in one or two fields, by syndicalism.

SECRETARY OF STATE OR PRIME MINISTER OF WALES?

When the Secretary of State for Wales visits a European 'Motor Region' like the German Land of Baden Württemberg, he usually meets — as his opposite number — the Prime Minister of that Region. If it is to be more than an executive authority like a County Council, the Welsh Parliament too should appoint a Prime Minister and a Cabinet of six or seven ministers, each heading a department or group of departments. Some might argue that each department should also be supervised by a committee but, if is to retain respect and avoid delay in deciding day-to-day matters, democracy requires a sharp cutting edge. The Welsh Parliament should legislate, decide broad policy lines, approve the budget and review performance rather than establish a network of executive committees like a local authority. An individual minister — or a small cabinet — is easier to hold to account than a committee and easier to identify from the point of view of the public and the press.

At present, the Secretary of State for Wales has a general co-ordinating role within Wales as well as specific responsibilities. Obviously, a Welsh Prime Minister could not make representations in the British Cabinet and its committees if, for example, the Ministry of Defence proposed to close an important establishment in Wales, or a new fiscal policy threatened to hit Wales particularly hard.

Informally, one could expect a good deal of consultation, not only with Whitehall, but with Edinburgh and Belfast. It would nevertheless be useful to have a particular cabinet minister nominated as an intermediary between the Welsh Prime Minister and the British Cabinet. Such a Minister would not need a large department and would doubtless be employed in some other capacity as well. He might even retain the title, Secretary of State for Wales, as envisaged in the 1978 legislation. If, however, the Welsh Parliament controls the greater part of government expenditure in Wales, and if — as they should — Welsh Ministers act as Whitehall's agents in spending most of the rest, the public should be left in no doubt that the Prime Minister of Wales is our principal public servant.

In recent years, it has also struck me that the post of Secretary of State has become progressively party politicised, with the result that the Welsh Office, originally nothing but a great asset to Wales, is now becoming something of a liability as well. Like a German *Land*, a Swiss canton or a North American state we should be able to manage without a nanny figure. Welsh Ministers would be not only accountable to their own Parliament but also empowered in their own right, in an executive capacity, by the Crown.

THE WEST LOTHIAN QUESTION

There remains the question of relations between the Welsh and United Kingdom Parliaments as such. Our present hard-pressed MPs should welcome the opportunity to concentrate on matters common to all four countries, and on Welsh affairs still administered from London.

During the last devolution debate, in the 1970s, much was nevertheless made of the unfairness of allowing an undiminished number of Welsh MPs to vote on domestic English matters corresponding to those devolved to a Welsh Parliament. By excluding the Welsh, Scots and Irish from voting on certain categories of legislation, there is nothing to stop the English from creating a sort of devolved parliament within a parliament if this really matters to them, and they are still not prepared to devolve power to their own regions.

The need for symmetry within the United Kingdom has, however, been challenged, not — as one would expect — from the Left but in a substantial Conservative contribution to constitutional debate, *The British Constitution Now* by Ferdinand Mount, who was head of Mrs.Thatcher's Policy Unit in 1982-84.[1] Having demonstrated how many halfway houses between unitary and fully federal systems have existed in the United Kingdom in the past, and exist today in other states, he concludes that over-rigid, mathematical symmetry may be a cause of friction rather than a solution to it, a negation rather than an enhancement of genuine democracy. According to Mount, the consensus in favour of a Welsh, as opposed to a Scottish, Assembly precludes legislative powers. However, he insists that the 'West Lothian question,' once pursued so ardently by Tam Dalyell MP (whose constituency gave the question its name), is answered by existing practice, for MPs are 'constantly voting on Bills which do not apply to them or their constituents' — as we in Wales know so well. Some of these anomalies are unjust but others 'follow from the uneven, asymmetrical nature of all existing societies.'

It is certainly not for the proponents of a Parliament for Wales to propose a diminution in the number of Welsh MPs at Westminster. After all, it is there that — subject to the development of the European Union — the most momentous questions of war and peace, finance and the economy will still be decided for the whole Kingdom.

THE EUROPEAN UNION

Constitutional settlements, it seems to me, should pay at least as much attention to the fate of minorities as to the legitimation of new arrangements by majorities. This was the element lacking throughout the breaking up of the old Yugoslavia.

While much of the opposition to a Welsh Parliament is unprincipled scare-mongering, we should have some regard for Welsh people who cherish a British identity and feel that a Welsh Parliament would threaten it. Such people should be encouraged that a Conservative of the calibre of Ferdinand Mount, a disciple of the greatest English Conservative thinker of recent times, Michael Oakeshott, should not only support Scottish and Welsh Assemblies but argue that 'the encircling European girdle makes the UK *safe* for devolution' [his italics].[8] Within the European Union, there can be neither isolation nor disintegration; instead of collision, the stage is set for creative dialogue.

Assuming that Wales belongs to the Union solely by virtue of the United Kingdom's membership, what scope is there for direct relations with the European institutions? On the face of it, the Committee of the Regions will give our representatives the opportunity to influence European policy without being under the inhibiting wing of the central government. According to Article 198a of the Maastricht Treaty, committee members 'may not be bound by any mandatory instructions' and 'shall be completely independent in the performance of their duties, in the general interest of the Community.' Both the Council and the Commission are obliged to consult the Committee on a wide range of matters outside regional policy in the narrow sense, while the Committee may also meet and issue opinions on their own initiative.

Again, according to Article 130b, member states 'shall conduct their economic policies and shall co-ordinate them in such a way as' to attain the Union's aim of 'reducing disparities between the levels of development of the various regions.' As a result of the Treaty and of the Single Market Programme, the range and significance of areas of interaction between Europe and sub-national government is bound to grow. Already, European institutions find it difficult to deal regularly with individual local authorities, while in the United Kingdom such authorities are due to become much smaller. In most other countries, the European Commission is able to deal with Regional governments which can ensure the conformity of all the participants in regional strategy and planning, governments which share much of the responsibility for economic policy with their central governments. The monitoring of the Structural Funds which provide grant aid, and the revision of fund regulations in the light of Welsh needs, in themselves require a strong and autonomous Welsh presence, not only formally and informally at Brussels, but in pressure groups like the Assembly of European Regions. Neither can we ignore the Council of Europe's Chamber of the Regions, whose membership extends to Central and Eastern Europe.

One of the strongest new arguments for a Welsh Parliament is, therefore, that the smaller nations and the regions of the United Kingdom now lack the capacity to take full advantage of the European Union. With the greatest respect to them, the local councillors who represent Wales on the Committee of the Regions lack both the clout and the credentials of their opposite numbers from Regions with their own parliaments. Apart from — for obvious reasons — Luxembourg and Denmark, and also Greece, all continental member-states include elected Regional representatives in their delegations to the Committee of the Regions.

Because of the way in which the German constitution diffuses power, the German *Länder* have insisted on direct representation at the European level, even at the Council of Ministers, whenever their collective interests are involved. Catalunya has a Foreign Minister, though his role is essentially commercial. The fact that Britain is an island has prevented many Conservatives from realising to what extent the old nation-state boundaries are becoming less sacrosanct in practice in mainland Europe, with multi-national associations of Regions sometimes taking the lead in economic development and — in the case of the *Arbeitsgemeinschaft Alpenländer* in the Eastern Alps — Swiss cantons and Austrian *Länder* being involved as well as European Union Regions of Germany and Italy. Yet it took about fifteen years to break down Whitehall's resistance to proposals by two Welsh County Councils, one English County Council, the Irish government, and the European Commission to grant aid railway improvements between Holyhead and Crewe in the interests of European integration.

In all this, the United Kingdom is out of step, while the views on Europe of both the majority and minority members of the Kilbrandon Commission in the early 1970s now seem positively antiquated. According to a recent study, the 'territorial management' of Wales and Scotland by their respective Secretaries of State still 'does not appear to be capable of moving outside of the parameters set by central government'.[9] I have myself had to fight a Whitehall Department trying to upset, and succeeding in amending, an agreement relating to the Social Fund between three Welsh Counties and the European Commission, which had the blessing of the Welsh Office.

Nevertheless, the existence of the Welsh Office does give Wales an advantage over the English regions, at least when the Secretary of State has no hang-ups over Europe. That advantage can only be consolidated when Wales acquires a directly elected Parliament. Without that basic evidence of political identity and will, we could well lose out as the expansion of the European Union gives rise to an unmanageable number of Regions, and the Committee of the Regions evolves into a second chamber of the European Parliament.

Such was the message of the Community Ambassador to Norway and Iceland, Aneurin Rhys Hughes, in two addresses given in Wales in 1992.[10] The message was all the more significant in that its bearer was fully involved in negotiations for the accession to the European Union of Norway and five other states, including Liechtenstein. If the

Welsh Football Association has to fight harder than the football authorities of Malta, the Faroe Islands, or Latvia to keep a stateless nation like Wales in the international arena, the least we can do for the Welsh economy is to give our representatives at Brussels credentials from a full blown Welsh Parliament comparable with the Catalonian *Generalitat,* or that of a German *Land* half the size of Wales.

NOTES

[1] Macaulay *The History of England from the Ascension of James II, 1848-61* (Everyman, 1946) Vol II, p. 280. This is his defence of the flawed and inconsistent Toleration Act of 1689 which 'most strikingly illustrates the peculiarvices and the peculiar excellences of English legislation.'

[2] See J.F. Aubert *La Constitution du Jura*; Thomas Fleiner, 'Die neue Vertassung des Kantons Jura, die Vertassung eines demokratisehen Rechts — und Sozialstaates'; and Daniel Thürer 'Grundzüge und Besonderheiten der Vertassung der Republik und des Kantons Jura' in the 49th *Annuaire de la Nouvelle Société Helvétique/Juhrbuch der Neuen Helvetischen Gesellschaft* (Bern, 1978).

[3] George Boyne, *The Reform of Local Government Structure in Wales: A Critique of the Case for Unitary Authorities*, Public Money and Management, (October - December, 1992)

[4] Ioan Bowen Rees, *Staffing Levels in Swiss Government*, The Journal of Federalism (Philadelphia, Winter 1983) Vol 13, p. 118-9.

[5] Joe Lee, *Ireland 1912 -1985* (Cambridge, 1989), p. 560 and sequence.

[6] Kilbrandon report: *The Royal Commission on the Constitution 1969 - 1973*, Cmnd 5460, October 1973.

[7] Ferdinand Mount: *The British Constitution Now* (Heinemann, 1992), p. 197-205 .

[8] Ferdinand Mount , ibid., p. 254-5.

[9] Peter Roberts, *The Role of Regions in the European Union* (ESRC Research Seminar Paper, London School of Economics, 1993).

[10] Aneurin Rhys Hughes, *Dechreuad Newydd i'r Gwledydd Bychain* (Transactions of the Honourable Society of Cymmrodorion, 1991), p. 318; *Cymru yn yr Ewrop Newydd* (Efrydiau Athronyddol, 1993), p. 70.

CHAPTER 3

SOVEREIGNTY, SUBSIDIARITY AND SUSTAINABILITY
The Scottish Experience

Canon Kenyon Wright

The referendum of 1979, far from settling the issue in Scotland, was a confused and indecisive affair, especially because the 40 per cent rule was used against us. This was the anti-democratic requirement that, regardless of turn-out, 40 per cent of those entitled to vote should say Yes. If such a provision applied to Westminster elections it would have deprived us of any government whatsoever in living memory.

It should be remembered that in the Scottish 1979 referendum there was a majority who voted in favour. On a 63.8 per cent turn-out, 1,230,937 voted Yes and 1,153,502 voted No. This meant that while 51.6 per cent of the votes cast were in favour, this amounted to just 32.9 per cent of the electorate. On that last reckoning the Scottish Assembly fell in 1979.

However, many voted No on the grounds that the scheme was badly conceived. Indeed, the Conservative government promised that if the vote failed a better scheme would be produced. Sir Alec Douglas-Home even said 'I would hesitate to vote against it if I did not believe that devolution will remain at the top of the political agenda'. Malcolm Rifkind pointed out in scorn: 'Scotland is the only nation on the face of the earth with its own legal system and no legislature to control and amend it'. How things change![1]

Since 1979 there has been a sea change in Scottish society. The late John Smith saw the establishment of a Scottish Parliament, not only as 'unfinished businesss' but as now being the 'settled will of the people of Scotland'. To understand why this is the case, we must see how the experience of the last few years has led Scots, irreversibly, to see that the problem is a constitutional system which was always unacceptable in principle, but is now intolerable in practice.

By 1987 the lost wilderness years were over, and the Campaign for a Scottish Assembly as it was then called, appointed a small constitutional steering committee of sixteen prominent Scots (but with no professional politicians) chaired by Sir Robert Grieve and with Jim Ross as secretary. Its report, presented in July 1988, *A Claim of Right for Scotland*, argued that the key issue was the sovereignty of the people, and that the impotence of Scotland within the present constitutional arrangements, especially when highlighted by the use of the royal prerogative to concentrate power in the last century as never before, was unacceptable. They said, 'The failure to provide good government for Scotland is a product not merely of faulty British policy in relation to Scotland but of fundamental flaws in the British constitution'.

The winter of 1988-89 was spent in intensive cross-party talks to implement the main proposal of that commission which was the setting up of a Constitutional Convention. To our sadness, but not our surprise, the Conservatives refused from the start to take any part despite repeated invitations. More surprisingly, the Scottish National Party also withdrew at the later stages of planning, chiefly in practice because of their fear of being committed to any consensus that fell short of full independence. The empty chairs for these two parties are still there in Convention meetings.

Despite the boycotts, the inaugural meeting of the Convention in March 1989 in the historic setting of the Church of Scotland's General Assembly Hall was a heady affair, the most representative gathering of Scottish society for many years. The convention comprises 58 of Scotland's 72 MPs, 7 of our 8 MEPs, 59 of our 64 local authorities along with the Scottish TUC, the major churches, the women's movement, ethnic minority representatives and significant sections of the business community. The Convention of Scottish local authorities, COSLA, provides an excellent and efficient secretariat for the Convention.

The first meeting in March 1989 adopted *A Claim of Right for Scotland* with these words:

> We gathered as the Scottish Constitutional Convention do hereby acknowledge the sovereign right of the Scottish people to determine the form of government best suited to their needs and do hereby declare and pledge that in all our actions and deliberations their interests shall be paramount.[2]

When those MPs and MEPs and local government people and others physically lined up to sign that declaration we crossed the Rubicon in Scotland. There was no way back from that point. The people are sovereign.

The very title *Claim of Right* put the Convention firmly in the mainstream of Scottish history. The seminal document was, of course, the *Declaration of Arbroath* of 1320. It denied the King of Scots (not the King of Scotland you'll notice) any divine right. He ruled 'subject to the consent of the realm' and could be replaced. In the unforgettable words of a parish minister at the General Assembly of the Church of Scotland in 1989 'They said to Robert the Bruce you may be the king but you do as you'r telt or you'r on the burroo' which translated into English says 'You may be the king but you do as you're told or you're on the dole'.

The Convention's founding declaration was actually the third claim of right in Scottish history. The first, by the Scottish Parliament in 1689, declared James II deposed 'because he had turned a legal limited monarchy into an arbitrary despotic power.' The second claim of right was made by the Church of Scotland in 1842. It rejected the right of the Westminster Parliament to impose patronage and claimed that the church had freedom from parliamentary control over its own internal affairs. That was finally granted in 1921, ending the great disruption.

In all cases, and this is the important point, the fundamental principle was the same. All the claims of right deny the English constitutional principle of the unlimited sovereignty of the crown in parliament and uphold the Scottish constitutional position that power is limited, should be dispersed and derives from the people under God. I add under God, but perhaps in secular language I would say that legislation can only derive its legitimacy from a more fundamental law constituting and thus limiting the state and its sovereignty.

In a report of the General Assembly of the Church of Scotland in 1989, these words appear:

> The crisis involves the clear conflict between totally opposing notions of sovereignty in English and Scottish constitutional traditions. From a Scottish constitutional and theological perspective this English constitutional tradition of state absolutism has always been unacceptable in theory; it is now intolerable in practice.[3]

The same report, which fully endorses the Church's commitment to the Convention, concludes:

> It is time for the Church of Scotland to add its voice in our generation to the historic call of the reformed faith in Scotland and Europe for constitutionally limited government under the rule of law.

I hope the Church of Wales will be as clear and bold.

The cracks are appearing in the Westminster ivory tower. The government has declared: 'The future of Ireland will be declared by the people of Ireland'. Can they with any integrity or plausibility say that of Ireland yet deny it of the ancient nations of Scotland and Wales? Indeed, if they do, they will send out a very dangerous message that bombs and violence can achieve what the consistent overwhelming democratic will of the people expressed in election after election apparently cannot. If the people of Ireland, and even the people of northern Ireland, have a sovereign right to determine their future, why not the people of Wales or Scotland? We must expose the double standards, we must reclaim the title unionist from those who are in practice unitarists. That is to say, those who want to preserve not the union which could thrive like most of the rest of Europe where power is genuinely shared, but the last remaining bastion of unitary centralised power in a Europe moving towards subsidiarity.

SUBSIDIARITY

In November 1990 the Convention presented to the people of Scotland a report *Towards Scotland's Parliament.* This followed twenty months of work, widespread consultation, and a genuine search for consensus. From the start the Convention agreed that no major decision would be made by majority voting, that no decision could be reached without the assent of each major party and group in the Convention. This concentrated the mind wonderfully and proved how much can be achieved away from the adversarial atmosphere of much of our politics. *Towards Scotland's Parliament* presented a detailed scheme for a directly elected Scottish Parliament within the United Kingdom which 'subject to the wishes of the people of Wales and the English regions would be the forerunner for Assemblies for these areas with a United Kingdom Parliament covering UK matters such as defence, foreign affairs and central economic and fiscal responsibilities.'

The document's listing of the powers of the Scottish Parliament is very extensive. It begins with the present Scottish Office powers and extends them quite substantially. It has powers over all major areas of policy including local government. Its powers are, in fact, exclusive rather than inclusive. It defines the Scottish Parliament as having control over all areas except those explicitly preserved to Westminster, to the UK parliament. The four areas mentioned are defence, foreign policy, macro- economic policy which we share, and social security policy but not implementation.

This Parliament is to be entrenched in its powers and its relationship with the UK and Europe 'in order that these would be incapable of being unilaterally amended at a later stage by the Westminster parliament'. This is crucial; it must be entrenched. It is of course an open question of how within the present British 'unwritten' constitution that can be done effectively.

The settlement establishing the Scottish Parliament is to include a charter of human rights. This would begin by making the European Convention of Human Rights justicable in the Scottish courts but going on to improve on that.

The fiscal arrangements are very clearly and carefully set out in *Towards Scotland's Parliament.* They seek an arrangement of financing Scottish expenditure which will give the Parliament the kind of independence and flexibility it will require while retaining an element of equalisation based on Scotland's needs and disadvantages in the context of the United Kingdom. This would be achieved through a system of assigned revenues, that is revenues assigned to Scotland's parliament as of right on the following basis.

First, all income tax collected in Scotland is assigned to the Scottish parliament along with all Scottish V.A.T. Second, there should be power for Scotland's Parliament to vary the income tax rate but only within a narrowly defined range. We actually propose tying the hands of Scotland's Parliament to about two or three per cent variation of income tax, within the assigned revenue system.

Thirdly, equalisation should continue for other taxation collected by the Westminster government. The equalisation principle, the Barnett formula as it is called, which has gone on for a long time, should continue based on a needs assessment. This would be reviewed on a regular basis, with the initial review taking place as soon as possible after the establishment of a Scottish Parliament.

Other important commitments made by the Convention in *Towards Scotland's Parliament* include a four-year fixed term and a fairer electoral system ensuring both broad proportionality and gender balance, though those are areas where a final decision has yet to be made. The document was amplified during 1991 by two working groups, one on the electoral system and the other on procedures and preparation for a Scottish Parliament.

Clear principles have been set out on how the parliament will work to make it quite different from Westminster — to make it more accessible, more accountable, more open, and more participatory in its expectation of what the MSPs (Members of the Scottish Parliament) will do. They will operate through an open committee structure and the Prime Minister and indeed all the ministers will be directly elected by and accountable to the Parliament .

Both the Labour party and the Liberal Democrats were committed to the implementation of the Convention's agreed scheme and remain so. The results of the 1992 election were, of course, deeply depressing and resulted in a kind of national numbness and even paralysis for a time. Scotland yet again voted clearly: in an election in which all parties made these issues central, including the government, 75 per cent of Scots voted for parties committed to a Parliament and 55 per cent for parties committed to the Convention scheme. There was not a single constituency the length and breadth of Scotland in which there was not a majority of votes for constitutional change. Yet, again, we were denied democracy.

At the start the Convention set three objectives: (i) to agree a scheme for a Parliament for Scotland; (ii) to mobilise Scottish opinion to ensure the approval of the people for that scheme; and (iii) to assert the right of the Scottish people to secure the implementation of that scheme. The first two have already been essentially though not completely achieved. The third, implementation, remains. But we have committed ourselves to keep the Convention in being 'until Scotland's Parliament is secured'.

There were, however, some weaknesses in the Convention's scheme which we are seeking to correct as rapidly as possible, and certainly before another general election. First, we did not bring out clearly enough the connections between the gut issues that trouble people, the day-to-day social and economic priorities, and the need for constitutional change. People need to see that Scotland's government would manifestly be better government.

Secondly, we failed to counter boldly enough the plausible lies spread by our opponents. These consisted mainly of the claim that Scotland would be 'the most highly-taxed part of the UK', that we would have greater bureaucracy and more government, and that the Union would be somehow under a terrible threat, the 'slippery slope' argument. All of these were not only totally untrue but could easily be shot down by the simple facts of our proposals about taxation or about local government or about a healthier, better union closer to the European vision. But we were not clear or bold enough in doing so.

Thirdly, on the issue of the electoral system, we achieved very substantial agreements on the principles but could not reach consensus on the best system to achieve the desired proportionality or on the most effective way of ensuring, from the start, gender balance in the new parliament. There was a commitment to the principles, but it was very difficult to come to a consensus in practice.

How are these now being tackled? The Convention appointed a Constitutional Commission consisting of twelve prominent Scots of differing persuasions but independent of the Convention, and asked it to report by the end of 1994 on the three major remaining issues of the gender balance, the electoral system and the constitutional implications of a Scottish Parliament for the local government of Scotland and for the UK as a whole. This was a device to see whether we can achieve consensus by another way when it was difficult to get it head on.

The question of gender balance in the Parliament illustrates well the work of this commission. It has said that there must be gender balance from the start or it will never be achieved. In other words, once you get bums on seats, you won't get them off very easily! More than this, however — and academic studies in other places have raised the issue — there is a threshold below which a gender balance becomes impossible to achieve. Unless from the start there are at least 25 per cent or 30 per cent of women in the Parliament the take-off towards achieving a balance is reckoned to be much more difficult.

Questions we still have to answer are: 'Can a gender balance be achieved from the start by voluntary means or does it require a measure of statutory provision and, if so, what measure?' On that, we have as yet no consensus. That is an example of the kind of dilemma we face .

Towards the end of 1994 the Convention launched another initiative, a programme called *Preparing for Change*. This comprises a series of consultations with key sections of Scottish society: industry, the arts, broadcasting, education, health and others, on how they will be affected by Scotland's Parliament and what their expectations and hopes for it would be. This is partly an exercise in preparing people mentally to see that change is inevitable, but partly a means of coming to Scotland's Parliament with the greatest possible clarity of expectation and agenda.

The Convention has also joined with other bodies in a new Coalition for Scottish Democracy which has the limited aim of campaigning for self-determination and is therefore able to include the SNP and others. This body has already taken Scotland's case with some success to the European Parliament and in June 1994 launched the idea of a Scottish civic Senate as a representative body of civil society.

A SUSTAINABLE SCOTLAND

Scotland's Parliament is not an end in itself, but a means to an end. The Convention has repeatedly stated its commitment to a Parliament which is open, participative, accessible and accountable. Establishing a Parliament for Scotland is an opportunity for the foundation of a new democracy which is participative rather than purely representative. Our goal is not just a new Parliament but a renewed Scotland which releases the latent energies slumbering in our people and restores our confidence and sense of purpose as a nation.

The growing disillusionment and loss of moral vision in all our nations within the United Kingdom must be channelled into an attack on the archaic constitutional system and its outdated vision and concepts. We need a new vision for the 21st century, and Parliaments for Scotland and Wales are an integral part of that renewed vision of who we are and where we are going. However, the problem is not just institutional; more fundamentally it is cultural.

A sustainable society demands both integrated strategies and policies and an aware and caring community. To leave everything to market forces while holding all power in Westminster is to have the worst of both worlds. It is to insist on ruling without governing, on power without policy. When you mistake reliance on market forces for a strategy, you get the grotesque lunacies of the coal industry today, and of the closure of the Ravenscraig steelworks.

Even in purely economic terms such policies make no sense whatsoever, but from an environmental and human point of view and terms of the quality of life, they are a madness that would be funny if they were not destroying the lives and happiness of men and women. The litmus test of any society is how it treats its poor and powerless, and how it plans for a sustainable future for us all. By that test can anyone seriously doubt that our own Parliaments would give us better government?

Those of us campaigning for improved democracy in Wales and Scotland should therefore keep closely in touch with one another. We have a common struggle. Ultimately it is for nothing less than for the destiny of our people and the soul of our nations, and I mean all our nations including England. The greatest threat to the United Kingdom is the attempt, like that of King Canute, to hold back the tide of European history by perpetuating a constitutional system which manifestly splits society, denies democracy, sanctifies secrecy and corrupts power.

Above all, our present system is incapable of producing the kind of long-term radical strategic thinking and planning which alone can build a just participatory and sustainable society for the next century, a society which enhances the quality of life for all and saves the environment for the future. I believe that our Parliaments in Scotland and Wales will inevitably lead to a demand for reform in England. We would be the promise or if you like, the threat, of a good example.

One thing is clear. History is on our side. In a Europe moving towards the Regions and towards growing subsidiarity, in a world gradually awakening to the needs for sustainable development, Britain cannot forever remain rooted politically in an age gone by. Scotland and Wales will have their own Parliaments, I believe, within a reformed, renewed and healthier Union. The question is no longer whether, but when.

NOTES

[1] For a full account of the 1979 Referendum campaign in Scotland, see John Bochel, David Davies and Alan Macartney (eds.), *The Referendum Experience — Scotland 1979* (Aberdeen University Press, 1981).

[2] *Towards Scotland's Parliament*, Report to the Scottish Constitutional Convention, November 1990.

[3] 'Report of Church and Nation Committee to the General Assembly', May 1989. It is re-printed in *Scottish Self-Government: Some Christian Viewpoints* (Handsel Press, 1989).

CHAPTER 4

A EUROPE OF THE PEOPLES
The European Union and a Welsh Parliament

David Morris MEP and Martin Caton

The goal of a democratic Wales playing its full part in a 'Europe of the Regions' is increasingly becoming a shared vision across the political spectrum. Yet it was not so long ago that this objective was derided by many as a 'slogan in search of a policy'. It was regarded as an emotional response to the experience of the most centralising government in British history and the recognition that in Brussels and Strasbourg, at least, they still believed in Regional Policy.

What is causing the shift from this sort of cynicism is a realisation that establishing a Welsh Parliament, as well as being essential to making Welsh government accountable to the people of Wales, also provides enormous opportunities and real responsibilities in the Europe of the future. People have observed what is happening in our partner countries within Europe and in the institutions of the European Union and have, rightly, perceived that a Europe of the Regions (and of the small nations) is in the process of construction. There is a growing realisation that without a Parliament Wales risks being left impotent on the sidelines unable to benefit from fully participating in the new Europe.

DEFINITIONS OF REGIONALISM

The primary driving force behind the pressure towards regionalism in the existing states of Europe varies from country to country and within countries. It ranges from assertions of linguistic and cultural singularity to a belief that more local and accountable institutions are pre-requisites for economic and social development. This has led, understandably, to differentiation by some analysts between the traditional, 'cultural regionalism' of Flanders and Wallonia in Belgium, Catalunya and Euskadi in Spain, or Scotland and Wales in Britain, and 'bourgeois regionalism' demonstrated in

Baden-Württemberg and the other German Länder and the French regions.

The Council of Europe definition of Regions is capable of embracing both these forms and all their various hybrids:

> A Region is a territory which constitutes, from the geographical point of view, a clear cut entity, or similar groupings of territories, whose population possesses certain shared features, and wishes to safeguard the resulting specific identity and to develop it with the object of stimulating cultural, social and economic progress. 'Shared features' can be taken to mean language, culture, historical tradition and interests related to the economy and transport. Not all of these elements need to be present in every case.

Of course, the demand for regionalism, even within this definition does not always take a positive form, or project progressive politics, as evidenced by the success of Lega Lombarda in northern Italy in recent years. That sort of narrow regionalism and nationalism — based on illogical hatred, jealousy, and fear — can be found to greater or less extent in most regions of Europe, just as the same sorts of prejudice associate themselves with most of the existing nation states.

However, when we look around at the established autonomous or semi-autonomous Regions and at the emerging Regions in the European Union the most apparent characteristics are not introspection, narrow-mindedness or bigotry. Rather, they give an impression of self-confidence that is outward looking and constantly searching for regional partners to co-operate with.

We believe that it is no coincidence that the most successful places in Europe, in terms of economic dynamism, are those Regions like Baden-Württemberg and Catalunya which have pro-active, decentralised governments that are democratically accountable. These Regions, through their democratic governments have created institutions for education and training, invested in research and technology, and established Regional banks that have fuelled their economic development.

Far from being an extra, unnecessary bureaucratic tier of government, Regional Parliaments in other European countries are proving a source of energy and initiative that respond to the needs of their people. One source of their vitality is through their relationship with the European Union and its institutions.

CONNECTING WITH THE EUROPEAN UNION

The German Länder present the best developed and oldest example of strong representation by Regions in the European Union. The Länder are responsible for all legislative and executive functions not expressly assigned to the Federal Government, whose responsibility is for international affairs, defence, passports, currency, air transport, customs and postal services.

The Länder have 'observer' status, dating from 1959, and automatic representation on member state delegations where their exclusive powers or interests are involved. The observer is appointed by the Conference of Economic Ministers of the Länder, attends meetings of the Council of Ministers and the Committee of Permanent Representatives, reports back to the Länder and takes part in meetings of the Bundesrat (the upper chambers of the federal parliament).

The Länder are also entitled to representation in matters which are exclusively their responsibility. They send two delegates to European Union representative bodies such as the Regional Policy Committee, the European Regional Development Fund Committee and the Standing Committee on Agricultural Structures. These all have well resourced information gathering and lobbying offices in Brussels, with many times the number of staff employed in the Wales European Centre, (set up by the Welsh Development Agency in recent years). They also all have Ministers of European Affairs.

The cumulative effect of this level of interaction between Region and European Union is that the German Länder are involved from the very beginning of the legislative and regulatory process in the institutions of the European Union across the range of issues that affect them, and not just concerning the grants and loans that become available.

In contrast, apart from the excellent but inevitably limited work of the Wales European Centre, Wales as an entity has to rely on the willingness of the UK government to involve the Welsh Office and for the Welsh Office to consult other agencies, like local government or special interest groups. In practice, this means that our voice is never properly representative and rarely heard early enough. We are also failing to monitor proposals in the systematic and comprehensive manner of the German Regions. That is why so often in Wales our interest in what is happening in Brussels or Strasbourg starts and finishes with the financial assistance that we can exploit. This is vitally important, of course, but it is far from being the only way that European legislation impinges on life in Wales.

INTER-REGIONAL CO-OPERATION

The holistic approach of the German Länder governments is not yet matched by any other member-state's Regions, but there are rapid moves in that direction by democratic Regional governments elsewhere, perhaps most notably in Spain where Catalunya is certainly making its presence felt in the corridors of power. The emerging 'Europe of the Regions' is recognised and welcomed throughout most of the European Union and most significantly in the Commission, the Parliament and amongst the majority in the Council of Ministers.

This is one of the main areas of thinking on the future of Europe in which the present British government is out of line even with most right-of-centre parties in our partner countries. What they understand in Strasbourg and Brussels, as well as in Paris, Berlin, Rome, Madrid and the other capitals, is that the larger member-states of the Union are not only *too small* to respond to the economic challenges of the decades ahead, hence the need for the European Union. They are at the same time *too big* as single, centralised entities.

Part of the reason for the growing awareness that we need Regional levels of government to act as the economic engines of progress is the recognition that in the international arena in which we now have to work and trade, old style 'regional policies' are becoming, on their own, less appropriate or effective. It is, incidentally, not surprising that British government ministers have not kept up with new thinking in this area of strategic economic development. For them Regional Policy has never moved far beyond Norman Tebbit's infamous 'On yer bike' approach.

Traditional Regional Policy has tended to consist of centre-to-periphery resource transfer to encourage centre-to-periphery relocation of industry and jobs. However, while this approach was reasonably successful in the past, it cannot meet the needs of the future. Certainly, there will be continuing need to provide financial assistance to disadvantaged areas, including investment in infrastructure improvements and other capital projects. Indeed, the current Structural funds should be massively increased to facilitate the agreed objective of 'cohesion' in Europe.

However, new policies need to be developed that enable deprived regions to break out of dependency and low competitiveness and encourage a culture of regional entrepreneurship. This means investing in education, training and skills; promoting indigenous economic activity; stimulating innovation and building on the strength of local communities. An important component of success will, in the future be inter-regional co-operation. This will need the development of regional networks that will allow small and medium sized enterprises to co-operate on research and development to enable them to compete with multi- national companies.

For a coherent new approach to economic development in the future, strategic regional planning will become even more important. Regions having democratically accountable governments, capable of producing such plans with a responsive approach that encourages the widest participation, will be at an enormous advantage. That advantage is likely to be increased as the European Commission continues in the direction of requiring far more integrated programmes for specific areas rather than packages of bilateral projects.

MECHANISMS FOR DEMOCRATIC PARTICIPATION

Alongside the perceived need for new economic approaches in and from the Regions, it is acknowledged in Brussels and Strasbourg that the process of European integration itself, especially if Economic and Monetary Union proceeds, risks alienating the peoples of Europe from the process of government, with all the dangers that presents. Regional government provides a counter balance in that process, as well as a democratic tier that complements the functioning of the whole Union.

The importance of the Regional dimension in the conversion of the European Community to the European Union was made explicit in Article 198A of the Maastricht Treaty. It was this that created the

Committee of the Regions. The Committee, now well underway, consists of representatives of Regional and local authorities. It has the right of consultation by the Council and Commission on regional issues and may submit an opinion on any matter where it believes specific regional interests are involved. The United Kingdom has 24 places, three of them from Wales.

At present Wales is represented on the Committee by local Councillors who are Conservative, Plaid Cymru and Labour nominees. However, there is no attempt to reflect proportionally the electoral support for these parties and no clear pathway of accountability to the people of Wales. This is an unacceptable way of representing the Regional interests of Wales in anything beyond the very short-term. Of course, if the Conservatives had not lost the vote in the House of Commons concerning the arrangement for appointments to the Committee of the Regions, Welsh representatives would not even have been required to be elected Councillors.

If the people of Wales want to be fully engaged in the Europe of tomorrow we need a democratic Parliament to provide the means for that participation. It goes beyond that, however. The 'Europe of the Regions' is under construction. We should be playing our full part in building it, yet we are prevented by a combination of myopia and mean-mindedness on the part of the present government.

Nonetheless, there is every chance that the next general election will produce a government much more sympathetic to Wales, along with Scotland, achieving the democratic self-government we need to enable us to participate fully in the emerging new Europe. Consequently, we should be debating now how we wish to see the new Welsh Parliament playing its full part in this Europe of the future.

The Parliament should appoint a Welsh Minister of European Affairs, who together with the Secretary of State for Wales would have the right to attend meetings of the Council of Ministers when issues of relevance to Wales are discussed. Representatives of the Welsh Parliament should, as a minimum, require the same rights and status as currently enjoyed by the German Länder.

The Welsh Parliament should establish its own adequately resourced and staffed office in Brussels, incorporating the existing Wales European Centre but with responsibility for promoting Welsh interests across the whole range of European legislation, regulation and provision that affects our country. It would work alongside the existing United Kingdom Permanent Representatives Office but articulate the distinctive concerns of the directly elected representatives of Wales. This office would also be responsible for establishing Inter-Regional links and involving Wales in Economic, Social and Cultural networks.

All Structural Funds (Regional Development, Social, Agricultural Guidance and Guarantee funds) provided to Welsh organisations, together with European Investment Bank loans, should be negotiated and administered by the Public Service of the Welsh Parliament (the new, directly accountable Welsh Office) contributing to a comprehensive strategic regional Policy for Wales. At the same time we should start fighting for a massive increase in the Structural Funds and the extension of their use into areas like health and education.

The Welsh Parliament should insist that it takes the majority of places allocated to Wales on the Committee of the Regions as the best and simplest way of providing a direct channel of accountability to the people. The interests and expertise of the new Unitary Local Authority tier of government could be protected by a minority presence.

SUBSIDIARITY AND THE DEMOCRATIC RENEWAL OF EUROPE

Its own birth being the remedy for the democratic deficit here in Wales, the Welsh Parliament should be pro-active in seeking to cure a similar condition in the European Union. It should argue for increased powers for the European Parliament, greater accountability of the Commission and more openness in the Council of Ministers. In particular, it should involve itself in the debate about the future role of the Regions in the structure of the new European Union as it becomes both 'wider' (including new members like, Norway, Austria, Finland and Sweden) and deeper (as European integration continues after the Intergovernmental Conference in 1996).

If, as we hope, the powers of the European Parliament will continue to increase until it fills the role of the primary legislative body for the Union, then the existing Committee of the Regions could develop into a 'Second Chamber' of that Parliament. Alternatively, as has been proposed by Scottish Labour MEP, David

Martin, the Council of Ministers itself could evolve into such a Second Chamber. If that were the direction we seemed to be heading in, it would be necessary for the Welsh Parliament, in co-operation with other Regional Governments, the Committee of the Regions and the 'regionalists' in the European Parliament, to fight to ensure that the Council included representatives of Regional Government, as well as nation-states.

Whilst the prospect of the existing Council of Ministers handing over power to the European Parliament and representatives of the Regions may seem difficult to imagine, recent history in Europe has shown that change sometimes takes place far faster than we can predict. It is, therefore, useful to have a destination to aim for and objectives against which to measure progress.

We believe that the people of Wales, like the peoples of all the other parts of Europe should now be engaged in the discussion about the democratic structures that govern them at every level. If that debate is reasonably and openly conducted then the importance of regional democracy to the development of a sustainable European future will become apparent.

In the long debates about the Maastricht Treaty, John Major on behalf of the British government, laid great emphasis on the principle of 'subsidiarity'. Quite cynically and quite typically the Tories have invented their own definition of subsidiarity. So, to them, it means stopping decisions being made at European Union level and keeping as much power as possible in Westminster and Whitehall.

Yet, subsidiarity really means 'decisions being taken as closely as possible to the people who will be affected by them'. It is an important principle, even if it is an ugly word. Perhaps the Welsh word *agosrwydd* (nearness) is better. It is an important principle, because at its heart is the belief that all power is rooted in the citizen and is passed to levels of government by consent in order to fulfil particular tasks.

It does not count as subsidiarity in our book if you dismantle European legislation that is working to protect the environment here in Wales and across Europe and replace it with weaker, less effective nation-state laws. Even less does it count as subsidiarity if you emasculate local councils and transfer their powers to central government and its Quangos.

For subsidiarity to work there must be the structures in place at the different levels to allow appropriate responsibilities to be held and exercised. For the requirement of 'nearness to the people' to have any meaning those structures must be democratic. Europe needs subsidiarity to function properly and to work at all subsidiarity needs democratic Regional government. Regional government, therefore, is essential to the healthy development of the European Union.

In Wales we need a Parliament to allow us to obtain the full benefits from membership of the European family. Even more important we need a representative Parliament , rooted in our culture of community and collectivism, to make the European Union far more than just a huge single market. We can help create a Peoples Europe and a Europe of the Peoples.

PART II

CONSTITUTIONAL MATTERS

CHAPTER 5

CALLING THE TUNE
Funding a Welsh Parliament

Stephen Hill and Jon Owen Jones MP

The primary economic argument in favour of devolved responsibility for public resource allocation is intrinsically simple: decisions are best made by those whom the decisions affect. This principle has underlined government policy for more than a decade, being readily identifiable in policy areas such as privatisation, the shift from direct to indirect taxes, and in the health and education reforms.

The same principle dominates conventional wisdom to the extent that all significant British political parties now wholeheartedly subscribe to it. Indeed, most politicians would consider the principle to be so obvious as to be hardly worth stating. The only accepted exceptions to this idea are potential conflicts of interest between different groups, the possible trade-off with efficiency, and potential economies in the provision of certain public goods with little local economic impact, such as defence or foreign policy. The equivalent principle of subsidiarity, or the delegation of responsibility to the lowest possible level, has widespread acceptance throughout Europe.

The economic case for a Welsh Parliament is equally straightforward: Wales has a distinct economic character that is inevitably poorly served by nation-state economic policies that seek to impose solutions on disparate regions. Devolved economic responsibility would mean that decisions on resource allocation are taken by people with both the greatest knowledge and awareness of local needs and priorities, and the greatest incentives to formulate policies to meet those needs. This is not just a question of being driven by electoral expediency but also a recognition that local communities must live with their mistakes with an intimacy that is unfamiliar to visiting politicians from outside.

Of course, the case for a Welsh Parliament requires rather more than just the simple re-statement of accepted principles of economic decentralisation. A Welsh Parliament would require funding to meet its devolved responsibilities. Equally, it is another tenet of the accepted wisdom of the age that public spenders be demonstrably efficient and fiscally responsible.

In this essay the funding requirements of a devolved Welsh Parliament will be analysed before briefly examining other European experiences and the detailed proposals that have been made for a Scottish Parliament. The vexed question of the fiscal relationship between Wales and Whitehall will then be considered, including some tentative estimation of the current flows of public funding and revenue between the two, providing a background to the funding debate.

We will conclude with specific funding proposals for a Welsh Parliament which, in our view, will best meet the basic principles of equity, efficiency and flexibility. However, no proposals can be set in stone. It must be recognised that the economic as well as political relationship between Welsh and UK Parliaments would be a matter of evolution as well as devolution, with the clear prior anticipation that fiscal arrangements would adjust over time.

FUNDING NEEDS

The level of funding received by a Welsh Parliament depends on the functions and responsibilities of that Parliament. It is presumed that a Welsh Parliament would assume the current responsibilities of the Welsh Office and hence need a similar level of funding, whilst extra responsibilities would necessitate additional funding.

Latest estimates suggest that public expenditure in Wales in 1992/93 was around £11billion [1], of which about £6 billion was within the compass and responsibility of the Secretary of State for Wales. Table 1 shows the distribution of this Welsh Office spending in 1992/93.

Over two-thirds of Welsh Office spending is on Health and Social Services and Local Authority Support, with a third of the remainder going on Housing. These areas would be the major funding responsibilities of a Welsh Parliament, with subsidiary responsibilities in Transport, Industry and Employment. It is to meet these responsibilities that a Welsh Parliament would need resources. It is noteworthy that in 1992-3 the Welsh Office spent £64,811,000 on administration, a figure that rose to £70,235,000 in 1994-5. [2] This

Table 1: Shares of Welsh office Spending (%), 1992-93

3.1	Agriculture, Fisheries and Forestry
5.3	Industry and Employment
5.0	Roads and Transport
10.5	Housing
3.2	Environment
2.9	Education and Arts
32.1	Health and Social Services
37.0	Local Authority Support
1.1	Administration

Source: Welsh Economic Trends, No. 14, 1993

offers some prospect that a Welsh Parliament, far from being a costly burden, may even be a cheaper option administratively.

Welsh Office funding is currently provided by Block Grant, calculated according to the Barnett formula using the ratios 10:5:85, for Scotland, Wales and England. In 1992-93, 94 per cent of Welsh Office spending was on education, roads and transport, housing, environmental services, health and social services and administration. Wales received 5/85ths of English spending, or 5 per cent of the British total (Northern Ireland being separately financed).[3]

The remaining 6 per cent of the Welsh Office budget is then subject to negotiation between the Welsh Office and Treasury. It is to the credit of successive Secretaries of State for Wales that Welsh Office funding has increased in real terms in recent years. As a result, identifiable spending per head in Wales in 1992-93 was £3,803, compared to a UK average of £3,411 and an English average of £3,290. Of course, the reason per capita spending in Wales is 11 per cent above the UK average is due to our relatively poor economic condition. Prosperity in Wales continues to lag well-behind the UK: average incomes are lower, the proportion of incomes from social security is higher, as is per capita spending on health, and so on.

Any funding arrangements for a Welsh Parliament will need to take account of this economic context. Wales is the poorest economic region in Britain. Hence our contribution to tax revenues will be relatively low and our need for public spending will be relatively high (of which more later).

Table 2 summarises some evidence of recent economic disparities between the British nations. In 1992-93 average weekly gross household income in Wales was just 86 per cent of the UK average whilst over 40 per cent of Welsh households had to manage on less than £175 per week compared to less than a third of English households. Finally, Social Security benefits as a share of household income was almost a half higher in Wales (at 18.5 per cent) than in England (12.4 per cent). Not only does the relative impoverishment of Wales influence the options for funding, it also helps to set the agenda for a future Welsh Parliament in seeking to improve living standards in Wales.

Table 2: Economic disparities between UK nations, 1992-93

	Average gross weekly income per household (£)	Share of households with average weekly incomes below £175 (%)	Social Security benefits % share of household income
Wales	294.6	42.4	18.5
Scotland	313.7	37.6	17.0
England	350.5	32.9	12.4
N. Ireland	281.3	43.2	19.1
UK	342.9	34.1	13.1

FUNDING MODELS OUTSIDE WALES

Most countries within the European Union have greater experience of political devolution than Britain, and hence have lessons to offer on the nature and scope of funding for devolved government. Similarly, proposals for a Scottish Parliament and its funding have received more attention over a longer period than has been the case in Wales. It is sensible, therefore, to consider the lessons we can learn from both.

The United Kingdom falls roughly into the middle of the European Union prosperity league. Its per capita gross domestic product (GDP) in 1991 was 98 per cent of the European Twelve average.[4] Wales had a GDP per head that was 85 per cent of the European average, rather closer to the Spanish (80 per cent) than the UK average. In terms of regional aid, spending per capita in Britain in 1989 was just £10 compared to £28 per head in Spain, £13 per head in Belgium, £54 in Ireland and £57 in Italy, but just £10 in Germany and £2 in France.[5]

Two examples of regional funding that are relevant to the Welsh debate are Spain and Germany. Spain is Europe's most recent country to have created Regional government, whilst Germany has a federal system of government that was established in the aftermath of the Second World War.

Spain

The death of Franco in Spain was quickly followed by regional devolution. Most taxation in Spain is levied and retained by central government, including personal income taxes, profits tax, payroll tax, VAT, excise and customs duties.[6] Regional governments are then funded by a tax-sharing grant and by ceded taxes including death and gift duties, wealth and property taxes, stamp duties and the gambling tax. Only customs duties are specifically allocated to central government under the Spanish Constitution, so that other taxes could in theory be allocated to any level of government. However, any regional power to levy tax on a particular tax base must be transferred with the approval of central government, requiring a decision by central parliament:

> The wealthier regions, the Basque country and Catalunya in particular, argue that poorer regions are a drag on their own economic development, and that indulging the autonomous aspirations of the poorer regions has established a series of parasitic mini-governments . . .
> Under this system Extremadura, the poorest region gets about thirty times as much per capita as Madrid, the richest area. These transfers have a high degree of visibility and are therefore the subject of intense political bargaining and controversy.[7]

The Spanish model is, therefore, a mixture of block grants and local taxes, which has provoked tension between richer and poorer areas. In contrast to Britain, the greatest degree of autonomy has been sought and attained by relatively rich regions — the Basque Country and Catalunya — who complain that their economies are held back by transfers to poorer regions. Within Britain on the other hand the loudest voices for devolution are within the relatively poor regions of Wales and Scotland.

Germany

A federal system of government has operated in Germany for almost forty years, with four types of taxes, three of which are paid directly to the appropriate level of government (federal, state or community taxes). Revenues from the fourth tax category, common or shared taxes, are allocated between levels of government according to specific formulae.

Central (federal) government accounts for some 45 per cent of all public spending with state (regional) government accounting for 35 per cent and community (local) government spending the remaining 20 per cent. The major difficulty is revenue sharing, with transfers between large financially strong states and smaller fiscally weaker ones:

> The question is whether the differences between states should be equalised in future (as in the past) by procedures of tax-sharing, or by a territorial re-organisation of the State.[8]

Transfers are determined by complex formulae which takes account of tax revenue per capita, population density, urbanisation and other factors. It also uses a quarter of VAT receipts to boost the tax income of poorer states. On the whole the German system has worked well in providing both financial support to poorer states (Länder) and a political consensus. It has been under some strain since unification, however, with mounting concern about the magnitude of transfers from West to East, posing some threat to the consensus.

In summary, Spain and Germany provide some contrasts, with Spain still evolving piecemeal solutions to emerging problems, whilst Germany has a well-ordered and long-established system which is beginning to creak under the weight of unification. The important lesson from both is that financing regional government is a complex and potentially divisive issue that needs to be considered with sensitivity, particularly with regard to the needs of neighbouring regions.

Scotland

Proposals for a Scottish Parliament are well-advanced, with a

Scottish Constitutional Convention preparing detailed plans for both revenues and expenditures.[9] These proposals recognise the need for fiscal responsibility and accountability, with a Scottish Parliament intended to have some power to raise revenue as well as incur expenditure. Hence funding arrangements are seen as needing to go further than the Barnett formula currently used to fund Scottish Office expenditure.

The Scottish Convention has therefore proposed that certain taxes be *assigned* to the Scottish Parliament as a right, which would then be used to finance a Scottish programme. This would necessitate annual negotiation with the UK Treasury about balancing adjustments, that is the say transfers. These could be positive or negative, depending on the relative needs of Scotland and the rest of the UK, the Scottish contribution to general UK public spending (that is, the public goods most efficiently provided centrally), and some principle of equalisation between relative tax bases and spending needs.

The Scottish Convention points out that both the United Kingdom and European Union are partnerships 'in which resources are pooled and burdens shared'. The assignation of certain tax revenues to a Parliament would be consistent with this principle, given a balancing transfer taking account of relative needs.

Given the scale of current Scottish Office spending, the specific proposals for Scotland would be to assign both income tax and VAT receipts paid in Scotland to a Scottish Parliament, which would then be subject to an annual adjustment with the UK Treasury. In addition, the Scottish Parliament would have the power to vary the standard rate of income tax payable in Scotland by up to plus or minus three pence.

This ability to vary income tax would give flexibility to a Scottish Parliament in its spending programme. So, for example, additionally raised resources could be used for specific projects such as an expansion of higher education. Those responsible for the additional tax and spending would then be directly answerable to a Scottish electorate.

A Scottish Parliament could also decide to cut income tax to stimulate the Scottish economy. Such a measure would have to be financed by reductions in the spending programme.

It is argued that whilst such tax changes would necessarily be marginal, they would give a Scottish Parliament both power and responsibility over its own affairs inside a limited range. The potential for a Scottish tax would certainly be denounced by defenders of the current status quo, but the democratic accountability of a Scottish Parliament would at least allow the electorate in Scotland to choose their own tax rate.

Finally, the Scottish proposals recognise that fiscal arrangements would adjust and mature over time. There would need to be a regular review taking account the changing relative needs of Scotland and the rest of the UK.

TAX REVENUES AND GOVERNMENT SPENDING

Governments raise tax revenue and incur expenditures in all the nations, districts and communities of the UK. Any imbalance is part of a general pool, with richer areas both providing higher tax revenue and requiring lower spending, and hence subsidising other areas. This section will make some estimates in order to illuminate the complex question of differences between government receipts and spending within Wales. In doing so it will consider the potential funding requirements of a Welsh Parliament.

It should be noted at the outset that accurate, comprehensive and timely figures on either government spending or receipts by country or English region are conspicuously absent. After pressure from MPs the Treasury now provides some estimates of spending by region, at least for the principal component of government spending defined as identifiable government expenditure, that is, money that can be associated with a particular territory.

Identifiable government expenditure represents around three-quarters of all government spending, with the rest principally made up of defence, overseas service, central government administration and debt interest. Whilst it may be argued that non-identified spending is incurred on behalf of Britain as a whole, rather than for any region, it is in the nature of this expenditure that it is predominantly (but not, of course, exclusively) incurred in the south of England. Moreover, whilst estimates of identifiable public spending by region are published by the Treasury and sensible estimates of non-identifiable expenditure not too difficult to make, a wide range of assumption and presumption is necessary to estimate government receipts by region.

Table 3 sets out Treasury figures for identifiable government expenditure by UK country for 1992-3. Not surprisingly, spending per head was slightly below the UK average in England and above in the Celtic countries, whilst per capita spending was over a third higher on average in Northern Ireland than for the UK as a whole. Identifiable government expenditure per head in Wales was 11 per cent higher than the UK average. It was just under £11 billion or a little over half of Welsh GDP, compared to about £150 billion and 37 per cent of GDP in England.

Table 3: Identifiable Government Expenditure by Country 1992-93

	£m	£/head	UK = 100
England	150,591	3,290	96
Scotland	20,267	3,968	116
Wales	10,997	3,803	111
N. Ireland	7,324	4,594	135
UK	197,179	3,411	

Source: HM Treasury, Statistical Supplement to FSBR, HMSO

That identifiable government expenditure per head in Wales should exceed the UK average is not surprising. Of more surprise is that it should be rather lower than in Scotland. Table 4 overleaf sets out this identifiable government expenditure by function. It reveals that although, as anticipated, spending per head on Social Security and Health were indeed higher than the UK average, it was per capita spending on Trade and Employment, Housing, Environment and Agriculture in Wales that far exceeded the UK average. In contrast, per capita spending on Law, Order and Protective Services in Wales was well under the UK average.

Of the £11 billion of identifiable government expenditure in Wales in 1992-93, almost £6 billion was within the control of the Secretary of State for Wales, covering all the functions listed in Table 4, except Law and Order and Social Security. Both of these are controlled by Whitehall spending departments which spent almost £5 billion in Wales in 1992-3. This makes up the vast majority of the difference

Table 4: Identifiable Government Expenditure by function, 1992-93

	£m Wales	£/head, UK=100
Agriculture	194	190
Trade and Employment	438	170
Transport	481	117
Housing	420	137
Environment	627	139
Law and Order	506	75
Education	1,643	101
National Heritage	58	88
Health and Social Services	2,235	109
Social Security	4,331	111
Miscellaneous [10]	64	430
Total	10,997	111

Source: HM Treasury

between total Welsh identifiable government expenditure and that controlled by the Welsh Office.

Remaining items of central government spending not identified in 1992-3 were some £29 billion on the Defence and Overseas Service, and around £18 billion of Debt Interest.

Identifying government expenditure in Wales is rather easier than estimating government revenue from Wales. Given UK totals for revenues collected from various taxes and duties, some assumptions can be used to generate tenuous estimates of Welsh revenues. Table 5 summarises these estimates for 1992-93. The three-decimal places relating to estimated Welsh receipts are a spurious indication of accuracy. With the exception of income tax receipts (published in Regional Trends), all of these figures are the product of using UK totals and estimated Welsh shares.

For example, receipts of VAT for Wales are estimated from Welsh shares of UK consumer spending, whilst estimated hydrocarbon tax receipts are based on estimated Welsh shares of fossil fuel consumption, and so on. In total our estimates suggest that in 1992-93 Wales generated total tax receipts of just over £10 billion, or 4.6 per cent of the UK total:

Table 5: Estimated Tax Revenue 1992-93

Source	UK total £ billion	Welsh Estimate £bn	Method
Income Tax	56.5	2.500	Published figure
Value Added Tax	37.4	1.702	Welsh share of consumer spending
Social Security contributions	37.4	1.558	Welsh share of earned income
Corporation Tax	15.7	0.885	Welsh share of trading profits
Oil duties	11.3	0.780	Welsh share of fossil fuel consumption
Tobacco/alcohol/ betting taxes	13.1	0.592	Welsh share of consumer spending
Vehicle Excise Duties	3.2	0.154	Welsh share of licensed vehicles
Community charge/rates	22.5	0.775	Welsh Office estimates
Taxes on personal capital	3.5	0.116	Welsh share of investment income
Other receipts	26.9	1.143	Welsh share of GDP
Total	223.9	10.205	4.56 per cent

Subtracting this estimated Welsh tax revenue from identified government expenditure in Wales leaves a deficit approaching £0.8 billion. However this excludes any Welsh contribution to or benefit from non-identified government expenditure, principally defence, overseas spending and debt interest. Any ultimate Welsh budget deficit in terms of tax receipts and government spending depends crucially on the allocation of this non-identified spending.

Suppose, for example, that this non-identified spending was

allocated pro-rata to population levels. In 1992-93 UK defence, overseas and debt financing expenditure incurred by the government totalled £46.5 billion. Taking the Welsh population share of 5 per cent means allocating £2.325 billion of this to Wales. Adding the deficit of £0.792 billion from identifiable government expenditure over estimated tax receipts gives a total Welsh deficit, therefore, of £3.117 billion.

However this certainly does not represent the level of any UK subsidy to Wales, since the UK as a whole had a government budget deficit in 1992-93 of £35.1 billion. Hence, on these figures, Wales was responsible for an estimated 8.9 per cent of the UK budget deficit compared to her 5 per cent of the UK total population.

There are of course a variety of possible alternative allocations of this non-identified government spending. For example, UK defence spending could be allocated on the basis of where this expenditure was incurred, with a great deal of evidence that the South East and South West of England received the lion's share. For example, in 1989 one specialist advisor to the Treasury and Civil Service Committee reported estimates that just 2 per cent of UK defence spending was incurred within Wales, with the South West and South East of England together claiming 62 per cent of all UK defence spending.[11] Allocating just 2 per cent of all UK defence spending to Wales would reduce the present estimate of a Welsh budget deficit by £0.71 billion, to just £2.41 billion, or 6.9 per cent of the UK's deficit. By the same token, allocating debt interest according to its regional payment distribution would, given that Wales is relatively poor, reduce the Welsh deficit still further.

The general conclusion to be drawn, from what are at best tentative estimates, is that the overall magnitude of any Welsh budget deficit is likely to be small in a UK context. It will arise from the economic circumstances of Wales, in particular the low levels of average income, reducing the tax take and increasing some items of public spending. In addition, the previous calculations take no account of the fact that the UK government both foregoes tax revenue through tax allowances and provides subsidies to some activities.

The most obvious tax allowance that will be regionally imbalanced is mortgage relief. The benefit of mortgage relief depends on borrowers' incomes and average mortgage advances, both of which are substantially lower in Wales than the UK average.

Consequently, the distribution of the benefits of mortgage relief must be highly skewed towards better-off regions. Although Budget changes will have reduced this imbalance by limiting mortgage relief, this imbalance will persist as long as the allowance itself.

Finally, if a Welsh Parliament were to assume the responsibilities of the Welsh Office, it is worth noting once again that in 1992-93 the Welsh Office spent a net £64.8 million in administration, scheduled to have increased to £70.2 m in 1994-95. Whilst a Welsh Parliament would undoubtedly need an executive arm and hence incur administration costs itself both directly and indirectly, the magnitude of these Welsh Office expenses provide considerable optimism that a Welsh Parliament need not be administratively expensive.

FINANCING A WELSH PARLIAMENT

Financing arrangements for a Welsh Parliament must be fair, efficient and responsible in providing resources that meet the needs of Wales, in avoiding complexity or excess administration, in providing the power to influence its own resources and hence spending, and in providing accountability at the ballot box that gives people in Wales the ability to make their own economic choices.

At the same time, overshadowing the funding needs of a Welsh, or for that matter a Scottish, Parliament is the economic reality that Wales, like Scotland, is, in a UK context, a relatively poor country that will continue to have fiscal requirements that exceed its tax raising capacity.

We therefore propose that there be two stages in an evolutionary process for funding the Welsh Parliament. The first stage would be the funding arrangement from the start. The second stage, an evolution of the first, would be considered after a period of perhaps five years, and in the light of the overall United Kingdom constitutional position then existing. This position would, of course, include the wishes of the Welsh Parliament itself which would — after at least two elections — reflect in a more mature way the wishes of the Welsh people.

First Funding Stage

The first stage would see the Parliament from the start being financed from two sources:

(i) The assignment of existing income tax and VAT raised in Wales to the Welsh Parliament as of right.

(ii) The annual negotiation of a Welsh equalisation payment between the Welsh and UK Parliaments that takes account of the relative needs and financing abilities of each.

The assignation of tax revenues would give a stature, legitimacy and sense of entitlement to a Welsh Parliament, whilst the continued UK collection of non-assigned taxes would be a direct manifestation of the Union and its continuance. The annual negotiation of a Welsh equalisation payment would establish the fiscal relationship between Welsh and UK Parliaments, providing scope for the recognition of relative prosperity or the lack of it.

These proposals have the advantages of simplicity, as well as consistency with the proposals for Scotland as agreed between the Labour and Liberal Democrat Parties in the Scottish Convention.

Estimates of current identifiable government spending and tax revenues within Wales provide some indication of the potential level of spending of a Welsh Parliament and hence its funding. As noted earlier, 1992-93 spending in Wales within the control of the Welsh Office amounted to almost £5.8 billion. The transfer of Welsh Office responsibilities to a Welsh Parliament would imply the need for roughly equivalent funding. According to Table 5 the assignment of income taxes and VAT to a Welsh Parliament would have raised some £4.2 billion, leaving a deficit of £1.6 billion to be met by an equalisation payment.

Non-assigned or ceded taxes, such as social security contributions, tobacco, alcohol and betting duties, would be explicitly recognised as contributing to those public goods provided by Westminster (including defence and social security).

In the context of devolved, democratic government the annual negotiation of Wales's equalisation grant would become a significant moment in the political calendar. A formula would need to be agreed to minimise potential conflict and ensure the maximum amount of continuity and forward planning. The existing Barnett formula which, as has been described near the opening of this essay, is currently used to decide the Welsh Office block grant, would be the best basis from which to start. There is little advantage to be gained in re-opening the debate on how this is calculated. At the same time it remains true, as has also been argued earlier, that Wales, Scotland and also the North of England, have a strong case to make where non-identifiable public spending is concerned, especially in the defence procurement field. This is the best answer to give to those who attack the Barnett formula.

For example, in a speech in a Scottish Grand Committee debate in February 1992 the Secretary of State for Scotland, Ian Lang, gave us a foretaste of the line of attack that the Conservatives will make on any funding arrangements for a Welsh or Scottish Parliament:

> I wonder whether the right Hon and learned Gentleman can guarantee that, given that position, those resources would be additional to the existing advantage that Scotland derives from the UK, whereby the UK Treasury continues to spend, for every £4 per head that it spends in England, £5 per head in Scotland. [11]

These figures only referred to identifiable public expenditure. Nonetheless, Ian Lang used them to make a thinly veiled threat to the Barnett formula. It is the level of debate we can expect on the funding arrangements for Welsh and Scottish Parliaments. Of course, in 1994-5, under the Conservatives, Britain experienced the largest tax increases in its history. A typical family had to pay an extra £1,330 a year.

The great advantage of these first-stage proposals for funding a Welsh Parliament is that they entail no new taxation, only a separate assignation of existing taxation.

Second Funding Stage

A vital characteristic of economic autonomy is the ability of a community to influence its own level of taxation and consequent public source provision. Our main proposal, therefore, for a Second Funding Stage for a Welsh Parliament would be, after a period of five years, for the Parliament to be able to vary the income tax rate in

Wales within a narrowly defined range of 3p either side of the standard UK rate.

It is unlikely to be long before a Welsh Parliament would desire the flexibility that such freedom would bestow. This is even more the case given the likelihood that a Scottish Parliament would already be exercising such a flexibility. The argument would be further strengthened if, as seems likely, there is a trend at the United Kingdom level to allocate specific taxes for specific purposes, for instance sales tax on alcohol and cigarettes to the health service, or extra income tax of perhaps 1p in the £ for education.

In reality, any economic distortion introduced by marginal changes in tax rates at the regional level would be very small. In reality, too, the ability to vary income tax rates would be circumscribed by both regulation and electoral necessity. If a Welsh Parliament sought future increased resources through minor variations in the tax rate on Welsh incomes (by up to plus or minus 3p in the £), justification would have to be accepted by the people of Wales or a price paid at election.

Even so, opposition to a Welsh Parliament would inevitably focus on the possibility of a Welsh tax rate in excess of the UK standard rate: a possibility that would presumably be described as a tax on being in Wales — or, as John Redwood has claimed, 'a tax for the privilege of being Welsh'[12] — and as a disincentive to future investment and employment.

It would be wise, therefore, to defer consideration of allowing a Welsh Parliament the freedom to alter the rate on taxes within its remit until sufficient time had passed to allow the new constitutional arrangements both to settle down in Wales and to evolve elsewhere in the United Kingdom. For example, a Welsh tax would be no electoral problem if, for instance there were also a Midlands Tax and a South West of England Tax.

At the 1992 general election both the Labour and Liberal Democrat Parties in Scotland agreed that a Scottish Parliament would be able to raise or lower Scottish income tax within a 3p band either side of the 25p basic rate. It would be helpful for a Welsh Parliament to see how such an arrangement first worked in Scotland. In a pamphlet produced in 1990 when the Scottish Convention was debating funding arrangements, David Heald described ways in which such a system might operate:

The Scottish Executive would be able to levy either 'additional' or 'subtractional' pence on income tax, subject to limits which might be, say, +3.00 per cent to - 3.00 per cent. Thus Scottish tax-payers would pay a cumulative rate of 22.00 per cent to 28.00 per cent. This is a relatively modest range though one can expect a Scottish Parliament would be under strong pressure to limit the 'additional pence' . . .

. . . the neatest solution would be to have two income taxes: a UK income tax and a devolved income tax levied upon the same taxable income. Instead of the present basic rate of 25 per cent, the UK basic rate might be set at 15 per cent and the devolved tax at 10 per cent. Thus, there would be two income taxes instead of one, but the total rate would remain at 25 per cent. One could safely predict that the opponents of devolution would attack such a plan, implying, if not directly saying, that two income taxes would be twice as burdensome as one. There would have to be confidence that, after an initial fuss, it would be recognised that it is the total rate that matters.[13]

CALLING THE TUNE

The main challenge in devising funding arrangements for a Welsh Parliament is to produce a scheme that is compatible with arrangements elsewhere in the United Kingdom while providing reasonable financial autonomy. It makes no sense to establish a legislative Parliament without also building into its structures fiscal responsibility. To do so would be a recipe for instability. They who pay the piper do, indeed, call the tune.

At the same time, it is clear that funding a Welsh Parliament should be an evolving process, developing in stages. This recognises the political reality that changing Wales's constitutional relationship with the rest of the United Kingdom has implications beyond Wales itself. What we do in Wales will affect, and be affected by, what happens elsewhere in the United Kingdom. In the financial field above all, there must be time for gradual change and adjustment. Creating a Parliament for Wales should be seen as part of a project for achieving constitutional change and devolution for the entire British State.

The proposals outlined here for financing a Parliament for Wales are not meant to be definitive or exhaustive. Rather they recognise the central importance of funding to the whole Welsh Parliament debate. We believe that, although far from simple, the funding problem is equally far from insurmountable. Experience from our European partners clearly demonstrates that funding possibilities exist which can meet the needs and aspirations of people to control their own activities. We believe that our simple proposals provide a platform that would allow a Welsh Parliament to begin to meet these needs and aspirations.

NOTES

[1] Identifiable Government Expenditure, from HM Treasury, Statistical Supplement to the FSBR, cm 2519.

[2] *The Government's Expenditure Plans 1993-4 to 1995-96, A Report By the Welsh Office*, HMSO, Cmnd 2215, p. 108.

[3] There are some indications that the Barnett formula is under increasing pressure. See *Independent on Sunday*, 11.9.94, p. 1.

[4] Regional Trends, 1994.

[5] Stephen Hill and Max Munday, *The Regional Distribution of Inward Investment in the UK*, Macmillan, 1994.

[6] See R. Bennett (Ed.) *Territory and Administration in Europe*, 1989.

[7] E. Mason Browne, *Political Change in Spain*, 1989.

[8] R. Bennett, op. cit.

[9] Scottish Constitutional Convention, *Towards Scotland's Parliament*, November, 1990. Available from the Secretariat, c/o Convention of Scottish Local Authorities, Rosebery House, 9 Haymarket Terrace, Edinburgh, EH12 5XZ.

[10] David Heald, *Territorial Expenditure, Asset Sales and the New Planning Total*, Memorandum submitted to the Treasury and Civil Service Committee of the House of Commons, February 1989. Published by HMSO as the Committee's Sixth report, July 1989. The memorandum was reprinted by the Scottish Constitutional Convention as an appendix to its *Consultation Document and report to the Scottish People: Towards a Scottish Parliament*, October 1989.

[11] H.M. Treasury enigmatically states that miscellaneous 'expenditures include net receipts of Land Registry in England and Wales and costs of the Central administration of the offices of the Secretary of State of the territorial departments'.

[12] Hansard, 24 February 1992, col. 5-6.

[13] Welsh Office Press Release, 5 August 1994, *The Prime Minister's European Policy Forum Speech - the Welsh Dimension, by John Redwood*.

[14] David Heald, *Financing a Scottish Parliament: Options for Debate*, July, 1990.

CHAPTER 6

PUTTING THE PEOPLE FIRST
Electing a Welsh Parliament

Tom Ellis

Democracy is the rock on which the people of Wales set their demand for an elected Parliament. It is essential, therefore, that the Parliament should be truly representative of Welsh society in all its ethnic, cultural, linguistic and social diversity. The word *representative* should be taken at its most democratically contributive. This implies a substantial extension of democracy from that experienced under the existing British political tradition which, as we shall see, is hardly democratic in the full meaning of that word. Indeed, if we cannot work towards new and enhanced styles of democracy in Wales, then the many unfortunate features of Welsh political life we now experience will be perpetuated in the new arena, and support for a Welsh Parliament will be diluted.

The system of electing the Parliament is therefore a matter of fundamental importance. This is so not only from a Welsh, but also from a British point of view. The beneficial effects on the British polity, as distinct from Wales itself, of a properly elected Welsh Parliament have so far been inadequately discussed. It is important to do so to demonstrate the interdependence of the various levels of political institutions within the modern Europe, and also to draw attention to the serious shortcomings of the existing unitary structure of the British nation-state.

Both subjects are complex, multi-faceted, and in many ways complementary. They can be conveniently approached, however, from a consideration of the principles lying behind the democratic election of representative governing institutions. The key role of an electoral system in a democracy, and the equally influential role of the political party, become apparent from such a consideration. This is especially the case in Britain where the political party has come to fill the constitutional vacuum within which the state functions. Electoral reform offers a crucial opportunity, not only to promote the democratic rights of the people, but also to improve the relationship between the political parties and the people.

AN OLIGARCHIC, ADVERSARIAL SYSTEM

The English, quasi-British, political culture, which developed after the so-called Glorious Revolution of 1688 when the concept of Crown-in-Parliament finally superseded that of the Divine Right of Kings, is at once 'oligarchic yet adversarial'. A handful of people at Westminster, organised into a government and opposition parties have wielded almost unlimited political power on the basis of 'sovereignty in Parliament'.

It so happens that the indigenous Welsh tradition, also for historical reasons, is different and worth noting. The Welsh tradition is that of dissent, the non-pedagogical self-help of the nineteenth-century Sunday school, the absence of a native patriciate, the lack of a class structure formalised by the trappings of State and enhanced by the influence of public school and London club, the non-differential role of accent, and of course the absence of a native governmental tradition. Together these characteristics have produced a society putatively more amenable than its broader British counterpart to the cultural demands of modern democracy.

Be that as it may, it must surely be reprehensible that, at the British level, one of the more pressing problems at the end of the twentieth century is still that of substituting for old oligarchic habits and their deferential presumptions, the mass-democratic values of advanced societies in which knowledge, initiative and responsibility are routinely demanded of millions of citizens. Such demands entail corresponding obligations for a country's constitution and its political institutions, a requirement that provides the impetus at the heart of the Parliament for Wales Campaign.

A basic democratic obligation is to enable and require citizens to make the most meaningful positive contribution possible towards their country's governance. It must be accepted that for a Britain accustomed to a long oligarchic tradition, such an objective is highly ambitious, not to say heroic. It is especially the case as the country's political institutions are wholly unsuited to that objective and, if left unreformed, will make its attainment virtually impossible.

In particular, the political party which, in a genuine parliamentary democracy, should form the impressionable interface between citizen and polity, in practice more closely resembles a stone boundary wall resisting democratic pressures from either side. This is precisely because the 'oligarchic yet adversarial' values are enshrined within it to an extraordinary degree. Furthermore, since for the most part they will be British political parties contesting seats in the Welsh Parliament, the objective of improving democracy in a Welsh context is equally forbidding.

Party exclusiveness and the unquestioning loyalty that a party expects of its members are prominent features of British politics reflecting these values. The political party in Britain is an essential instrument of parliamentary democracy. Yet the public at large, the people, are excluded from it. Whatever its ideology and background its mores are bound to be elitist and oligarchic. Thus, successive governments, according to their colour, have indulged their oligarchic instincts with penchants for benevolent paternalism, social engineering or market rigour. At the same time, the constant adversarial reflex, a useful safeguard against autarchy in the small closed society of a century and more ago, in its modern party manifestation is a source of divisiveness within society.

It is true, of course, that anyone can become a member of a political party, but that is to miss the point. Few people have the time, energy or disposition to pursue an active political career. The plain fact is that the only opportunity open to the majority of people to influence the character of a party is to take it or leave it at an election once every four or five years. In a complex industrial democracy that is too crude an opportunity to be of great value.

TYRANNY OF THE POLITICAL PARTY

In Britain, therefore, the political party, essential instrument of parliamentary democracy that it is, is paradoxically an obstacle to full scale democratisation. And as party is the citizen's one formal point of contact with the polity, albeit an uncertain one confined to the casting of an occasional and often ineffective vote, one can argue plausibly that party is the prime obstacle to democratic reform. It follows that the initial requirement of contemporary British politics is reform of the political party.

Astonishingly, however, the autonomous nature of party within the political system has never seriously been questioned. Party remains inviolate and beyond the reach of political and constitutional reformers. It has acquired an unchallenged institutional authority, setting it apart from the electorate. It has overriden democratic obligations except in the crudest — and ultimately anti-democratic — sense of occasionally appearing willing to bribe the electorate.

The instinctive commitment of politicians to the autonomous status of party as a political institution was demonstrated vividly during the short life of the Social Democratic Party (SDP) and its alliance with the Liberal Party. A shrewd leadership at the launch of the new party would have allowed for long-established institutional loyalties, misguided in the circumstances or not, within the rank and file membership of the Liberal Party. Such leadership would have presented the SDP as nominally the junior partner within the alliance, for example in terms of numbers of parliamentary candidates.

This in fact was the course advocated unavailingly by the Welsh section of the SDP — an interesting manifestation perhaps of at least the vestiges of a different cultural inheritance. The practical consequence for policy and political stance would have been little different but the enterprise almost certainly would have been electorally more successful. The surprising reality, however, was the espousal by some experienced SDP politicians of a fierce and far from spurious institutional loyalty to the fledgling party that evoked an ambiguous attitude to their Liberal allies. The ambiguity and atavistic institutionalism from self-proclaimed 'breakers of the mould of British politics' damaged public confidence in what initially had been seen as a promising new beginning in British politics.

TWO PROPOSITIONS

So dramatic an example underlines convincingly two theoretical propositions that are worth advancing at this point. They are first, that in a parliamentary system claiming to be a mass democracy, party exclusivity is a perversion; and second, that party loyalty taken to excess can be a blockage to reform. Each is proffered as a relative rather than an absolute rule but it appears that neither is yet accepted by most politicians.

A passage from Pandit Nehru's book *The Discovery of India* is of relevance to the argument here. 'The creative minority', says Nehru, 'is always small in number but if it is in tune with the majority and is always trying to pull the latter up and make it advance so that the gap between the two is lessened, a stable and progressive culture results. Without the creative minority a civilisation must inevitably decay, but it may also decay if the bond between a creative minority and the majority is broken, and there is loss of social unity as a whole, and ultimately the minority itself loses its creativeness and becomes barren and sterile'.[1]

In the realm of politics, if one likens the creative minority to the political party at its best, Nehru can be paraphrased in the following terms: in a stable and progressive society there are political parties and an electorate, and there is a gap between the two linked by a bond. If the gap becomes too small and the bond withers — or in other words, if parties become irresponsible and fail to inspire — society decays. On the other hand, if the gap becomes too large and the bond breaks — that is to say, if parties become exclusive and remote and again fail to inspire — society again decays, including the parties themselves.

SYMBIOSIS

On this reading a fruitful relationship between party and body-politic is a symbiotic one. In contemporary British politics, however, the symbiosis can scarcely be said to exist and there is a need to regenerate it. The task is made more urgent because of a significant change of electoral mood over recent years. Up to the end of the sixties the electorate clung to old habits, and was reasonably confident of its allegiances. Two distinct adversative parties shared the bulk of the votes at general elections, and a swing of a few percentage points produced a change of government in conformity with the so-called electoral cube law. The political and electoral processes continued to function under the momentum of 'our glorious past', and the electoral certainties including 'the swing of the pendulum' reflected corresponding convictions, or at least lack of misgiving, about Britain's place in the world.

Gradually, however, the convictions began to crumble in the minds of voters. Public opinion has at last become aware of the seriousness of Britain's decline. Many political and social problems stem from that awareness, as does the growing demand for constitutional reform. However, the political parties — the erstwhile creative minority — remain trapped in old habits and attitudes. It is now a platitude to say that they fail to inspire. Nor is it an exaggeration to say as a consequence that fifty years after World War II and loss of Empire, Britain has still to 'find a role'. The damaging political, social and economic outcome, and the deep public cynicism about politics and politicians, denote a country in serious difficulty. Nehru's prosaic 'loss of social unity' is manifest, and its ominous consequences for the future can hardly be overstated.

REFORM

Radical reform of British politics is urgently required, the prime objective being that of providing government at all levels with genuine democratic legitimacy. The establishment of a Welsh Parliament is, of course, a specific and major part of that reform. An even more specific reform, common to the Welsh and British context, is the introduction of a new parliamentary electoral system. This is the most immediate means towards developing a more democratic, less oligarchic and less adversarial parliamentary system at both levels. That is because in the first instance the political party — 'the primary obstacle to democratic reform' — must he made more accessible to the electorate. It must become less autonomous as an institution. The bond linking party to electorate has to be reforged to the right dimension otherwise Nehru's social decay will inevitably worsen. In practical terms the key to that change lies in reforming the electoral system — the one constitutional bond linking elector to polity, although at present a fragile and unsatisfactory one — so that party might once again gradually become a 'creative minority' symbiotically linked to its majority.

That is the principal justification for changing the electoral system. It is therefore important constantly to keep it in mind as the overwhelmingly significant criterion against which to choose a new system. Most electoral reformers, however, ignore that criterion for reasons outlined below. Indeed, in the context, many, if not most, of the usual criteria which are advanced from time to time in the electoral reform debate, even including proportional representation itself, lose much of their significance. It cannot be over-emphasised therefore, that the crucial requirement is for discretion and choice to be made available to the individual voter so that he or she can gain greater access to, and influence the character of the political party. The degree to which it is achieved will determine how successfully party becomes 'the impressionable interface' between electorate and polity, and provides the creative lead for a genuine democracy.

ELECTORAL SYSTEMS

Apart from the existing Simple Majority or first-past-the-post system, there are three broad types of electoral system which are generally acknowledged as being suitable for parliamentary elections:

* List Systems (LS).
* Additional Member Systems (AMS) which are a compound of list systems and the existing first-past-the-post system.
* The Single Transferable Vote System (STV).

All produce, when properly applied, a satisfactory degree of proportionality, that is the number of seats won by a party is broadly in proportion to the percentage it gets of the votes cast. Expert opinion on the merits of the different systems divides into two camps which reflect two points of view, that of the political party and its managers, and that of the electorate. Parties, in so far as they are prepared to accept electoral reform, for the most part favour LS or AMS type systems, while non-partisan bodies like the Electoral Reform Society favour STV. The difference between the two points of view is crucial since coming down on one side or the other will determine whether democratic input into the political system will be enhanced or not.

Unfortunately, public debate has been dominated until recently by the party point of view. A consequence has been to equate electoral reform uniquely with the introduction of *proportional representation for parties*. This limitation has done a major disservice to the wider cause of reform, even allowing for the importance of proportionality.

Reformers seem to have been unaware that there might be more to electoral reform than fair play for parties. Their myopia has influenced the language of the debate to the extent that the terms 'electoral reform' and 'proportional representation' have become synonymous in the public mind.

This error is compounded when, as so often in studies sponsored by the political parties themselves, the recommended choice of system is dependent on its ability to serve narrow party purposes. Some list systems, for example, have been favoured because they place control of the party ever more firmly in the grip of the party leadership, a possibility which is hardly conducive to reducing party exclusivity.

Furthermore, the error of equating electoral reform with proportional representation has led to a distortion in the application of criteria when making a choice of system. It is easy to devise a system resulting in a high degree of proportionality. The Israeli system, for example, in which the whole country is a single constituency, is an almost perfectly proportional one. However, it has many serious drawbacks, not least because it makes it possible to vote only for a party, with all the candidates for election being placed on lists drawn up in order by the parties themselves. In addition the system results in a multiplicity of minor parties and hence unstable government. Few reformers would want to introduce this system to Britain.

The tendency, therefore, has been to search for a system giving, like the Israeli's, a high degree of proportionality but without the obvious defects. The approach has been unremittingly negative. Each system is first checked for proportionality, and is then studied for its defects. A system is finally recommended or rejected according to the number and relative importance of these. Any contribution it might make to the polity beyond proportionality, especially its democratic input, which should be the point of the exercise, is ignored. This is despite the fact that a single such contribution might outweigh all the system's drawbacks.

It has become necessary, therefore, to emphasise the importance of choosing a system 'warts and all' against properly weighted criteria, and to base that choice on an assessment of the system's net positive contribution to the political culture, and not on the negative reasoning of choosing the system with the smallest number of defects.

That is why, in the context of British political culture with its lack of democratic content, proportionality, important though it is, is not the sole or even most important criterion. More important is the degree of opportunity provided by an electoral system for the individual voter to influence the character and political stance of a party, and hence ultimately the quality of his or her democracy.

THE SINGLE TRANSFERABLE VOTE

A practical way of enabling the electorate genuinely to influence the character and stance of a political party is through the choosing of its public representatives, in particular its members of parliament. An electoral system which enables a voter in his or her constituency to choose between two or more candidates of the same party, and to give weighted fractions of his or her vote to candidates of more than one party if so minded, enables influence to be brought on the character of the parties.

At a stroke exclusivity is ended and parties become inclusive of society. Individual voters gain access to the parties. A direct symbiotic relationship develops between the voter and the party with all the advantage that that entails.

This is the great virtue of the STV electoral system which, as it happens, is also a proportional system. It is doubly blessed so to speak. Constituencies under STV are multi-member, usually with four or five members each. So for example the City of Cardiff would form a constituency of four members while the County of Clwyd would have five. Continuing the example in the case of the County of Clwyd, each party at an election would adopt three or four candidates (no party is likely to receive 100 per cent of the vote so there would be no point in adopting five candidates) and voters would express their preferences for the candidates in numerical order simply by marking each name 1, or 2, or 3, and so on.

In British circumstances these two features provided by STV of cross-party voting and choice of candidates within a party — which can be summarised as Voter Discretion — represent a substantial increase of democratic input to the political system. Experience in the Irish Republic and elsewhere shows that the exercise of voter discretion tends over time to weaken party exclusiveness. This is the essential first step towards a more refined democracy than one in which the opportunity is periodically given to change the vivid colour of one government for the equally vivid but different colour of another.

STV puts political discretion into the hands of the voter in a way that is both powerful and mischievous. For instance, empowerment became more than just a popular epithet when STV was used in the mid-1980s for elections to the short-lived Northern Ireland Assembly. It was a joy to see voters choosing which of 'that lot' they wanted, and in which order. The political parties endeavoured to hold on to control by distributing mock ballot papers to 'help' the voters. Nevertheless, the shift of power from the vested interests of the parties to the individual voters once they entered the polling booths was almost tangible. The feeling that they were taking power to themselves, and so bringing about fundamental change, was clear.

Unfortunately, in that example vested party interests proved too strong for the empowerment to last. The Unionist parties withdrew co-operation and the elected Assembly was wound up. Even so STV is still used in local government elections in Northern Ireland, specifically because of its robustness in confronting party domination and manipulation. It is significant, for example, that following the 1989 district council elections no fewer than 11 of the 26 councils had Unionist chairmen and non-Unionist vice-chairmen or vice-versa. The failure of extremist candidates to gain election reflected the desires of the general public for moderation, and provides one of the few hopeful signs in Northern Ireland politics.

PRACTICALITIES

There are, of course, other criteria, of greater or lesser importance, which can be used for judging an electoral system. A not unimportant one, which might well have a practical bearing on establishing the multi-member constituencies of a Welsh Parliament, is that of the territorial connection between a member of parliament and his or her constituency. This connection, much trumpeted by supporters of the existing first-past-the-post system, stems from the admirable concept of the representation of communities as such. It has traditionally been a feature, grossly abused at times, of the Westminster Parliament. For example, the 'member for Denbigh' (the seat was disbanded in 1983 as it happens) reached back to the time when there was a 'member for Calais' in the same Parliament. In Denbigh's case the continuity extended even to the name of the member himself. Sir Watkyn Williams Wynn sat for the constituency for an unbroken period of over 300 years up to 1868.

The point, however, is a serious one. It is especially so for Wales where *brogarwch* (affection for locality) is a more significant phenomenon than it is in England. In Wales, as in Ireland and most other countries of continental Europe, there exists a highly developed sense of localism. Unlike much of continental Europe, Wales along with the rest of Britain, has been unable to develop a significant political role for that localism. It is no surprise that the Westminster description of 'a good constituency member' is applied to less distinguished members of parliament.

It is ironic, therefore, that STV, which greatly strengthens the link between members and their constituencies, should be criticised by supporters of the first-past-the-post system on the grounds that it weakens the accountability of the member to the constituency. For example, the report of the Labour Party's Working Group on electoral systems, chaired by Lord Plant, claimed explicitly that 'under STV in multi-member seats it is difficult for an MP to be accountable to the whole electorate if, say, the seat has five members.' [2]

One might be permitted to point out that associated with the concept of accountability is that of retribution. In articles in a recent issue of the journal *Representation* both a former Irish Taoiseach and a former Irish Minister for the Public Service complained of the ability of electors under STV to override party leaders and to punish or reward, as they saw fit, members of parliament of the same party in the same constituency.[3] The practical application of accountability can hardly be clearer, except of course that it is accountability to the electors rather than to the party bosses.

Another example of this kind of criticism comes from Ferdinand Mount's book *The British Constitution Now*. Mount puts his case as follows: 'In particular, it would, I think, be a bizarre way of increasing the independent-mindedness of members of parliament to break the constitutional link (with the constituency) which at present does give them a genuine (if vestigial) sense that their duty is to represent all the people of their constituency and not simply those who voted for the party. It is this sense that the member is 'returned' for Loamshire by a spontaneous act of the people of Loamshire which we surely wish to reinforce'.[4]

The parenthetic 'if vestigial' in this last quotation is an exquisitely delicate aside to be savoured while pondering in the harsh light of reality the genuineness of the member's representational function in the Westminster Parliament. Four-fifths of parliamentary constituencies constitute 'safe' seats. The member's loyalty in each — human nature being what it is — is to the party, or more especially to the constituency association or management committee. They selected him or her for the job and they can de-select. That may be why the habitual independent-mindedness of the overwhelming majority of members of Parliament is hardly a self-evident phenomenon. It is also one of the principal reasons for the exclusivity of the political party.

A less disingenuous criticism, and one rarely expressed in public by MPs, is that under STV all the MPs from the one multi-member constituency, including those of the same party, are obliged to compete with each other in serving their constituents. That is precisely why the professional politicians object to it. The voters are able to make contact with more than one constituency MP. At elections they can hold each of them individually to account as well as their respective parties. All this is not to the liking of most politicians apprenticed to their craft in the oligarchic British tradition. It is, in a word, too democratic a concept, and one for which they believe the public is not mature or responsible enough. The validity of the criticism depends, of course, on the validity or otherwise of the premise.

A further practical point arises both from STV's predisposition to strengthen localism and from the need in any case to strengthen local government. To ensure proportionality between parties it is important that the multi-member constituencies should have four or five members. If, after reorganisation, Welsh local government were composed of 25 unitary authorities, all of approximately the same size, then each authority would form a natural multi-member constituency of four members for a Welsh Parliament. This would result in a parliament of 100 members. The most compelling advantage of this arrangement would be the unequivocal democratic link established between local, community, and national government. Furthermore, such a connection between the Welsh national and local levels lends itself happily to an European Union in which 'subsidiarity' has become an increasingly important principle of government.

A final question arises of whether it would be advantageous for elections to the Welsh Parliament to coincide with local government elections? An immediate objection, stemming from existing British practice, is that under such an arrangement the electorate might be swayed by all-Wales considerations as against those of local concern, and vote for its local authorities accordingly. It is, of course, notorious that, at present, low turn-outs are a feature of local government elections and that, to an increasing extent, electors vote at those elections principally to register their views on central government.

Both traits confirm the oligarchic nature of the British polity. Indeed, one can argue that Britain has in fact never experienced local government, only local administration of central government. That is precisely one characteristic of the undemocratic culture and practice which have led to the creation of the Parliament for Wales Campaign. Whether or not one supports the argument for simultaneous elections — granted appropriate constitutional and institutional structures — depends ultimately, therefore, on one's faith in the Welsh people's aptitude for democracy and its responsibilities.

CITIZEN OR PARTY? THE KEY QUESTION

The electoral reform debate during the past twenty years has been a flawed debate. It has avoided the democratic question and has been notable for its lack of intellectual honesty. In his book *Citizens and Subjects* Dr Tony Wright M.P. argues convincingly that the institutions and political culture of the British State have never seriously concerned themselves with democratic values.[5]

That profound insight into the British condition is reflected by the manner in which participants in the electoral reform debate unwittingly assume inappropriate criteria for choosing a new electoral system. Three recent statements by eminent participants illustrate the point.

Firstly, Stuart Weir writing in the journal *Representation* argued that out of several possible electoral systems reformers should select 'realistic front-runners, without the distortions of . . . dogmatic belief'.[6] Secondly Lord Plant speaking at a symposium organised by the journal *New Statesman and Society* said that he had been depressed at the 'shoals of letters' he had received 'from people who would prefer first-past-the-post to any alternative other than their favoured system'.[7] And thirdly, Dr David Butler also writing in *Representation* pointedly claimed that as a young man he had been 'put off the idea of electoral reform' 'by the certainty with which supporters of STV held to their belief that it 'was the one and only way to elect a legislature'.[8]

All three reject what they regard as dogmatism because they believe that the choice of electoral system is bound to be a finely balanced one, made from a number of contending systems, each having advantages and disadvantages, but none having an overriding quality irresistibly justifying its right to be chosen.

Within a culture conditioned by the absolutism of British-style parliamentary sovereignty that attitude is understandable for the following reason. It arises from the belief that the key to improving the quality of parliamentary governance is fairness for the political parties, crucial parliamentary role players that they are. Hence the important characteristic of a new electoral system is that it should produce proportionality between parties. However, since many systems possess that characteristic, the debate inevitably revolves around their secondary characteristics. In those circumstances it would of course be foolish to be dogmatic; indeed a justifiable criticism of the general debate in any case is that too often too much trivia is allowed to obfuscate it.

Hence appeals for a balanced judgement and for an absence of dogma are not only to be expected but carry with them an aura of detachment and objectivity. Consequently, electoral reformers who unswervingly proclaim their devotion to a particular electoral system are open to the charge of dogmatism. The charge is sustained no matter how powerful the reasons for that devotion may be, and especially if they lie outside the prescribed parameters of the debate. And since the debate is dominated by the political parties, as might be expected given the British political culture, those parameters are not surprisingly confined to party interests which for the most part are directed towards maintaining the constitutional status quo.

It is worth noting this adroit example of an insidious constitutional incrementalism by which, over the years, as Dr Wright shows, the British State has purported to accommodate demands for democratic reform while all the time remaining intransigently undemocratic. The insidiousness is pervasive. It dominated the *New Statesman* Symposium for example. There the insidiousness was made translucent in the advice which Lord Holme was prepared to give his party leader on electoral systems. 'STV is the best system', he said, 'but the best should not be the enemy of the good'.[9]

Some reformers, however, appreciate that since the basic criterion for choosing an electoral system on the party lines outlined above, depends overwhelmingly on the interests of the parties, it is therefore a narrow and so unsound criterion. If, as they believe, the democratic deficit resulting from the ritual dance around the totem pole of parliamentary sovereignty is at the root of Britain's problems, then the issue at stake in the search for improved parliamentary governance becomes, above all else, the extension of democracy.

One notes that the assertion that democracy is the rock on which the people of Wales set their demand for an elected Parliament is augmented at the level of electoral principle. The democratic objective becomes not only the motivation for a Welsh Parliament but also the crucial criterion against which to measure the merits of electoral systems.

A key principle arises here. When 'democratic input' becomes the overwhelming criterion for an electoral system, a radically different situation arises in which the word 'dogmatic' is simply not applicable, at least in the above usage, for a splendidly practical reason. The reason is simply that only one of the potential electoral systems — STV — can claim to be able directly to introduce an increased democratic input to the political system. It does so by dramatically extending the range of options available to voters, enabling them to project their views much more pointedly through the ballot box. The effect of the refinement on the representativeness of the political parties, rendering them much more inclusive of society, is ultimately such as to justify describing the system as being different in kind from other systems.

It might then be argued, of course, that dogmatism can arise at a deeper level from a refusal to consider the respective merits, not of a score of electoral systems, but of the two alternative premises on which the whole argument can be based, namely democratic input or fair play for parties. It is necessary in that case, however, to appreciate that the difference between the two is not one of degree but of kind. If this were not so then the original charge of dogmatism by the three commentators might be well founded. Furthermore, this difference is extraordinarily important in Britain's idiosyncratic circumstances where, as has been pointed out, the political party fills the constitutional vacuum within which the state functions.

Fortunately the two premises are not mutually exclusive; it is possible to enjoy the merits of both by adopting the STV electoral system. That is why its supporters are devoted to it. It is worth recapitulating that when properly applied STV produces a satisfactory degree of proportionality for parties, and at the same time extends the discretion open to voters to such an extent that over a period they are able directly to influence the character of the political parties. This is a significant increase of democratic input providing some answer to *quis custodiet ipsos custodes.*

THE REAL DEBATE

The real debate therefore is whether an extension of democracy should be regarded as imperative. There are many people who believe that it should. The following passage by John Dunn, from his book *Democracy: The Unfinished Journey* speaks for an increasing number. He is in fact quoting contemporary feminism as a dramatic example of the democratic need. Precisely the same argument can be applied to Wales:

> We can hear it clearly in the words of the American feminist Catherine MacKinnon:
> 'My issue is what our identifications are, who our community is, to whom we are accountable. If it seems as if this is not very concrete, I think it is because we have no idea of what women as women would have to say. I'm evoking for women a role that we have yet to make, in the name of a voice that, unsilenced, might say something that has never been heard.'
> Its careful aesthetic resonance locates this firmly within the modern academy. But it carries the voice of democracy across the ages: the demand to speak for oneself, to be heard, and to make what is said effective in the texture of lives lived together. That voice has never gone unchallenged, and it has often been very thoroughly suppressed. But two and a half millennia after Kleisthenes it is clearer than it used to be just how hard it is to keep it suppressed. The democratic hope is that, for as long as there continue to be human beings, it will never again be silenced.[10]

The working group on electoral reform at the Llandrindod Democracy Conference unequivocally insisted that the Welsh Parliament should be a truly democratic one, and that to this end it should be elected by as democratically contributive a method as it is possible to implement. The group considered several electoral criteria, for example the six adopted by the Scottish Constitutional Convention. These were as follows:

(i) The system must be a proportional one;
(ii) it must help to produce a gender balance in the Parliament as well as fair ethnic representation;
(iii) it must preserve the link between the member and his/her constituency;
(iv) it must be simple to understand;
(v) it must ensure adequate representation of less populous areas;
(vi) it must be designed to place the greatest possible power in the hands of the electorate.

The working group concluded that, of these, the first and the sixth were the most important, and that especially the sixth was essential. Both, of course, point to the choice of STV as the most appropriate electoral system.

So, too, does the Scottish Convention's second criterion. The mechanics of STV make it especially appropriate in promoting a gender balance in a Parliament for Wales. The ability of the voter to number the candidates in order of perceived priority enables a choice to be made for all the women candidates standing, or for preference to be given to the available women candidates. This would be regardless of what the parties' attitudes to the selection of women candidates had been.

If, in a four-member seat it had been agreed that women should hold two seats and men two, then when two men had been elected the remaining votes to be counted would be transferred to women candidates; if two women candidates were first elected the remainder would be transferred to the men. In this way STV can be the vehicle for significant and desirable cultural changes, precisely because of its ability to reflect political views quite separately from party views.

Of course, this outlook is not held by everyone. There are people who believe that an extension of democracy is not imperative. They include some members of so-called democratic political parties —

for obvious reasons dare one say? They also include commentators who acknowledge, to their credit quite openly, Britain's traditional political culture. For example Ferdinand Mount writes as follows:

> One may call parliamentary government 'democratic' in the sense that its procedures maximise those satisfactions which politics can supply for as many people as possible; but, if it does so, it satisfies people very largely as consumers of government rather than as its producers; it is outcomes rather than inputs which are maximised; political participation will be accorded a lower priority than getting government off people's backs, happiness put before power as a desideratum.[11]

One dares, in the context of a campaign for a Welsh Parliament, to venture the opinion that Ferdinand Mount's view, as expressed here, is more an English than a Welsh sentiment. There is yet another group of commentators who see themselves as realists. They insist that a new electoral system, whether it enhances democracy or not, must be acceptable to Westminster MPs because it is they who will make the final decision. In other words a new system must be acceptable to the political parties. That is the most perfidious argument of all, not least because, in the context of Britain's democratic shortcomings, the so-called realism of its proponents is in fact a dogma serving the party-oriented, undemocratic nature of the British polity. Parliaments for Wales and Scotland, and Assemblies for the English regions, despite the resistance of Westminster, would in due course destroy that dogma and release energies held captive for too long. The process would be greatly helped if the right electoral system were chosen.

It is significant, however, that the Scottish Constitutional Convention, which is campaigning for a Scottish Parliament and which includes formal representation from the Labour and Liberal Democrat parties, has unfortunately already decided on an Additional Member System (AMS) for elections to that Parliament. Furthermore, the Welsh Labour Party has published a consultation paper in which it offers a choice of three types of electoral system, namely first-past-the-post, AMS and regional list systems.[12] The one system designed to increase democratic input into government, while at the same time allowing for proportionality between the parties — that is to say, STV — is notable by its absence. It is time vigorously to insist on our democratic rights and put the people first.

NOTES

[1] Pandit Nehru, *The Discovery of India* (London Meridian Books), 1946.

[2] *The Plant Report* (Labour Party) Vol. 3, p. 30.

[3] *Representation - Journal of Electoral Record and Comment*. (Available from The Arthur MacDougall Fund, 6 Chancel Street, London SE1 0UU) Vol. 30, p. 42 and 49.

[4] Ferdinand Mount, *The British Constitution Now* (Heinemann, 1992), p. 174.

[5] A. W. Wright, *Citizens and Subjects* (Routledge, 1994)

[6] *Representation* No 32, p. 20.

[7] Ibid. No 32, p. 19.

[8] Ibid. No 31, p. 77.

[9] Ibid. No 32, p. 77.

[10] John Dunn (Ed.) *Democracy: The Unfinished Journey* (Oxford University Press, 1992) p. 265.

[11] Ferdinand Mount, op. cit., p. 167.

[12] *Shaping the Vision: A Consultation Paper on the Powers and Structure of the Welsh Assembly*, Labour Party Wales, July 1994.

CHAPTER 7

DEFENDING THE HIGH GROUND OF DEMOCRACY
Local Government and a Welsh Parliament

Mari James

There are at least three fronts on which local government should be considered alongside the question of a Welsh Parliament. Local councils are the main democratic participants in a largely undemocratic system of government. There are a range of issues raised by the reorganisation of local government. Not least is the role of local government in the campaign for a Parliament for Wales.[1]

Since the repeal of the Wales Act 1978 there has been substantial devolution from Whitehall to the Welsh Office together with an increase in the number of unelected Non-Departmental Public Bodies — the NDPBs or Quangos. Together these have augmented a real and very influential all-Wales level of government.

In the devolution debates at the end of the 1970s, and in the 1979 referendum campaign, the main issue was giving an elected Assembly jurisdiction over the transfer of numerous functions of government from Whitehall to Wales. The introduction of the democratic element was regarded by the Yes Campaign in the referendum as the main strength of the proposals.

Yet transference of government functions from Whitehall to Wales does not by itself need legislation to be implemented. Thus since 1979, and despite the result of the referendum, there has been a more extensive transfer of functions than the Wales Act would have brought about.

A consequence has been to change the character of the Welsh system of government from that which applied in the 1970s. It was described at the time as 'Government by Consultation', a product of informality and close working relationships between the Welsh Office and local authorities.[2] In its place, during the 1980s, developed instead a system of government by consultation and networking between the Welsh Office and the Quangos.

THE LOCAL DEMOCRATIC DEFICIT

This burgeoning Welsh state apparatus produced by the mid-1990s a system whose only common thread was its lack of a mechanism for democratic accountability. Compounding that position the government introduced legislation to reorganise local government in Wales, essentially by abolishing one tier, the counties. Other government institutions in Wales are also undergoing reorganisation, but without the same glare of public attention.

The new local councils being created by the Local Government (Wales) Act 1994 are being termed Unitary Authorities. This is a misnomer, however. Within the formal local authority system, even when the counties are removed, there is a lower level of Community and Town councils which exist throughout much of Gwynedd, Powys and Dyfed and are increasing in Clwyd, Gwent and Glamorgan. The existence of these truly local councils make the remaining tier more accurately described as most-purpose rather than unitary. Furthermore, there are now a whole range of government functions carried out below the all-Wales level by bodies other than elected local councils. All these should correctly be considered as part of the local government system now operating in Wales.

Many of these unelected bodies are responsible for functions previously handled by elected councils, functions over which the councils have some duty of care and oversight. They represent areas of responsibility that could logically be included in a future democratic local government structure. Hence, the total local government system in Wales now includes, alongside the elected councils, the following:

- health authorities
- local hospital trusts
- water companies
- Governing Bodies of Further Education Colleges
- Governing Bodies of Grant Maintained Schools
- Boards of Training and Enterprise Councils (TECs)
- Urban Development Corporation (in part of Cardiff)
- Regional Arts Associations (now formally part of the Arts Council of Wales)
- National Parks
- economic Joint Venture Initiatives
- Housing Associations.

In addition to such bodies that have specifically local responsibilities, some of the all-Wales Quangos also exercise their functions at local level. The decentralisation of the Welsh Development Agency is likely to enhance its interaction with local councils. If councils do not welcome its overtures, the WDA will interact with companies at a local level in a way that currently only happens in areas specifically targeted for regeneration in south Wales.

The deficit in this unelected part of the local democratic system remains its lack of legitimate accountability. The Welsh Unit for Local Government at the University of Glamorgan has identified four principles by which the democratic content of a system can be measured. [3] These are:

- The extent of public representation in decision-making through the electoral process.
- The opportunity for direct public participation in policy-making.
- The capacity of local authorities for responsiveness to public demands.
- The dispersal of political power within and across areas.

This is a damning checklist of the democratic deficit in Welsh local government when applied to the organisations listed above. On the first principle of public representation through the electoral process, all the bodies fail.

On the second principle — opportunities for direct participation in policy-making — the non-elected organisations might argue that they have people participating in their governing bodies and boards who would not be there if open election was the only route for involvement. Equally some organisations, such as TECs and Grant Maintained Schools, might argue that they are trying to develop mechanisms for wider participation in their policy-making. Certainly, it is the case that meeting the first criterion does not guarantee an organisation will meet the second. In some local councils in Wales there is only limited opportunity for any real public participation in policy-making. [4]

The third criterion, responsiveness to public demands, is equally elusive on anything resembling a frequent basis in any of the local organisations, elected or otherwise. Elected organisations have an in-built responsiveness in the electoral process itself. Policies are adopted and implemented in response to public demand as expressed in the ballot box or, at least, to the perception of that demand. Elected politicians are 'held to account' by the electorate every few years. This certainly prevents councils straying too wide off the mark of local opinion, since fewer votes and thus lack of position will result for councillors.

The danger in some parts of south Wales, however, is that one party has come to dominate local elections to such an extent that this responsiveness to public demands has been blunted. If a party is sure of continued election year in, year out, there is a danger of it becoming complacent and thinking its repeated election is evidence of complete support for all its works in every shape and form. In such circumstances there can be other indicators of public dissatisfaction and so of inadequate response mechanisms. Reduced participation in elections is one such indicator, as is reduced membership of the political party in question and support for other non-party causes such as pressure groups, whether they be to save the planet or a local school.

It may be anathema for many people in the public sector to admit, but the other organisations with effective mechanisms for responsiveness to public demands are private companies. Whether their 'public' is defined as shareholders or customers, the demands of these 'publics' can have an immediate impact on the behaviour of a company.

Unfortunately, however, this is not one of the facets of the private sector that has been transferred into the public sector in the various moves that were initiated in the 1980s to bring the best of the two sectors together. The TECs, for instance, were set up as private companies. Yet they receive nearly 100 per cent of their income from government grants. They experience no impact from customer satisfaction with their products, nor competition from other suppliers, nor support or rejection from shareholders, either individual or institutional. If there is anyone to whom the TEC companies are responsive in the conduct of their business and delivery of services it is not their customers, or the local electorate, but rather the central civil servants and politicians who control their annual grants. Thus, rather than enhancing any responsiveness to the public, the introduction of private companies into this arena of local government has served to reduce its democratic element still further.

The least responsive form of organisation is one in the public sector that has its income guaranteed, or at least does not have to earn it by the sale of goods or services, and is not elected and so has no formal contact with a public testing ground. There is little, short of fundamental change in central government, to prevent such organisations carrying on for years pursuing policies they have generated internally and for which they have never had to seek any mandate. Their policies may become increasingly out-of-date and irrelevant but the juggernaut will trundle on obeying its own rules. This recalls a classic Weberian definition of bureaucracy more than any definition of democracy.

The fourth criterion for assessing the democratic content of a system is the dispersal of power within and across a geographical area. Again it is the case that elected status does not necessarily carry with it compliance. There are an increasing number of initiatives of decentralisation within local councils in England, but few examples yet of any such good practice in Wales. The existence of Community and Town councils within a local authority's area can militate towards the dispersal of power, yet how effective this is in practice depends on the vigilance of the Community Councils themselves.

The debate around the decentralisation of power from Whitehall to Wales has often floundered on this problem of centralisation of power within Wales rather than its dispersal further downwards. Decentralisation is an instructive tool for considering the degree of democracy that is involved in both the elected and non-elected aspects of local government in Wales. It shows that lack of elected status goes hand-in-hand with a shortage of the other democratic criteria.

Equally, elected status alone is not sufficient to guarantee observance of the other democratic criteria. Local councils and other local organisations which aspire to serve their populations could do a lot worse than treat these four criteria as the basis of a democracy audit of their practices to monitor their performance as effective, open, democratic and participatory organisations.

A CLASH OF STANDARDS AND STATUS

Many councillors and council officials have experienced instances of local Quangos which have handled public money in a way that, had it occurred in their council, would have made them eligible for surcharge by the district auditor. Different standards concerning probity in the management of public money and service delivery apply to elected and non-elected local government. It is overwhelmingly the view of councillors who serve on both elected bodies and the Quangos that the more stringent standards generally apply to the elected bodies.

Of course, a balance has to be struck between efficiency and professionalism on the one hand, and democracy and accountability on the other. Quangos are often able to act with a speed unavailable to councils which have timetables dictated by committee schedules and preparation of reports. Most councillors, however, would judge that they should improve their efficiency by better management rather than curtail their democratic practices of accountability. They would argue that it is the Quangos that should change with, as a minimum, putting in place the same criteria for accountability for public money as set down by statute for local councils.

This clash of standards came into public view during 1994 when the member of the Quango, Health Promotion Wales, who brought the failures of its accounting procedures into the open was also a local authority officer: David Griffiths, Gwent County Council's Director of Education.

More insidiously, however, the growth and elaboration of the network of Quangos across Wales has led to a shift in perceived status of their members as compared with local elected councillors. It is almost as if the appointment by the Secretary of State for Wales of a member to a local unelected board conveys with it some of the pomp and grandeur of central government. This is seen by some as a stark contrast with the grubbiness of the electoral process.

The feeling that local councils have developed a second-class status in the government of Wales compared with unelected local bodies is widespread. At a public meeting on the Quango system held during the National Eisteddfod in Glynneath in 1994, attention was drawn to the position of public housing in Dwyfor. The local Housing Association in the area was being funded by the national Quango, Tai Cymru-Housing for Wales, to build new houses in large estates. This was not in accord with the planning policy of Dwyfor District Council which was giving priority to developing smaller packages of land with clusters of new housing and refurbishing below-standard older housing. In accordance with these policies the Council refused planning permission to the Housing Association. As a result, however, the Council was being severely criticised and held up as obstructing money coming into the area. The elected council was coming under pressure to change its policies and bring them into line with those of an unelected Quango.

The dual system of elected and unelected bodies operating at local level, of the kind illustrated here, is inimical to an open and democratic system of government. It undermines the normally accepted values of civic society and does not promote public participation.

In terms of efficiency it is also counter-productive to have bodies responsible for public money which are not bound by conventions built up over many years to ensure transparency of decision-making and reduce the likelihood of corruption. The handful of instances that have come to light of failures in accounting, profligate spending, and ineffective central monitoring should be understood as inevitable illustrations of the local Quango system, rather than the occasional personal slip-ups that they are sometimes depicted as being.

Within such an imperfect public sector, elected local councils in Wales occupy the moral high ground in a largely undemocratic system. It remains the case, however, that whichever way it is measured, the spending of elected local government and unelected sector government through the Quangos is currently almost exactly equal.

This position will become worse. The democratic deficit is due to increase. While Quangos multiply, the erosion of the functions and responsibilities of elected local councils continues apace. Consideration of just one area, education, makes the point. Post-16 education has already been hived off into locally incorporated but centrally-funded colleges. In the mandatory period of education, for 5 to 16 year-olds, local authorities increasingly have an enabling, rather than a direct administrative and co-ordinating role over locally-managed schools.

And, as we have seen, new legislation is removing a whole tier of local government or, as the Conservative's Welsh representative on the European Union's Committee of the Regions, Cllr. Lord Kenyon, put it in the debate in the House of Lords, a 'layer of democracy'. He actually said:

> I do not believe that it is an exaggeration to claim that at the grass roots the political parties in Wales largely support the establishment of unitary

authorities, although I recognise that for some this is within the context of an elected Welsh Assembly or Parliament. That of course I do not support. To me, that is just introducing yet another layer of democracy, which we were trying to remove. [5]

We have also seen, however, that the very fact that an authority is elected does not guarantee accountability, scrutiny, or openness of decision-making. Several have recently been questioned by a number of Ombudsman judgements critical of their decisions and decision-making processes.

Yet, while undoubtedly there have been occasions when elected local government has fallen short of required standards, how much more is this likely to be case in the unelected sector where the same standards are not enforced? Shortcomings should not be used as an excuse to heap public criticism on the elected bodies and at the same time give increased funding and reduced red tape to the unelected bodies. Rather, we should build on the values of a participatory democracy that still exist, restore functions to elected bodies, and introduce elected bodies where they do not yet exist.

Local government is not just a matter of geographical boundaries, but also of functions and most important of all, a matter of democratic culture. In its much publicised criticisms of Welsh Quangos the House of Commons Public Accounts Committee has concentrated on trying to return the public bodies to the basic standards of proper conduct established a century ago in the Northcote and Trevelyan reports on the Civil Service.

That was a period of cleansing the civil service of the nepotism and corruption that had become rife. It was also a period of extensive political reform in all levels and sections of civic life in Wales. The expansion of local democracy went hand-in-hand with the establishment of high standards of governance and public service.

The size and illegitimacy of Wales's Quangoland has been extensively documented.[6] It is not, however, just in the big scandals involving the bosses of the all-Wales Quangos that these standards are slipping. They are falling as well in the everyday, local infringements of public behaviour in the unelected sector of local government. Only when these functions are absorbed by elected local government will the behaviour be brought under effective democratic control.

Local politicians are increasingly exercising their democratic obligation to 'blow the whistle' on such practices. The frustration for these people who are willing to speak out is that having blown the whistle on specific cases, the iniquities in the overall system continue.

THE REORGANISATION OF LOCAL GOVERNMENT

One effect of the Local Government (Wales) Act 1994 has been to promote the case for a Welsh Parliament and to bring about some of the conditions that are required for a new political settlement.

The passage of the Bill threw a spotlight on the lack of responsiveness of Welsh central government. As with the proposed local government changes in England, much of the opposition to the Bill in Wales was not against the so-called unitary structure being introduced. Rather it was against some particularly inept gerrymandering of boundaries. This led to a revolt even amongst Conservative backbenchers, most notably the Brecon and Radnor MP Jonathan Evans.

To accommodate the pressure in England, a Local Government Boundary Commission was set up. Such a move has the advantage to central politicians that it keeps them at arms length from unpopular decisions. It also affords them the opportunity to overturn recommendations of the Commission that may prove too unpopular with the troops in what used to be the Tory shires until the 1994 English county elections. Not only that, the process ensured that any firm decisions could be postponed until after those elections. The Commission also allowed for different treatment of different areas of England.

All this is the stuff of the normal checks and balances of a pluralist political system that, throughout the ages, politicians and democratic philosophers have found effective in preventing authoritarian rule. It was not, however, the process that was used in the consultation process in Wales. Yet there was nothing intrinsically different about the local government structure in England to make a Boundary Commission appropriate for one and not the other.

It is hard not to draw the conclusion that so far as Wales is concerned the Government, by refusing to allow a Commission, stopped even trying to maintain a facade of democracy. This could be because democracy does not give the Government the answers it wants to hear in Wales. For if an objective Commission had been part of the process it would have been impossible for it not to have considered, if not recommended, that some sort of all-Wales elected tier should accompany local government 'reform'.

All authoritative voices of local government in Wales are united, at least on this point. The Assembly of Welsh Counties has called for 'a Welsh Regional Council to be created as soon as possible . . . responsible for all the executive functions of the Welsh Office and some executive functions of the Home Office and Department of the Environment.' The Council of Welsh Districts 'supports the establishment of an elected Welsh Assembly . . . (believing) that the policies of the Welsh Office would be more responsive to the needs of Wales if they were debated and determined by a Welsh Assembly.' The Welsh Association of Community and Town Councils have also insisted on the establishment of a Welsh Senate to assume responsibility for all Welsh Office functions and to be a strong voice for Wales in the European Union.

MAINTAINING THE MORAL HIGH GROUND

Although Welsh local councils would not have started from the Local Government (Wales) Act 1994, they can still use some of the provisions being enforced upon them. Many of those involved in local councils are feeling exhausted and battleworn. They have had a lot thrown at them since the implementation of the 1980 Local Government, Planning and Land Act. They have had to accept a fundamental change from being involved in real government of local affairs with significant revenue raising powers, to operating a limited administration of drastically reduced functions with mere grant distribution powers. The effect has been to turn local government from having any pretension of autonomy to being merely a matter of local administration of central government. Many may not consider it worth bothering to attempt being elected to the 22 new authorities that take over from 1996.

Nevertheless, it is crucially important that when the new councils are established they begin with provisions for openness and access, for public consultation, clear accountability and efficient scrutiny. Their policies and practices of democratic decision-making must be of the highest standards. When the democratic deficit grows, it makes the responsibility on those remaining in democratic positions even greater. The moral high ground has not yet been captured from elected Welsh local authorities. They should not be willing to surrender it.

The opportunity for establishing a new order of local democracy has been recognised by Labour's Spokesman for Wales, Ron Davies. Speaking to an all-Wales Local Government conference in Cardiff in early 1994, he said:

> The new authorities can demonstrate their own commitment to the highest principles and thereby ensure that they gain both the confidence of their own communities and, by demonstrating their own integrity and competence, gain for themselves a secure and expanding future . . . Councillors, be they majority, minority, or no party have a constitutional role to play in representing their own electors and in playing a full part in the corporate decision-making process of the council . . . If politicians seek to govern by secret meetings, stifled debate, or rigid caucus they will serve neither the interests of local government nor much beyond the shortest term, their own. If the judgements made are sound the decision-makers will have nothing to fear from public scrutiny. When decisions are taken they are on behalf of all the community and must be exposed to the full light of public debate. Finance or policy, budget or expenditure, management or programme must all be, in the Euro-jargon, subject to transparency. That will be good for democracy, and good for the political parties with the integrity and confidence to take those decisions. Above all it will be good for local government, and I hope that's the route we will follow in Wales. [7]

LOCAL GOVERNMENT AND THE CREATION OF A WELSH PARLIAMENT

The provisions of the 1994 Act will affect strategic functions such as economic development and transport and will give the new councils some scope for developing innovative means of service delivery. Plans are being made in some areas for joint bodies to deliver functions previously administered by national Quangos. The prime example is in the area of economic development where the reorganisation and lack of clarity in policy direction of the Welsh Development Agency and Development Board for Rural Wales has encouraged the local councils to develop their own policies for economic and industrial development.

There can be good and less favourable results from this process when seen in the context of the future establishment of a Welsh Parliament. The benefits will be in the innovations undertaken in service delivery and structure of government. The new authorities will not only be organising their own existing strategic functions, but also operating in liaison with other local bodies such as health authorities.

That such experimentation is being undertaken in a period leading to the establishment of a Welsh Parliament can only be of assistance to the process of determining the optimum system of local government below the Parliament. Those involved, however, must beware of the trap offered by the current legislation of enabling local councils to set up bodies without direct paths of accountability to the electorate. Joint bodies between councils need to have specific mechanisms for openness of decision-making, accountability and for scrutiny.

Local councils also have an important role in the establishment of a Welsh Parliament in maintaining their moral high ground of democracy, and fostering and promoting a democratic culture. That moral high ground should only be relinquished to a democratically elected Welsh Parliament in a partnership where powers and functions are shared in an effective and imaginative way.

There are fears that the democratisation of the all-Wales tier of government is somehow inevitably synonymous with centralisation within Wales. For instance, researchers at the University of Glamorgan's Welsh Unit for Local Government have observed:

> Greater responsiveness to public demands might be achieved if the Welsh Office were to be democratically accountable through a Welsh Assembly. However, this argument overlooks the threat that a Welsh Assembly might pose to local democracy. The establishment of an Assembly might devolve power from London to Wales; but if the Assembly takes over responsibilities from local authorities then it will also centralise power within Wales. This would be a difficult balance to strike. The choice, if it ever arises, would test the commitment of the Welsh people to genuine decentralisation. [8]

This analysis fails to recognise the overwhelming democratic deficit that exists at the all-Wales level, quite apart from the arguments in favour of democratic decentralisation at the Regional level within the European Union. These provide the essential context for ensuring and promoting local democracy. Both make the case for an all-Wales Parliament. The keyword is subsidiarity. Functions are best carried out at the lowest possible levels of government closest to the people. A Welsh Parliament set up within that European context, but in the teeth of Whitehall centralism, is hardly likely to deny subsidiarity so far as local government within Wales is concerned.

The principle of subsidiarity should be applied not only to elected local government but also to non-elected local government as well. Only the establishment of a Welsh Parliament will enable this to be achieved. In the same way as the boards of national Quangos should be replaced by specialist committees made up of elected members of the Parliament, scrutinising the relevant departments of the Welsh government machine, so local Quango boards should be replaced with elected local councils. This is the only practical way for their functions to be incorporated, and in many cases returned, to local elected control. There are no known plans to transfer functions from local councils to a Welsh Parliament, as the University of Glamorgan researchers suggest. The only reference to such a possibility was made by the anti-Assembly campaigners in the 1979 referendum.

There are proposals for elected local councils to have their powers entrenched in a new constitutional settlement. For instance, Labour's spokesman Ron Davies has said:

> We must break up and devolve the centralist state that the UK has now become, and an essential part of that is that local authorities must be set free from the constraints imposed by central government. Local government must be made constitutionally independent of the executive and within that context local government now needs to state its vision and to reclaim the powers accrued by the executive. The proper objective of all political parties now should be to ensure that duly elected local authorities are guaranteed their independence beyond the reach of even a Labour government. [9]

To entrench such powers is not strictly possible within the context of the unwritten British constitution. It would be more workable, however, if the United Kingdom signed the European Declaration of Local Self-Government. This is another example that shows that the European rather than the Westminster model is more appropriate for seeking good practice for decentralised democracy.

THE RELATIONSHIP BETWEEN WELSH CENTRAL AND LOCAL GOVERNMENT

It has been recognised that with the establishment of a Parliament an opportunity would be lost if there was not an integration between the local authority and the Welsh central administration. Article 9 of the Llandrindod *Democracy Declaration* states:

> Public and civil servants working for all tiers of government in Wales will belong to an integrated Welsh Public Service responsible to the Welsh Parliament.

It may well be that a seamless web of a Welsh public service will take time to develop. Nevertheless, what is needed is a structure within which individuals can transfer between parts of the service, whether in central government, local councils or any other publicly-funded bodies in a way that is as trouble-free as possible. This is important for career development as well as for more mundane aspects such as pension rights. This policy is important to ensure the best use of the cumulative skills and experience for the various levels of Welsh government.

Again, and contrary to the perspective offered by the University of Glamorgan researchers, the policy can only enhance the status of the officials working for Welsh local government in the context of a Welsh Parliament. The complex development of the public sector in Wales in the last decade has resulted in public servants currently being employed by central government, national Quangos, private companies, individual schools and colleges, local Quangos, hospital trusts, elected councils and other organisations with no formal links between them. Good government is not well served by such a plethora of public servants. Neither is there much evidence of the much vaunted economies of scale.

One important way of ensuring that the structure and functions of government below the all-Wales level are as decentralised and democratic as possible is to involve the councils themselves in their evolution. A clause the Liberals had inserted into the Wales Act 1978 as part of the Lib-Lab Pact of the time, was one imposing on the Assembly the obligation to set up a review of local government in Wales in liaison with the existing local authorities with a view to recommending reforms. There is equal need for a similar provision in the establishment of a Welsh Parliament in the 1990s.

One of the first tasks of the new Parliament will be to develop a new system of local government to restore accountability to all local government functions, whether they currently come within the remit of the elected or non-elected spheres. Moreover, there is no need to create a system that is uniform throughout Wales. The regions of Wales, very broadly described by the present county areas, have been likened by Ioan Bowen Rees, former chief executive of Gwynedd county council, to cantonal areas. They all have different requirements in fulfilling the effective and accountable delivery of public services.[10]

A HISTORY OF EVOLUTIONARY CHANGE

It is sometimes assumed that constitutional change is only effective when it happens in one integrated piece of legislation. History and experience show us that this is rarely the case and that effective constitutional change is more likely to be an evolving process over a period of time. In Wales a century ago series of profound political and social changes that were taking place in parallel to the equally profound economic 'renaissance' of the booming new coal and iron industries. Amongst the relevant and formidable statutes and *de jure* advances of the period were the following:

1867 Suffrage Act
(Together with the 1884 Act this enfranchised the wage earners and peasantry of Wales)
1870 (and 1891) Education Acts
(Established free primary schools throughout Wales)
1880 Creation of the National Eisteddfod Association
1880 Welsh Parliamentary Party formed
1881 Welsh Sunday Closing Act
(First distinctively Welsh piece of legislation)
1881 Welsh Temperance Act
1881 Welsh Rugby Union established
1883-4 Creation of the University Colleges at Cardiff and Bangor

1883 Committee of Investigation into Local Government set up by Gladstone
(This was the forerunner of the County and Parish Councils legislation)
1883 Corrupt Practices Act
('Helped Wales send men born and bred among the people to Parliament')
1888 Local Government Act
(Established County Councils)
1889 Welsh Intermediate Education Act
1893 Incorporation of the University of Wales
1894 Local Government Act
(Established parish councils)

The excitement engendered by these changes is evident in the numerous speeches, newspaper articles and writings of the time which are still widely available. A whole new group of people became involved in Welsh political and civic life, most prominently David Lloyd George, T. E. Ellis and Sam Evans. All were products of a series of reforms without which they would have still been excluded from the political and increasingly democratic processes in Wales. With hindsight we can see a logical and inevitable pattern being put together. At the time, however, each step of the way had to be fought for and there were footsteps backward as well as forward.

The ultimate achievement of political 'freedom' for the people of Wales was seen as freeing the majority nonconformist population from the shackles of the minority Church of England with its established, privileged positions on the local Quangos of the time. The opposition to the Church's position was not least in the area of taxation, where the tithes were compulsory for all to pay and yet were only used for services provided by the Church such as Church schools.

It was argued by the forces of conservatism that the proposed new civic authorities would have an irresponsible attitude towards collection and distribution of taxes. Despite the avowed support of the Liberal Governments under both Gladstone and Roseberry at Westminster, there were three abortive attempts at legislation to achieve Welsh Disestablishment before the implementation of the successful Act in 1920.

While parallels between the constitutional changes taking place towards the end of the nineteenth century and those in progress and anticipated at the end of the twentieth are of interest, they should not be taken too far. Nonetheless, it is heartening, to a degree, to realise the amount of time taken to achieve reform and the many pitfalls on the way. At the very least, it puts into some perspective the 1979 Referendum result and the repeal of the 1978 Wales Act.

THE CAMPAIGN FOR A DEMOCRATIC CULTURE

In a political society where democracy is reduced but where public services are still provided, it is too easy for the populace to overlook the lack of democratic accountability. It can become an issue only for the commentators and political activists. It is the task of those involved in democratic local government in Wales to ensure that this complacency is not allowed to take hold. Parish Councils, today's Community and Town Councils, celebrated their centenary in 1994. The Parish Councils Act of 1894 was described by T.E. Ellis in the following terms:

> The Local Government Act of 1888 transferred the government of the counties of Wales from the plutocracy to the people. The still greater Act of 1894 creates local democratic assemblies, parochial and municipal, with large powers throughout the length and breadth of Wales. [12]

The Community and Town Councils that have joined the Parliament for Wales Campaign in such large numbers are the successors of those 'local democratic assemblies' and as such are well placed to give a lead. Through their right to consultation these most local of councils can exert pressure on higher levels to ensure participation and the generation of a democratic culture.

It is not the purpose of this chapter to prescribe the structure, boundaries or functions of any new system of local government for Wales under a Welsh Parliament. That is the job of an elected Welsh Parliament with the active participation of the elected local councillors of Wales. It is sometimes argued that a new system of local government cannot wait the establishment of a Parliament since some system has to be in place for the Parliament to operate. This is no more true than it is of the precise structure of the Parliament itself.

A two-stage process is becoming increasingly accepted. An

elected Parliament can be established which has one of its main initial responsibilities the review and reform of local government, with the specific remit of bringing the unelected sectors of the current local government system under the control of elected councils.

The various arms of local government are well-used to burying their day-to-day and party political differences in the cause of the maintenance and promotion of local democracy. This tradition needs to be deployed in the crucial preparation phase of the establishment of a Welsh Parliament. Only when that is achieved can local government rest content with everyday political wrangles and the moral high ground of Welsh democracy with a Parliament for Wales.

NOTES

[1] This chapter is based on a paper presented by the author to the local government workshop of the Llandrindod Democracy Conference, on the issues which emerged at the workshop and subsequent consideration of those issues. Particular acknowledgement is due to Cllr. Janet Davies, leader of Taff-Ely Borough Council, who acted as both Chair and Rapporteur of the workshop session and has assisted with helpful comments on the preparation of this chapter.

[2] P. J. Madgwick and Mari James, *The Network of Consultative Government in Wales*, Gower, 1980; and *Government by Consultation: the Case of Wales*, Centre for the Study of Public Policy, University of Strathclyde, 1979.

[3] George A. Boyne, Paul Griffiths, Alan Lawton and Jennifer Law, *Local Government in Wales: Its Role and Functions*, Joseph Rowntree Foundation, 1991.

[4] For instance, the Widdicombe report on *The Conduct of Local Authority Business* (Cmnd. 9797, HMSO, 1986) found that 54 per cent of Welsh councillors were over 60, compared with 20 per cent in England; 95 per cent were male compared with 80 per cent in England; and 50 per cent had a manual working background compared with 30 per cent in England.

[5] *Hansard,* 14 December 1993, Vol 55, No 15, col. 1296.

[6] See, for example, Kevin Morgan and Ellis Roberts, *The Democratic Deficit: A Guide to Quangoland*, Department of City and Regional Planning, University of Wales, Cardiff, 1993.

[7] Ron Davies MP, *Strengthening Local Democracy*, paper given to a Conference on 'The New Unitary Authorities', University College of Wales, Cardiff, 19 January 1994.

[8] George A. Boyne et al.p. 69, op. cit., note 3.

[9] Ron Davies MP, op. cit., note 7.

[10] Ioan Bowen Rees, *Government By Community*, Charles Knight, London, 1971, p. 228-230.

[11] Kenneth O. Morgan, *Rebirth of a Nation: Wales 1880-1980* (University of Wales/Oxford University Press, 1982).

[12] T. E. Ellis, 'Wales and the Local Government Act 1894', speech made on 22 November 1894 and re-printed in *Speeches and Addresses by the late Thomas E. Ellis (*Hughes and Son, 1912*).*

CHAPTER 8

INCLUDE US IN
Women and a Welsh Parliament

Siân Edwards

The establishment of a Parliament for Wales offers us the chance to create, from the start, an institution that will eliminate the barriers to women's participation in decision-making. Women are grossly under-represented in both the Westminster Parliament and in local government. A Parliament for Wales, with a fairer gender balance in its membership, would be a great step towards achieving democratic government in Wales.

There is not a democracy in the world in which women are fully represented in the decision-making processes or adequately able to participate. There are, however, examples of countries where positive action programmes have significantly increased participation in legislative bodies. Within the European Union work is underway to create a better balance between women and men in politics, via the European Union Network on Women in Decision Making.

A number of countries have been taking steps to increase the representation of women in their Parliaments. In Italy a compulsory quota of a minimum one third of candidates of each sex must be on every local election list, representing 25 per cent of seats in Parliament. In Belgium, the ruling party have adopted a positive action programme, including reserving one third of places on the electoral lists for the communes (local councils) for women. Momentum in Europe has built up around a campaign to 'Vote for a Balance of Women and Men' in European elections. A declaration adopted by the European summit on 'Women and Power', in Athens in 1992, has been taken up by a number of political parties. It states that:

* Formal and informal equality between women and men is a fundamental human right.
* Women constitute more than half the population; equality

requires gender balance in the representative and administrative apparatus (organs/agencies) of Nations.
* Women represent half the potential talent and skills of humanity and their under-representation in decision making is a loss for society as a whole.
* The under-representation of women in decision-making prevents full account being taken of the interests and needs of the population as a whole.
* A balanced participation of women and men in decision-making would produce different ideas, values and styles of behaviour suited to a fairer and more balanced world for all, both women and men.

These five principles provide the basis on which to build practical progress in equal representation for women. It is instructive that the world's newest democracy is beginning to build these principles into its operational practices. The African National Congress required that at least one third of candidates for the first multi-racial elections in South Africa should be women.

WOMEN IN THE WELSH IMAGINATION

In Wales the image of women has always been ambivalent. On the one hand traditional social patterns are strongly matriarchal, while on the other the role afforded women in public and civic life is minimal. The image of the Welsh *MAM* has been transferred occasionally into radical protest roles as with Jemima Nicholas, who supposedly fought off the last invasion of Britain at Fishguard in 1797, and Rebecca whose effigy led the anti-tollgate riots in west Wales in the 1840s. These images, however, concern defence of the homeland and of the basic values and lifestyle of the Welsh home and hearth. They reinforce rather than challenge the idea that woman should only have a domestic and family status.

The Laws of Women in indigenous mediaeval Welsh law, as codified by Hywel Dda, also recognised a woman's role in society solely in terms of her position in a family, or more specifically, in marriage. The much vaunted special status of a woman of property with rights equal to men only became valid after seven years of recognised marriage.

So also, the right to inherit land and property through the female rather than the male line was only applicable in certain special circumstances. These were where there was no recognised legitimate heir but an offspring of a woman from other than a recognised marriage. This later right stemmed less from acknowledgement of the woman's position and more from the different interpretations of marriage and of legitimacy of children in Welsh Law as opposed to that in the encroaching ecclesiastical law. In Welsh medieval law, 'No one is a bastard through their mother.' [1]

Such traditional images of women are still prevalent in Wales but are increasingly at odds with the reality of life for today's Welsh women. According to Jane Aaron and Teresa Rees the identity of women in contemporary Wales is in a state of transition:

> The turmoil of the nineteenth century seems to have left Welsh women with only two lasting — indeed, painfully persistent — images of themselves: the Welsh-costumed figure in her tall black hat and shawl, smiling for the tourist trade; and the Welsh 'Mam', the staunch mother who gives her all to her hard-beset family, a figure immortalised on celluloid in the Hollywood version of *How Green Was My Valley*. Some of us may have very different pictures in our minds of contemporary Welsh woman: we may visualise women marching from Cardiff to Greenham to set up the first 'benders' outside the US airbase; women on picket lines during the miners' strike of 1984-5; activists in the Welsh language movement in prison in England due to the lack of gaols for women in Wales; Welsh Women's Aid establishing refuges throughout Wales; Valleys' Initiative women establishing their own co-operatives, and bringing new life to depressed areas in south Wales; business women in Cardiff side-stepping the exclusionist old boys' networks by setting up women's business clubs. And yet the vitality of change in Welsh women's lives which such images denote still seems to lack general credence; 'macho' Wales is still the norm in terms of public representation. [2]

The debate on the role of Welsh women in political life is taking place within a new context. The feeling is growing that it is totally inappropriate for the image of the 'Welsh *MAM*' to persist when the reality is one of increasing prominence and a high profile for women in all walks of life. It is against this background that efforts must be made to ensure that, from the start, a Welsh Parliament gives women unqualified equal status.

THE EXCLUSION OF WOMEN

A successful political initiative in Wales would attract considerable attention and interest elsewhere. The starting point, however, has to be an understanding of the current position and the barriers to women's participation:

* The Westminster Parliament currently has 60 women MPs out of 651.
* Only 164 women have been elected to Westminster since 1918.
* Seventy-five years after women got the vote 90 per cent of MPs are still men.
* Britain has a lower percentage of female MPs than any European Union country except France and Greece. Denmark has 33 per cent.
* The Labour party has the largest share of women MPs but still only 37 out of 271 (13 per cent).

If the presence of women at Westminster for the whole of the United Kingdom is poor, the position in Wales itself is worse:

* Only four women have ever been Welsh MPs, and there is currently only one: Megan Lloyd George (Anglesey and Carmarthen, variously between 1929 and 1966), Eirene White (Flint East, 1950 to 1966), Dorothy Rees (Barry 1950 to 1951) and Ann Clwyd (Cynon Valley, since 1984).
* Four women have been elected members of the European Parliament from Wales: Beata Brookes, Ann Clwyd, Eluned Morgan and Glenys Kinnock (the latter two in the June 1994 election).
* Of the 37 district councils, two have women leaders: Janet Davies (Plaid Cymru) in Taff-Ely, and Sue Essex (Labour) in Cardiff.
* There are no women leaders of the eight county councils.
* Currently only eleven per cent of county councillors in Wales are women.
* In 1989 only twelve per cent of candidates for the county councils were women.

These facts are evidence that if the existing structures and practices of local or central government are replicated in a Welsh Parliament, then undoubtedly the same pattern will persist. As one electoral commentary on Wales has observed: 'In Wales at least, the triumph of the suffragette movement is yet to come, as far as general elections are concerned, although the pattern in the European Parliament may be different.' [3]

The near exclusion of women from representative politics has been recognised by all the political parties in Wales to some extent. We may see some improvement as a result of the following initiatives currently being taken:

* The Labour Party has introduced a series of quotas governing numbers of women and men to be elected on to all its internal decision making bodies. Their 1993 Conference agreed to set a target of fifty per cent women candidates in all seats where a Labour MP is retiring and in fifty per cent of the most winnable seats.
* The Liberal Party has issued a consultation paper on policy for women and are working on a series positive action measures.
* Plaid Cymru has had a policy of equal representation at all levels within the party since 1981, but has largely failed to implement it in practice. A decision to reserve five seats on the National Executive for women was rescinded in 1986. However, the party has now established a high-level 'Gender Balance Commission' with a brief to make recommendations on improving the position of women.
* There are no specific initiatives to improve the position of women within the Conservative Party although there are a number of women arguing for a greater acceptance of women's potential contribution and attempts to recruit more women candidates.

Within all political parties the picture is very similar, with considerably fewer women than men selected and rarely in the most winnable seats. There is a growing realisation that a shift of attitude and intention by the political parties is a necessary condition for change. But will that be sufficient by itself? The evidence indicates that it will not. For instance, in examining the recruitment of more women and black MPs to the House of Commons, political scientist Pippa Norris has estimated that if current trends are projected forwards on a linear basis, then the number of women MPs would be only 100 (from a total of 650) by the year 2,000. Women would not achieve parity with men until the middle of the 21st Century.

Pippa Norris has also analysed the Labour Party proposal that there should be all-women short lists in half the Labour inheritor and strong challenger constituencies, and calculated the effect on the number of women likely to be elected at the next general election. On the basis of post-war electoral trends (in relation to retirements and marginal seats), the effect would be to increase the number of women Labour MPs from 37 to about 63, or at most to 75. This would increase the representation rate of women in the House of Commons from 9 to 15 per cent. As Pippa Norris says:

> This does represent considerable progress, but at the same time this would remain below the average in most comparable European parliaments, and far below the 30 to 40 per cent in most Scandinavian countries. The Labour proposal might therefore sound quite radical, with the promise of introducing an extra 50 per cent of women MPs at a stroke, but its overall impact on women's representation in Parliament would probably be far more modest. [4]

WHY WOMEN DON'T TAKE PART

There are a number of practical, interacting factors which militate against women participating in political activity as it has evolved in our present political parties and institutions. Among the most important are the following;

* **Childcare and other domestic responsibilities:** this presents a physical restraint on the time available to women to participate. Those women who are involved in full-time politics tend to be either single and without children, or married or divorced without young children.

* **Lack of education and training opportunities:** although on average girls achieve better at school than boys, lower aspirations mean fewer women achieving at Higher Education level; employers are considerably less likely to offer training opportunities to women than to men.

* **Traditional attitudes and social pressures:** women who do seek to achieve and enter non-traditional occupations often meet opposition and come under pressure from parents, partners and peers. Often they find it difficult to fit into a 'male oriented' culture in the workplace or organisation.

* **Lack of confidence:** many studies have demonstrated that women generally undervalue their own skills and abilities and, consequently, are less confident than men at taking on new tasks, or taking risks in work or political life.

* **Low wages or dependence on benefits:** women earn substantially less than men, are often economically dependent on a man and are more likely to be dependent on state benefits. Often they do not have transport or financial resources, for instance money to pay baby-sitters that would enable them to participate in external activities.

In politics, these barriers have been found to come together to create an underlying alienation of women from legislative institutions, and in particular what are generally perceived as male institutions, male agendas and male political methods. Politics is identified by many women as an area of 'hard' decision making, involving tough and aggressive speaking. In practice, while this is often the case, there is an equal but rarely recognised need in politics for the skills of co-operation, diplomacy, practical problem-solving and tenacity. All these are perceived as typically 'female' qualities.

However, given the alienation described, and the more practical issues of lack of time and money, it is little wonder that so many women opt out of the political process altogether. Indeed, addressing these practical issues has been highlighted by some feminist commentators as the main barrier to overcome for women in a new political culture:

> With the prospect for a Welsh parliament more promising than it has been for over a decade, some women in Plaid Cymru were beginning to argue that such a body must not be a replica of Westminster. If women were to be treated fairly under the new constitutional arrangements then changes such as flexibility of working hours, provision of childcare and an end to the confrontational style of debate would be necessary. [5]

The challenges have been comprehensively considered by those tackling the issues involved in setting up a Parliament in Scotland. They were well summarised in the submission from the Scottish TUC's Women's Committee to the Scottish Constitutional Convention:

> The present political system is constructed in such a way as to virtually exclude women from participation. In a society where the main domestic responsibility for child and dependant care lies with women, it is not surprising that there are so few women MPs or local government elected representatives. This responsibility, or assumption that the responsibility is a woman's is unlikely to disappear in the next few years, if even within this century. A Scottish Parliament should therefore, from the outset, make itself accessible to women. This means that the hours of the Parliament should be suitable to allow women maximum participation . . . We believe that the work pattern for elected representatives should be such as to allow them to bridge the diversity of their responsibility and workload. [6]

THE NEED FOR POSITIVE ACTION

In meeting the need to make a Welsh Parliament more appropriate for women than the Westminster model, there are a number of obvious strategies:

* Hours of working must be within a five-day Monday-to-Friday week, with morning and afternoon sessions. The Parliament's recesses should follow the pattern of the Welsh school holidays.
* Support must exist for child care and other caring needs, including the provision of a crèche at the Parliament, available to the Parliament's members and staff, together with additional child and carer allowances for members of the Parliament
* Membership of the Parliament needs to be a properly waged activity, with realistic travelling, subsistence and secretarial and research allowances.
* The Parliament should operate through a committee and working group structure in which informal procedures and the aim of seeking consensus predominate. Adversarial formal debates would be kept to a minimum. To further the creation of such an atmosphere the Parliament's layout could be horseshoe or circular.

The model would be the European Parliament's hemicycle, rather than the Westminster Parliament's parallel, and confrontational layout.

* The Parliament should establish an Equality and Democracy Committee to further examine its own procedures to see how they can assist equality of opportunity for all groups. The Committee should also be charged with examining all legislative proposals to assess their impact on equal opportunities.

THE QUOTA DEBATE

While undoubtedly improving the potential for women to participate — and, incidentally, improving the working conditions for men as well — such strategies are unlikely to have the impact that is required to ensure equal gender balance in a Welsh Parliament. Changes in the political working environment may make a contribution but are unlikely to be sufficient on their own to challenge the deep-rooted cultural bias and strong vested interests that characterise Welsh politics. Moreover, such changes will improve the situation in the medium rather than in the short term — that is, when women are already better represented.

It is difficult to find any examples of a significant increase in women's membership of legislatures without such strong interventionist positive action. Nor does any particular electoral system in itself produce improved gender ratios, although the Additional Member System or the Single Transferable Vote system can operate on rules designed to ensure that quotas from various groups, such as gender groups, are elected.

From experience of legislatures around the world, all the evidence is that until women have representation in a legislature of at least between 25 and 30 per cent, they are unable to make a significant impact either on its working environment or the character of the laws that flow from it. This implies setting a quota for women's representation of at least 25 per cent. This was the essential background to the debates that preceded agreement on the the second clause of the Llandrindod *Democracy Declaration* . It states:

> A Welsh Parliament will ensure, from the start, that there is a gender balance in its elected representatives and will ensure that its procedures

and operation enable women and men and minority groups to participate to the fullest extent.

To pursue this policy effectively its advocates must first address the main, principled objection of its opponents: that quotas are fundamentally undemocratic because they discriminate between men and women. The opponents of quotas, both men and women, argue that they limit the freedom of political parties to choose candidates, and also limit the freedom of choice of the voters. Setting quotas, it is claimed, is patronising to women. Some women who have already succeeded in the present system say that to be transferred to a quota election would diminish their achievement. Instead of positive action in favour of women, it is argued that recruitment in politics, as in other areas of life, should be on the basis of merit alone.

What such views ignore, however, is that in practice, without some form of quota system women will be denied equality of participation in the Welsh Parliament. The starting point for women in elections to the Parliament will be the substantial disadvantages of the gender imbalance that discrimination against women has produced. Discrimination against women penetrates deep into our culture and history and is so endemic as to be itself deeply undemocratic. So long as men dominate the governmental and political decision-making processes to the extent they have in the past, and continue to do so in the present, then practices, let alone culture, are unlikely to change substantially. There is a process of change underway as we have seen. Nevertheless, it is limited and very gradual. It is likely to prove so slow that the only way to make a significant impact in the Welsh Parliament will be by positive action through some form of quota system. There are three basic arguments [7] in favour of such a course of action:

1) Democracy is based upon the participation of all in political decision-making. Women constitute at least half of any population and it is axiomatic therefore that they should be represented proportionately.
2) Political participation requires the articulation and defence of the interests of the group or groups that are represented. Women are more aware of their own needs and interests, and are therefore better able to press for them.

3) Involving women in a gender-balanced Welsh Parliament will improve the culture of the decision-making process itself.

All these issues were examined during the workshop and plenary debates on the involvement of women in a Welsh Parliament at the Llandrindod Democracy Conference. The debate at the plenary session, which agreed the *Democracy Declaration*, was won by the words of George Crabbe, of Cowbridge, who said, 'I would like to say, very briefly, that I support this clause. I am totally in favour of positive discrimination; after all, it has served us men very well down the centuries'.

ACHIEVING A GENDER BALANCE

It should be possible to achieve a consensus on the following six propositions:[8]

1) The current level of representation of women is unacceptable.
2) We cannot allow the under-representation of women at Westminster to be reproduced in a new Welsh Parliament.
3) A system of government which claims to be democratic cannot deny the right of both men and women to enjoy full participation in political decision-making.
4) Action needs to be taken to ensure the desired gender equity in a Welsh Parliament.
5) The desire for gender balance is not threatening or unusual, but a reflection of broader changes in the roles of men and women in society and in the labour force, and is in line with trends in other European countries.
6) We should seek agreement on a proposal which does not alienate the broad constituency in support of gender balance, and which attempts to meet the needs of all the legitimate interests involved.

In Scotland there have been two main approaches in the debates inside the Constitutional Convention to achieving a gender balance for the Scottish Parliament. The first places the onus on the political parties, but with penalties in the event of their failing to make progress. The proposal that was agreed at the time of the 1992 general election was to require the political parties to put forward equal numbers of male and female candidates, and if they failed to do so they would be subject to the following sanctions:

1) A party failing to do so would forfeit its right to top-up seats in the Additional Member System that was the agreed form of proportional representation for elections.
2) The deposit system would be used to penalise parties which did not produce a gender balance in their candidates, rather than to penalise parties with few votes.

Parties could, therefore, choose to reject gender equality but at a significant cost. It would be left to the parties to decide how they organised the distribution of seats. Choice would be improved for the electorate since there would no longer be an overwhelmingly male slate of candidates. The obvious drawback of this approach is that it would not automatically produce gender equality in the Parliament. The top-up section of members would have an equal gender balance but the parties would have to tackle internally the problem of distributing winnable and unwinnable seats. Nonetheless, the proposal could result in significant progress towards gender equality. [9]

This approach was broadly agreed between the Scottish Labour Party and the Scottish Liberal Democrats as a compromise position at the time of the 1992 general election. Labour wanted to go further, in the direction of the Scottish TUC policy described below. In the wake of the election, however, the Liberal Democrats' discomfort with the compromise became clear. They claimed the approach was undemocratic since the law should not interfere with the internal organisation of political parties by imposing legal obligations. This argument has been opposed by Isobel Lindsay, Chair of the Parliament for Scotland Campaign, in a paper drawn up for the Convention's Constitutional Commission:

> The argument which has been put forward that the law should not interfere with political parties is clearly a nonsense. At the moment the law interferes extensively with political parties through electoral law. It restricts the age of candidates, how much they can spend, what they can call themselves on ballot papers, what they can and cannot do to gain support, etc. If the law can intervene to equalise the position of the rich and poor in regulating election expenditure, why should the law not

intervene to help equalise the position of men and women participating in the electoral system? [10]

The position of the Scottish TUC's Women's Committee on the mechanism for achieving a gender balance in a Scottish Parliament, endorsed by the General Council, was more likely to achieve the desired aim. It offered an electoral reform option based on the premise that 50 per cent of elected representatives should be women and 50 per cent men, as follows:

> Each constituency would be entitled to return two elected representatives to the Parliament: one woman, one man. Voting could be facilitated by introducing two voting papers — a category for women, which would reflect the different political parties; and a category for men, which again would reflect the different political parties. If current Parliamentary constituencies were changed, this principle could still apply, and could be made to work under virtually any system of proportional representation. [11]

It is clear that rules can be built into some systems of proportional representation to ensure the counting process produces an equal gender balance of representatives in the Parliament. The success of achieving gender balance in this way would be conditional only on the political parties not disenfranchising voters by failing to field sufficient women candidates.

Even given the advance that has occurred in the thinking in Wales regarding women's concerns and rights, such a position would be bound to have a dynamic and innovative effect on Welsh politics. While both the Welsh Labour Party and Plaid Cymru have policy commitments to equal representation for men and women, it is difficult to see how this can actually be achieved in practice other than through a mechanism of the kind advocated by the Scottish TUC. It could be that such a device would be subject to review after two, or perhaps three elections. There could be a so-called 'sunset clause' in relation to the legislation establishing the electoral arrangements for the new Parliament. Nevertheless, as Isobel Lindsay has put it in Scotland:

> Any suggestion of waiting until we see how bad the situation is before we act is a recipe for conflict. Once bottoms are on seats, it is very

difficult to shift them. If we are to get change, the time to do it is at the start before personal interests have become entrenched.[12]

Establishing a Parliament for Wales will provide a unique and exciting opportunity to improve dramatically the representation of women in Welsh life. To be successful, as the Llandrindod *Declaration* states, that opportunity must be seized from the start.

NOTES

[1] R. R. Davies, *The Status of Women and the Practice of Marriage in Late-Medieval Wales*, in Dafydd Jenkins and Morfydd E. Owen , *The Welsh Law of Women*, University of Wales Press, 1980.

[2] Jane Aaron and Teresa Rees, 'Identities in Transition', in Jane Aaron, Teresa Rees, Sandra Betts and Moira Vincentelli, *Our Sisters' Land. The Changing Identities of Women in Wales*, University of Wales Press, 1994.

[3] Arnold J. James and John E. Thomas, *Wales at Westminster. A History of the Parliamentary Representation of Wales 1800 - 1979*, Gomer, 1981.

[4] Pippa Norris, *Party Strategies for Bringing Women into Power*, Edinburgh University, 1993.

[5] Charlotte Aull Davies, 'Women, Nationalism and Feminism' in *Our Sisters' Land* Aaron, Rees, Betts and Vincentelli, 1994.

[6] Statement on 'Scottish Constitutional and Electoral Reform' adopted by the 1990, 93rd annual congress of the Scottish TUC, and re-submitted to the Scottish Constitutional Commission in February 1994.

[7] These arguments closely follow those in an article prepared by Monique Leijenaar and Evelyn Mahon for a workshop of the European Consortium for Political Research in 1992 on women in political elites.

[8] These points follow those made by Alice Brown and Joan Macintosh in a paper, *Gender Equality* produced for the Scottish Constitutional Commission, October 1993.

[9] This description outlines the 'thinking' behind the compromise between the Labour Party and Scottish Liberal Democrats in 1992 and is contained in a 'Note on Electoral System and Gender' prepared for the Scottish Constitutional Commission by Isobel Lindsay in November 1993.

[10] Ibid.

[11] Scottish TUC, op. cit., note 6.

[12] Isobel Lindsay, op. cit., note 9.

PART III

ECONOMY AND THE ENVIRONMENT

CHAPTER 9

DEVELOPMENT FROM WITHIN
Economic Renewal and a Welsh Parliament

Kevin Morgan

In framing a new economic development strategy for Wales the most important ingredient of all is credibility. In other words it will have to be credible to the public at large and to the professionals who work in the various bodies involved. Failing this, we will have neither the popular support nor the professional commitment which are necessary for success. In short, we need to tap the skills and energies of as wide a constituency as possible because no amount of government support — be it from Cardiff, London or Brussels — can ever compensate for the absence of political will and social commitment within the nation.

We also need to recognise the limits of what can be achieved at the Welsh national level. Many of our social and economic problems are international in scope and character and therefore cannot be solved at the level of the Welsh economic region alone. The past decade of Thatcherism has been an all too painful reminder of the fact that British policies are too intrusive, too influential and, ultimately, too powerful a force to overcome at the Welsh level. Even so, an animating principle is the belief that the task of renewal must begin within Wales, utilising our existing resources. Whatever the limits on our sphere of action it is imperative that we do more, much more, to help ourselves.

Our existing resources may seem modest, but they are certainly not insignificant. In political terms, for example, a mini-state system has evolved in Wales which is nowadays quite significant, especially when one considers the paucity of regional institutions in England. Whatever the weaknesses of this state system, it is as well to remember that the English regions would dearly love to have institutions like the Welsh Office and the Welsh Development Agency. In cultural terms we continue to set a high premium on collaborative action and this, too, is a resource which has yet to be fully mobilised for economic purposes. These non-economic resources play a very important economic role in all the more dynamic European Regions. Wales would do well to look at, and learn from, these more politically robust Regions.

Many of the key economic and political elements of a renewal strategy for Wales can be described by drawing on the experience of some of the more successful Regions in Europe. As we shall see, the question of regional economic renewal inevitably involves a political dimension because the form of governance is, potentially, a very significant component of economic development.

ECONOMIC RENEWAL: HARNESSING OUR RESOURCES

If we set aside the symptoms of our economic weakness (for example, low wages and high unemployment) and focus instead on the underlying structural causes, then we find that the key problems in Wales are no different to the problems that have bedevilled the wider UK economy for more than half a century. Most industrial experts agree that the acute problems in the UK economy are: a low commitment to research and development (R & D); a woefully inadequate system of vocational education and training; the relative absence of 'patient money' for long term investment; and a weak government-industry partnership. Taken together, these are the chief causes of the UK's poor post-war record of industrial innovation. With the exception of government-industry relations (which have been productive in Wales), these are also the key problems of the Welsh economy.

If we are going to overcome these problems we must make a decisive break with the traditional regional policy approach, geared as it was to advance factories, land reclamation and foreign inward investment. This approach may have been appropriate at an earlier age — the age of low quality mass production — but it is hopelessly inadequate at a time when the accent elsewhere in Europe is upon quality production, technological innovation and skilled labour. The European Commission, for example, is firmly of the view that the most effective regional development strategies in the 1990s will be those which succeed in forging a more integrated approach to regional, technology and training policies (Cooke and Morgan, 1991; 1993).

What we need in Wales, therefore, is not a regional policy geared to reproducing the past (with low skill, low paid jobs), but an innovation strategy that can begin to chart a more rewarding form of economic development in the future. This process is already well underway in other more self-conscious parts of Europe — like Baden-Württemberg, Emilia-Romagna, Catalunya and the Basque Country for example — and it is high time that we in Wales followed a similar path.

If we look at Baden-Württemberg, a strong industrial Region in Germany with a high degree of self-governance, we soon discover that there is no real mystery about its success. Among other things it has a robust regional innovation system, some of the main features of which are:

* A well-developed research and technology transfer system, which hosts over one hundred decentralised technical support centres, each of which affords small and medium sized firms access to advanced technologies, expert advice and problem-solving facilities.
* A highly effective system of vocational education and training, which tries to ensure that sufficient skills are available so that employers do not have to rely on labour poaching.
* A strong networking culture within the corporate sector, the main feature of which is strong buyer-supplier linkages between large and small firms in the Region.
* A deep commitment to public-private sector collaboration, which makes for a more collective and consensual approach to the problems of regional development.
* A high degree of political self-governance, which allows certain policies — in education, culture, training and technology, for example — to be tailored to the needs of the Region, a facility which is becoming ever more important in an era of rapid and economic change (Cooke and Morgan, 1990).

In contrast to the UK, where innovation is left almost entirely to market forces, the German approach recognises innovation for what it is, namely a collective social endeavour. That is to say, the burden of innovation is shared to a much greater extent than it is in the UK. Although firms are expected to shoulder the main burden, there is a dense network of supporting institutions to assist them in the process, and this enables even the smaller firms to stay abreast of the latest technologies.

The guiding principle of the Baden-Wurttemberg support infrastructure is to provide help for firms that are willing and able to help themselves. And, as often as not, the most stimulating forms of assistance are information, knowledge and expertise rather than the capital grants which dominate British regional policy thinking.

The fact is that Britain should no longer be considered the benchmark for regional economic development since neither its policies nor its performances warrant such a privileged status. If we want more inspiring models or more challenging benchmarks then we have to broaden our horizons and look to continental Europe. Fortunately, the task of absorbing the very best practices from the continent has been rendered that much easier now that Wales has signed inter-regional co-operation agreements with some of the more dynamic European regions like Baden-Württemberg and Catalunya for example.

It is not as if Wales is starting from scratch. There is still a strong industrial culture, with innovative firms which could function as exemplars to others. Moreover, bodies like the Welsh Office and the WDA are beginning to recognise the poverty of the traditional regional policy model; so that they, too, are looking for a new and more effective regional development strategy. In other words the combination of pressing problems and bankrupt policies has begun to produce a new intellectual climate in the nation, a climate which is more receptive to fresh ideas than at any time in the post-war period. A consequence is that a combination of new trends are struggling for air in two fields which are crucial to the future health of the Welsh economy: technology and skills.

On the technological front Wales is often deemed to lack enough firms which have a strong research and development base. This is hardly surprising when one considers that branch-plants, specialising in low level production activities, have been the main form of investment since the war. However, in the engineering industry — which plays a major role in south Wales — some encouraging trends have emerged in recent years. Among the more hopeful signs of renewal is a new trend towards occupational upgrading, which is especially strong in the electronics industry. In the period between 1978-90, for example, the key category of professional engineers, scientists and technologists increased by 1,157 per cent in Wales compared to an increase of just 115 per cent in the UK as a whole (Lawson and Morgan, 1991).

This technical upgrading suggests that the stereotyped branch-plant image, with its accent on assembly-only jobs, needs to be revised. The picture is reinforced by a recent survey which showed that Welsh firms are spending more on research and development than ever before (Cooke and Morgan, 1992). What this survey also showed was that these firms needed much more technical support than they were able to get from existing government schemes, for example information about key technologies and potential research partners, not to mention better tailored innovation grants. In other words there is a demand for innovation-inducing services, the kind of services that are provided through a subsidised network of technology transfer centres in Baden-Württemberg.

However, Wales is not totally bereft of technical centres which provide innovation services and research expertise. In addition to the innovation service centres which already exist — mainly in the further and higher education institutions — the WDA has helped to create seven centres of expertise within the University of Wales. These centres have specialist expertise in a number of advanced technologies, such as microelectronics, new materials, and information technology. (Cooke and Morgan, 1992).

This is the kind of infrastructure which should be built up if we are to pursue a more successful industrial vocation in the future. However, these centres are starved of resources and, with very few exceptions, their services have not been marketed at all well to Welsh firms generally. Indeed, most firms are probably not aware of the existence of these innovation service centres.

So it is not enough to create a new innovation system, geographically well located though it is. The system has to be sold and publicised through a more concerted development campaign, otherwise it simply won't be used. We need to mobilise our technological resources and put them to work in the cause of economic renewal. This is one of the key tasks of a new innovation strategy for Wales.

On the skills front a number of promising initiatives are underway, but these need to be more widely understood and more firmly anchored in the mainstream of our thinking about economic development. If the technological base of the Welsh economy is to be improved this can only be done through a workforce which is far better educated and trained than it is today. In the long term, of course, there is nowhere better to start laying the foundations of a new skills base than in the schools.

The greatest tragedy of the school system in the UK is that, unlike most other European nation-states, a large proportion of our 16-19 year old population are defined as failures if they cannot succeed in purely academic subjects. In other words, the UK has miserably failed to develop a vocational education and training (VET) system that can engage the energies and the talents of a swathe of young people. There is a bitter irony in all this because it is now generally acknowledged that the UK's skills deficit relative to Germany, France and Japan, is most acute in the category of intermediate skills, the very skills which are produced by a VET system. Like the UK as a whole, Wales has to redress this deficit as a matter of urgency.

No country can aspire to a viable industrial future if its children eschew careers in industry in general or in engineering in particular. In educational terms one of our greatest tasks is to persuade young Welsh people that a career in industry would be rewarding. Indeed, in this regard there is currently an interesting initiative underway in Wales, in which 70 schools and 3,000 students have been invited to explore innovative projects in the field of design and technology. The aim being to raise the status of engineering in our schools (Jenner, 1992). This kind of initiative has more chance of succeeding the more the Welsh economy plays host to firms like Bosch, Sony, and Pirelli, firms that do not conform to the dirty image of industry which is so prevalent in our classrooms.

Beyond the schools the most important task is to recognise the potentially significant role which the Further Education (FE) colleges can play in the process of re-skilling and in economic development more generally. For far too long the FE sector has been the Cinderella of the UK's elitist education and training system. The real significance of the FE sector lies in the fact that it is the primary delivery vehicle for the very intermediate skills which both the UK as a whole and Wales in particular have so signally failed to nurture.

As so often happens, it has taken an external influence to bring home to the various Welsh agencies the true significance of our FE colleges. For example, Bosch, one of the most training-conscious firms in Europe, is tapping the resources of three of Wales's FE colleges in an exacting programme to develop high quality apprentices. Other quality-conscious firms, like Sony and British

Airways, are also using the FE sector to good effect. But, as critics have rightly argued, while the FE sector was able to meet the demands of these blue chip firms, largely because such firms command a special status, it is not equipped to provide a more generalised level of training because of the years of under-investment in equipment and staff development (Rees and Thomas, 1992).

Two of Wales's most far-sighted FE principals have called for urgent action to reverse the attrition of the FE sector (Wilmore and Cocks,1992). This call should be heeded, otherwise we shall never be able to launch a re-skilling exercise on the scale that is now needed. Like technology policy, the key task here is to integrate skills provision into the mainstream of our economic development thinking.

Raising the quality of the technology infrastructure on the one hand and the skills base on the other would do more to promote inward investment and indigenous development than anything else. The linkages between the foreign and indigenous sectors of the Welsh economy also need to be developed much further. In the past the authorities seemed to think that once a foreign firm had been lured into Wales then the developmental job had been done with respect to that firm. A low premium was accorded to 'aftercare'. However, the Welsh Office and the WDA should keep the lines open to these foreign firms to ascertain what their component needs will be over the medium term. This information could then be broadcast to a number of indigenous firms so that they could adjust their plans accordingly.

As it happens the WDA is beginning to adopt a far more pro-active stance. Its most important initiative is the supplier development programme. This tries to identify potential indigenous suppliers so that more of the foreign sector's purchasing budget is retained in Wales. The next step ought to be to tap the foreign sector's expertise for the benefit of local suppliers by, for example, encouraging the former to act as 'tutors' to improve managerial and technical skills within the indigenous sector.

The supplier development programme is just one part of a wider strategy which the WDA is trying to develop for the 1990s. This strategy will make some amends for the past in the sense that it focuses as much on indigenous firms as upon inward investment, a welcome new departure.

Even so, although the WDA is now more alert to the need for

innovation than ever before, it labours under too many constraints to be able to develop the complete innovation system that is needed. While financial constraints do not help of course, the most important constraints of all are the lack institutional cohesion together with the lack of a commonly shared innovation strategy for Wales as a whole.

As things are we have a plethora of institutions — the Welsh Office, WDA, Training and Enterprise Councils, Enterprise Agencies, local authorities, further and higher educational institutions to name only the main players — all of which could perform a much more forceful role in promoting economic development if there was a general sense of national purpose. As it is, however, the energies of these dispersed centres of expertise are sapped as each institution pursues its parochial ends. A Welsh innovation system requires, above all else, a network approach, a disposition to collaborate to achieve mutually beneficial ends. In such an environment where knowledge circulates much more rapidly, the best practices of one part are broadcast to all. This, in short, is the challenge we shall have to meet if we seriously want to promote sustained and balanced economic development in Wales.

Deliberately, little has been said here about key problem areas within Wales, like the Valleys, because their economic future is inextricably tied to the fortunes of the wider economy. However, there is a distinctive role for the Valleys to play as places to live and work, and this role would be fortified by an economic development strategy that stated this as an explicit commitment. The Valleys need their own distinctive economic agenda and this can be achieved through a greater effort to promote these communities as industrial villages based on small and medium-sized firms.

Regions which exist on such a basis in Europe have made strenuous efforts to ensure that such firms have access to high grade skills and advanced technologies, and this is precisely what we should seek to do for the Valleys. The innovation system that has been sketched here — combining economic, technology and training policies — could provide the framework in which to pursue this strategy.

However, even this will not be sufficient to engage the entire labour force of the Valleys. As a result many people will continue to be dependent on employment opportunities in Cardiff and along the M4 corridor. This means that a much better public transport infrastructure will need to be developed, especially with respect to new rail systems. Unless this happens the opportunities along the coastal belt will be restricted to those with cars, a form of transport that hardly needs to be encouraged (Davis and Morgan, 1993).

THE GOVERNANCE QUESTION

To begin the process of economic renewal some key political issues need to be addressed as a matter of urgency. These include the structure of the state, the role of the Labour Party, and the potential for political collaboration in and beyond Wales. Such issues tend to generate more heat than light. Sensitive though they are, however, they deserve to be discussed in a much more open and democratic manner, not least because Wales has fallen way behind Scotland in terms of the quality and vigour of its internal political debate.

Just two of these key issues will be highlighted here: the need to reform the state-system in Wales and the need for a wider political consensus, two intimately related concerns. As regards the state system more and more people are beginning to recognise the enormous centralisation of political power which has occurred in Wales since 1979. This process continues apace, as is all too apparent in such spheres as education and health, where the Conservative government is actively replacing local authorities with unaccountable Quangos (Morgan and Roberts, 1993). Centralised political power on this scale is not just an affront to a modern democratic society, it is also inimical to a modern and efficient economy in the sense that innovative firms benefit from having political discretion close to hand. This is well understood in dynamic economies like Baden-Württemberg in Germany.

In the face of an ever more centralised UK nation-state it is imperative that we begin to challenge this debilitating trend. We need to re-examine current state structures in Wales to make them as *democratic* and as *efficient* as possible. In broad terms the state system in Wales embraces a wide array of institutions, including the Welsh Office, local government, and a whole series of unelected Quangos, many of them economic agencies like the WDA. The most unacceptable feature of the present regime is the fact that we have a Welsh Office, deploying an annual budget of more than £7 billion, which is controlled by a minority political party in Wales. Political authority in no way reflects the dominant political culture, a phenomenon which would be impossible in the federal systems of Europe.

The reform of this state system should be carried out in the name of basic democratic principles, which is the principal case for a Welsh Parliament. However, in view of the urgent economic need for a more effective and coherent institutional structure, the reform of the state system should also be driven by a desire to make our institutions better equipped to pursue an effective economic development strategy. In short, this requires far more political co-ordination than we have today. The problem of co-ordination has been compounded by the enormous institutional changes of recent years. Consider the changes that have yet to be fully digested:

* The devolution of Welsh higher education from the Whitehall Department of Education and Science to the Welsh Office.
* The consequent creation of a Training, Education and Enterprise Department inside the Welsh Office.
* The creation of two new Quangos, the Higher and Further Education Councils, the latter involving the incorporation of FE colleges, removing this sector from local authority control.
* The advent of the Training and Enterprise Councils (TECs) the private-led and publicly-funded bodies which are now responsible for training and enterprise.
* The radical overhaul of the Welsh Development Agency and the creation of three devolved sub-regions for its operation — north, south, and west Wales.
* The reorganisation of local government, which will see the arrival in 1995-6 of 22 most-purpose authorities.

All of these institutions have a crucial role to play in promoting Welsh economic development, yet there is little or no framework in which they can operate. The result is an absence of shared common purpose so that their efforts can be focused in the same direction. Such a framework is especially important in the case of the most-purpose authorities because, on present indications, these will be too small to execute strategic functions like planning, transport, economic development and environmental control let alone the major function of the old eight counties, education. Indeed, there are signs that a number of 'super-councils' — operating, perhaps, through joint boards — may have to be created to address these strategic functions, thus creating an even more crowded institutional area.

The Welsh Office, which is now in charge of education, training, enterprise and economic development generally, is ideally placed to orchestrate these disparate sources of institutional expertise. To date, however, it has shown neither the will nor the appetite to play such a role. Such inaction is totally unacceptable when Wales is at such a critical juncture: so much so that we need to insist that the Welsh Office starts as wide a process of public consultation as possible with the aim of building a new national planning framework.

The second key issue — the need for greater political consensus in Wales — turns the spotlight outwards, to the political parties and the people of Wales generally. In other words, we have to ask ourselves a simple question: can we muster sufficient political support across Wales to create a new political agenda for the 1990s? A new agenda would embrace a series of new initiatives to address our pressing problems — economic, social, environmental. It would be that much easier to deal with these problems if we had a more democratic system of government in Wales, a system that was physically and politically closer to the people it sought to serve. What we have at present is a thoroughly undemocratic regime, at the apex of which stands the Welsh Office, whose forbidding fortress-like building is both uninviting and inaccessible to the general public.

As the dominant political party in Wales, the Labour Party has a key role to play in creating a new political agenda, one of the main items of which should be a directly-elected Welsh Parliament. If Labour continues to refuse to entertain cross-party talks on the constitution, together with its negative stance towards the Parliament for Wales campaign, that will be seen as further symptoms of a tragic loss of purpose. Opinion polls have shown a rising tide of support for a more democratic system of government in Wales and this popular sentiment, which is not confined to any one party, could be given a decisive boost if the Labour Party in Wales lent its full weight to what is manifestly a progressive and democratic undertaking.

The Welsh Labour Party's timid attitude to constitutional reform stems in part from its fear that such support might give credence to Plaid Cymru and, inadvertently, fuel demands for an independent state. This stance displays a profound lack of confidence in Labour's own capacity to win the hearts and minds of voters in Wales. Instead of being in the forefront of the campaign to create a new and broader democracy, the Welsh Labour Party is now perceived, even by many of its own supporters, as too defensive in spirit and too conservative in outlook. However, there is still time for it to re-consider its position. It would be a very positive step indeed if the Labour Party took the lead in the campaign for a Parliament for Wales.

A directly elected Welsh Parliament would provide a more robust forum for political debate within Wales. Equally important, it would serve as a democratic mechanism through which Wales could engage more productively with the rest of Europe, with the institutions of the European Union, and with our growing band of partner regions in the Union, all of which have strong elected bodies. More direct links with Brussels will become ever more important in the 1990s because, in the European Union view, Regions themselves will be expected to play a much more forceful role in promoting economic development in the future.

Better and more effective links with the rest of Europe may be important, but the true significance of a Welsh Parliament lies closer to home. It should be seen first and foremost as a democratic forum for publicising and redressing our most pressing social, economic and environmental problems. Even though a Parliament will not of itself solve these problems, it would certainly help us to address them in a more open and forceful manner. Far from being a diversion from the 'bread and butter' issues, the demand for a directly-elected Parliament signifies an added determination to solve our problems in a more democratic fashion, and in a way which resonates with our own distinctive political culture.

Theory and practice tell us that democratic and accountable institutions are essential for social and economic renewal. Why? Simply because no institution — be it a firm, a development agency or a government body — can give of its best if it is held in low public esteem.

NOTES

Cooke, P. and Morgan, K. (1990): *Industry, Training and Technology Transfer: The Baden-Württemberg System in Perspective*, Department of City and Regional Planning, University of Wales College of Cardiff.

Cooke, P. and Morgan, K. (1991): *The Intelligent Region*, Department of City and Regional Planning, University of Wales College of Cardiff.

Cooke, P. and Morgan, K. (1993): *The Network Paradigm: New Departures in Corpoprate and Regional Development,* Environment and Planning, D, Vol 11, pp 543-564.

Davis, F. and Morgan, K. (1993): 'Line up the Metro', *Western Mail,* 26 October.

Jenner, P. (1992): 'Building into Youth a Zest for Industry', *Western Mail,* 9 June.

Lawson, G. and Morgan, K. (1991): *Employment Trends in the British Engineering Industry, Engineering Industry Training Board,* Watford.

Morgan, K. and Roberts, E. (1993): *The Democratic Deficit, A Guide to Quangoland,* Papers in Planning Research, No 144, Department of City and Regional Planning, University of Wales College of Cardiff.

Rees, G. and Thomas, M (1992): *Inward Investment, Regional Development and Labour Market Adjustment,* School of Social and Administrative Studies, University of Wales College of Cardiff.

Wilmore, T. and Cocks, J. (1992): *Skilling for Engineering in Wales,* Barry College.

CHAPTER 10

SUSTAINING THE HEARTLAND
The Rural Economy and a Welsh Parliament

Neil Caldwell

Wales may be famous for its (almost-extinct) coal mines and heavy industries, and its close-knit urban communities, but it is, in truth, still a very rural country. Agriculture and related activities have traditionally dominated the landscape, despite the natural disadvantages of mountainous terrain, poor soil and high rainfall.

About 90 per cent of rural Wales is designated as a Less Favoured Area, and farm holdings are fairly small and family-owned, though that is changing. Whilst the number of people employed in agriculture in the European Union as a whole is 7 per cent (only 2.8 per cent in England), in rural Wales the figure is much higher: 8 per cent in Gwynedd, 14 per cent in Dyfed, 15 per cent in rural Clwyd and 18 per cent in Powys.

Land-based industries are responsible for both the creation and more recent degradation of the rural environment, which is still of a remarkably high quality. There are three national parks covering over one fifth of Wales, five Areas of Outstanding Natural Beauty, 400km of Heritage Coast, 40 National Nature Reserves, 684 Sites of Special Scientific Interest, twelve internationally protected wetland and bird sites, plus a Biosphere and a Biogenetic Reserve. Not only are these places of immense value in themselves, but they also contribute to the attractiveness of Wales for tourism and as a base for other economic activities.

Rural Wales is described in the draft (1994) Welsh Office Rural Strategy[1] as suffering from 'extreme peripherality', though such a description would really be more accurate for places like Donegal or Galicia. Nonetheless, the scattered communities of rural Wales and the mountainous topography do create problems for inhabitants, particularly in the remoter areas. Vehicle ownership is high. There are almost half as many cars as people, despite low average incomes. Meeting this need reduces already low disposable incomes.

Public transport provision is poor, despite the efforts of local authorities and the development agencies to extend the limited services. Bus deregulation has reduced rural services, and few small villages are on a regular route. Trains provide a vital lifeline in some areas, but most people have to depend on a car to get around, which is why rural dwellers oppose measures to constrain their use. The growth in car use has, however, led to centralisation causing the loss of local shops, schools and other essential services, so that people must travel further afield, whether or not they enjoy easy access to a car.

Straighter, wider and faster roads are as seen as vital to the economic prospects of rural areas, despite the fact that transport costs are only a small component of total business costs. Moreover, improved access to markets cuts two ways. It may help local firms reach a wider market. However, it also extends the range of major providers of goods and services that benefit from large economies of scale and centralised structures, enabling them to move in from outside, undercutting small businesses on the periphery.

The distance and isolation of much of rural Wales (until fairly recent times) from large, English-speaking towns helped nurture strong Welsh-speaking communities. In those places where Welsh is still widely spoken, it is closely associated with the farming community. Even in these areas, however, rapid in-migration is undermining linguistic and cultural traditions and causing social tension.

Low population levels in rural Wales led to the formation of a dispersed, 'Celtic' settlement pattern. The resulting communities are very small. Throughout Powys, Ceredigion and Meirionnydd, for instance, three-quarters of the population live in 'towns' or villages of less than 2,000 people. Powys is the least populated county of any in England or Wales, within which Radnorshire has a density of just 19 people per square kilometre.

There has been recent controversy over the way in which 'local needs' housing should be provided in rural areas. The decline in local authority built 'council housing', the 'right to buy policy' and the failure of other providers, such as the housing associations, to meet the increasing but highly variable demand for social housing, has tempted planning committees to permit sporadic development in the open countryside. This misguided strategy was criticised by the Welsh Affairs Committee for doing little to meet real social housing needs.[2] The Welsh Office responded thus:

There is no reason to suppose that a pattern of settlement which historically met the needs of an area is still appropriate today. Economic conditions, transport facilities, telecommunications and environmental priorities have all changed. The need to provide and maintain rural services and the principle of sustainable development both point to the advantages of focusing development in existing settlements. Nor is it most logical to provide affordable housing for low income households in places where it is difficult and expensive for them to acquire the services, including transport, that they require . . . the Government remains of the view that further sporadic development will damage the appearance of the countryside, increase the cost of providing services, and encourage the use of cars and other vehicles. [3]

THREATS TO THE RURAL ECONOMY

For over a century, depopulation was a predominant trend in rural Wales, with people of working age leaving the remoter parts to seek employment in more prosperous areas, both within and beyond rural Wales. Whilst population growth has occurred in all districts since 1971, this has been due in the main to in-migration of older people, who have chosen to spend their retirement years in attractive surroundings. Younger people, however, are continuing to migrate because of the dearth of employment opportunities, poor leisure and social facilities, and the difficulty of securing affordable housing in their own communities.

The economy of rural Wales suffers from low output and earnings, high under-employment, low female activity rates, decline in some traditional industries and low gross domestic product. Whilst unemployment in rural Wales as a whole is low, this is partly because the countryside exports unemployment to urban areas. Out-migration and seasonal employment, in both agriculture and tourism, serve to keep long-term unemployment low.

It is has been argued that past policies and practices have not always given sufficient priority to the need to improve the self-sufficiency of the rural economy; that in some ways they may have actually made rural Wales less able to fend for itself. The finger has been pointed at one-sided development initiatives which have tended to emphasise one particular sort of outcome while ignoring other possible effects.

For example, attracting inward investment without building links to local firms, induces vulnerability to a 'branch plant' syndrome, or creates jobs without much regard for the quality of skills involved or the level of wages paid. In turn that contributes to a low wage, low skill labour force.

The 1991 Census showed that there are many people of working age in rural Wales who are neither working, nor officially seeking work, nor claiming unemployment benefit, and who therefore do not count as unemployed. Estimates of economic activity rates for 1991 show Gwynedd and Dyfed as having the lowest female rates of any of the 64 counties and regions of Great Britain. In general, rural workers receive markedly lower wages than those in urban areas. The importance of agriculture is one factor, but the economy is becoming increasingly dependent on the services sector, particularly tourism and public administration.

Rural Wales is experiencing an accelerating rate of economic change. Basic structural problems, such as the decline of the agricultural industry, the narrowness of the area's manufacturing base and over-dependence on a small number of large employers, make the economy particularly fragile. The run-down of defence establishments and the closure of Trawsfynydd nuclear power station are two major threats which have led to the adoption of special measures.

Less visible are the threats posed by a poor skills base, low levels of self-confidence and entrepreneurialism, and the lack of a modern telecommunications network that could do much to overcome the traditional communications problems of rural Wales.

LOCAL EMPOWERMENT

The Welsh Office has been often criticised for its apparent inability to develop an integrated approach to rural issues, despite being a multi-functional department. The response to a specific concern has traditionally been to create a Quango. Thus we have a kaleidoscope of Quangos, each with its narrow, 'sectoral' remit, jostling to gain the attention of decision-makers. In the current Quango-hostile climate, however, a trend towards greater collaboration between them can be discerned. This is reinforced by the need to demonstrate the adoption of integrated rural development strategies in order to obtain European Union funding.

How far the concept of integration permeates the thinking of Welsh Office ministers is hard to guess. They have enjoyed the opportunity to 'divide and rule' whenever inter-sectoral disputes have arisen — especially those between development, planning and the environment. As a result they have managed on numerous occasions to dodge the responsibility of mapping out a clear direction for all agencies to follow.

In a lecture on the environment, presented to the Countryside Council for Wales at Margam Park, in December 1993, the Prince of Wales said:

> I don't think it is unreasonable to look to the Welsh countryside as a crucible of new ideas and the best solutions are local solutions. The low-key, bottom-up approach may not be the most spectacular, nor provide material for glitzy press releases, but in my experience it does tend to work best in the long run. Indeed many people now recognise it to be essential for what is increasingly being called 'sustainable development'.

There may be irony in quoting a member of the Royal family in a book dedicated to the need for a Parliament for Wales, but the message is an important one. One way of ensuring that development brings lasting benefit is to enlarge the scope for local people to exercise self-determination and leadership. This ensures that the pace and nature of development is dictated by their needs, rather than by external perceptions of their needs. The purpose of working with communities is to enable them to overcome barriers in their own way, and at their own pace. In this way they are more likely to assume ownership of, and responsibility for, developments. This leads to greater awareness of the scope for using local skills and resources, and the possibility of keeping a greater share of the benefits within the locality.

Much can be learned from countries like Switzerland where power is decentralised and local communities have the confidence and authority to make their own decisions. Such a system is more likely to retain young people in their home communities and encourage the development of self-sustaining local economies.

SUSTAINABLE DEVELOPMENT

The Government now says it is important to ensure all future development is environmentally sustainable. All policy documents therefore include a reference to sustainability, and the Welsh Office's Rural Strategy is no exception:

> . . . realisation of sustainable development will require the achievement of broad objectives which meet the economic, social and cultural aspirations of the people of Rural Wales, whilst at the same time maintaining and enhancing the rural environment.[4]

This is certainly the aim, but vague statements do little to explain how to ensure that development decisions lead to a reduction in energy and resource demands, less wastes and harmful emissions, while enhancing biological diversity and landscape quality. Few robust measures or indicators of sustainability are in regular use, and those supportive instruments that exist, such as Environmental Assessment, Appraisal or Audit, remain largely unfamiliar to business, administration or services in rural Wales.

The Secretary of State for Wales has resisted calls for greater guidance and support to be made available, in contrast to his Scottish counterpart who recently decided 'to create a Scottish body of experts to advise on the practical steps needed to ensure that future development is productive and sustainable'. In his defence the Secretary of State might point to the establishment in March 1994 of his Welsh Economic Council which has put these isues on its agenda. However, the Council is not a gathering of experts as such, but rather a meeting point for the heads of the leading Quangos (such as the Wesh Development Agency and Higher Education Funding Council), with representatives from the Wales CBI, Wales TUC and local government.

It remains the case that the Welsh Office has a poor record in providing a clear and integrated rural development strategy. This failing has been exacerbated by the existence of two separate development agencies, the Development Board for Rural Wales and the Welsh Development Agency, supporting different areas of Wales with different statutory powers. Although both agencies have similar business support services, the Development Board alone has a 'social development' remit. The WDA's Rural Unit (now disbanded) tried to offer its areas similar support for the development of community facilities, but did not find it easy. The transfer of social development powers from the DBRW to mid-Wales local authorities, coupled with the appointment in July 1994 of David Rowe-Beddoe as chairman of both agencies, suggests the ground is being prepared for a future merger.

Some people hanker after a unified Rural Development Agency with powers like those of England's Rural Development Commission. This, it is suggested, would foster a stronger identity for rural Wales, improve and simplify the provision of development grants and advice, and co-ordinate the work of all bodies and agencies involved in rural Wales, including the Welsh Office, the Countryside Council for Wales, the Wales Tourist Board, the Training and Enterprise Councils, local government and the voluntary sector.

Local government is also a focal point where a whole range of services, regulations and aspirations can be integrated in a development plan based on sustainability. Land-use planning and development control functions are powerful tools, if used properly. The current emphasis on plan-led, rather than development-led, planning is welcome, though many Welsh rural authorities have shown a marked reluctance to adhere to their planning policies in the past.

RURAL DEVELOPMENT AND THE DEMOCRATIC DEFICIT

Local government has a vital role to play in the attainment of sustainable and integrated forms of rural development. Its political and administrative capacity has, however, been deliberately weakened over the last decade. Now the eight counties, which deliver the majority of services, and which together have formed a serious political counterforce to the Welsh Office, are to be reorganised out of existence in the name of local democracy.

The 22 new most-purpose authorities being created may seem closer to local communities than the counties, but the extinction of some 'old counties', the welding together of others and the often controversial boundary decisions, have aroused, rather than mollified, local loyalties.

At least two major failings will quickly become apparent under the new system. First, the new authorities will be too small to deliver effective services without joining together with others. Second, many services will be contracted out, leaving slimmed down committees little to do other than approve and renew contracts. This is the so-called 'enabling authority'.

The Secretary of State is known to be opposed to excessive joint working. Without it, however, it will be very difficult to deliver services requiring a strategic overview and a reasonable degree of specialism. This particularly applies to planning and other 'environmental services'.

In other fields, such as education, housing, training and enterprise support, much of the responsibility has already been devolved to a local level or to county-based Quangos. For that which remains, collaboration between authorities could take a whole variety of forms, but it will be difficult to lever agreements above the lowest-common-denominator.

The low priority given rural affairs, in relation to their importance to Wales, is partly a reflection of the lack of a cross-party political focus. The most recent attempt to set up a Wales Rural Forum, bringing together groups like the Womens' Institute, the churches, the farmers' unions, local community initiatives and environmental groups, has been fraught with difficulties. Initial suspicion of the Forum by the statutory sector is slowly evaporating, however. The Forum has published its own Rural Strategy but its capacity to present a clear agenda and influence the political process is still quite limited.

To what extent would a Welsh Parliament make a difference? It would at least offer an important public focus for debate on rural affairs, which would get more attention than they are given at present by the Welsh Office. However, it would still be necessary for those most concerned to devise and promote innovative, integrated and community-based solutions through bodies like the Rural Forum, to which the politicians could respond.

The strategic vacuum created by the fragmentation of local government into a system of small unitary authorities, could be ably filled by the Parliament. Institutional structures, policy objectives, spending priorities and statutory powers could all be fashioned to address Welsh conditions and needs far better than at present, just as they presumably are in the Regional Parliaments of the decentralised

European Union nation-states — Germany, Spain, Belgium, Italy and, since the mid-1980s, even France. It could off-set the parochial tendencies of small local authorities by establishing a broader policy framework and hopefully some vision.

Even so a Welsh Parliament could hardly be a panacea for all the weaknesses and failings of the rural economy. It is far from certain that it would recognise the centrality of environmental sustainability, for instance. How much better it would be at ensuring agencies worked more collaboratively, within an integrated rural strategy, would have to be seen. The structure, status and powers of our democratic institutions are clearly of importance, but so too is the ability of grassroots opinion to speak with coherence and conviction. Nowhere is that more necessary than in rural Wales. Yet a Parliament could not hinder that process. Rather, there is every chance it would be a catalyst, enabling the voice of rural Wales to be heard more clearly.

NOTES

[1] *Rural Wales: A Strategy for Development*, a strategy to guide future European Structural Funding, being prepared by a working group supported by the Welsh Office's European Affairs Division.

[2] Welsh Affairs Committee: Session 1992-3, Third Report *Rural Housing*, House of Commons Paper G21-I, HMSO.

[3] The Government's Response to the Third Report of the Welsh Affairs Committee, Session 1992-3, CM 2375, HMSO.

[4] *Rural Wales: A Strategy for Development*, op. cit., note 1.

[5] Department of Environment News Release, 25 January 1994, issued to coincide with publication of the 'UK Sustainability Strategy'.

CHAPTER 11

LOOKING AFTER OUR LAND
Farming and a Welsh Parliament

John Osmond

Welsh farming in the 1990s is confronted by falling demand, falling incomes and falling land values. The result is that many people are leaving the land. Children are not inheriting a farming tradition from their parents. Instead, they are selling their land to the highest bidder. Many farms are being amalgamated into larger holdings. Traditional farming communities are breaking up.

This is an economic problem. But deeper, and more important it is a cultural dilemma that goes to the core of Welsh values and identity. In the process it is highlighting yet again the democratic deficit that exists near the heart of so many Welsh policy concerns. It is extraordinary how little the Welsh land issue has been remarked upon, or policies to deal with it debated. Exposed in this key area of the Welsh economy and culture is an empty silence at the heart of the Welsh administrative state machine.

That there is such a machine cannot be doubted. At its apex is the Secretary of State for Wales who, according to a Welsh Office Press notice of 20 August 1993, as well as having 'overall responsibility for the department takes a special interest in' the following: economic matters; industry; regional policy; the Welsh Development Agency; the Citizen's Charter; local government reorganisation; the Programme for the Valleys; financial and revenue support grant issues; European Community issues; constitutional issues; Cardiff Bay; the West Wales Task Force; and also agriculture, the Rural Initiative and environment policy.

That one person should have oversight of so many issues of central concern to an entire nation is a key question that underlines the demand for a Parliament for Wales. The answer is that the Secretary of State for Wales cannot have a continuous, detailed command of every brief. In practice, for instance, his agricultural responsibilities are handled inside the Welsh Office by an Agriculture Department split into three divisions: Grants, Subsidies and Land; Commodities and General Agricultural Policy; and Fisheries and Animal Health. In turn these operate through the key economic Quangos and privatised utilities, including the Countryside Council for Wales, the Development Board for Rural Wales, the Welsh Development Agency, the Welsh Water Authority, the National Rivers Authority, and the Wales Tourist Board.

Beyond such agencies are a plethora of specialist agricultural advisory bodies and tribunals such as the Agricultural Advisory Panel for Wales, the Hill Farming Advisory Sub-Committee for Wales, the Agricultural Tribunal (Wales), six Agricultural Wages Committees, six Agricultural Training Boards, and six Agricultural Dwelling House Advisory Committees. A farmer working in rural Wales can receive advice from eighteen separate official sources.

There may be plenty of advice to hand, but it is not being given within an overall context of forward planning for Welsh land management as a whole. The various agencies are stumbling towards a future in which management of the land will have to be brought into an ever closer relationship with environmental requirements. This offers some hope to a farming community whose financial security is now under unprecedented attack. Wales's farmers are of crucial importance, not just for the maintenance of a beautiful and ecologically rich countryside, but because they embody an irreplaceable part of our cultural inheritance. As yet however, and in the absence of a democratic forum to mobilise opinion around it, there is little strategic thought being given to this central concern of the Welsh polity, and even less strategic action.

BREAK-UP OF THE FAMILY FARM

There is clear evidence of a trend towards the break-up of medium-sized holdings in Wales, farms between 50 and 250 acres. Those below tend to be sold off as residential 'small-holdings' — put on the market at relatively high prices— and those above merged into very large holdings, typically sheep ranches. It is now increasingly common for the land of a newly bought farm to be amalgamated with that of its neighbour, and the house sold off either as a holiday home or as a smallholding to people from outside the area. In one case in the early 1990s a 144-acre farm in Dyfed was sold in four lots of land for a total of £479,000, that is over £3,329 per acre. [1]

During the 1980s the number of holdings in Wales between 50 and 125 acres began to fall precipitously. Between 1982 and 1987, for instance, they dropped from 9,753 to 9,159 — a reduction of 593 holdings. [2] There is no doubt that the trend has continued since then and is accelerating.

The result is the destruction of the Welsh family farm, the kind of holdings that can in the right circumstances offer a reasonable living to a young family. Small farmers form a cultural enclave that has an importance far outstripping their numbers. Together they are the last community in Wales which naturally uses the Welsh language in their everyday working lives.

Hitherto, these people have not responded to purely market forces. Rooted to the land in which they work, they have held on to their land regardless of whether its price has gone up or down. They have passed it on to their children who have done the same. Moreover, they have done this through all manner of vicissitudes, conserving resources against bad times, generally living frugally with few outgoings.

The historical threat now facing Welsh agriculture is that this pattern is being dislocated if not destroyed, with potentially catastrophic consequences for the rural economy and Welsh culture as a whole. There is an undeniable case for a minimum level of activity within the farming industry below which, for a range of reasons — strategic, environmental, and cultural — it should not be allowed to fall. Yet with the impending reduction, if not removal of price supports, there is an unanswered question of how the decline of Welsh farming can be stopped from at its present spiralling rate.

In March 1993, 48-year-old Cyril Lewis, who has farmed all his life in Gwynedd, gave evidence when the Commons Select Committee on Agriculture met in Wrexham. He outlined a pessimistic vision of his future. He farmed 200 acres at Penmachno in Snowdonia and was facing the prospect of selling up and severing his family's links with the land: 'My farm has been in the family for two generations but neither of my sons are interested because they say I have to work too hard for too little money,' he said.

One of his sons worked for the National Westminster Bank in Dolgellau, while the other was a pharmaceutical representative in Manchester. 'Its difficult to look to the future,' Cyril Lewis added. 'If my sons don't come into farming then I will sell up and that will be the end of the line of farmers in my family.'[3]

PRESSURES ON FARMERS IN THE 1990s

Statistics for the first two years of the 1990s showed the numbers making a living on the land in Wales falling from 63,600 to 61,000. [4] Commenting on the decline a spokesman for the Farmers Union of Wales said: 'It is the smaller, family farms and smallholdings that are disappearing. When smaller farms come up for sale the land is bought by a neighbouring larger farm and the farmhouse is sold off separately with around four acres of land.' [5]

The figure of 60,000 or so people are employed in the industry, is reckoned to amount to only 43,000 full-time equivalents. This means that a large, and growing, proportion of farmers work part-time on the land. It is estimated that during the 1980s the number of full-time, regular workers fell by 30 per cent, signalling a trend that seems bound to continue. Nonetheless, farmers still represent 5 per cent of the workforce for Wales as a whole (the United Kingdom figure is 2.8 per cent), and 18 per cent in mid-Wales, the area covered by the Development Board for Rural Wales. These figures do not assess the employment multiplier effects in supplying industries or in the marketing and processing of agricultural produce. They are, however, considerable. When taken into account the 5 per cent directly dependent on agriculture in Wales as a whole rises to between 8 and 10 per cent, and more in rural Wales itself.

In Wales, agricultural output consists of three main products. These are milk (33 per cent of output); cattle and calves (26 per cent); and sheep and lambs (26 per cent). Together, they account for 85 per cent of all Welsh agricultural output. Given the physical constraints against producing alternatives, this makes Welsh farming particularly vulnerable to adverse change. [6]

During the 1980s a decline in farm-gate prices resulted in a steep decline in the value of the output of Welsh farming (by 14 per cent) and an even steeper decline in farmers' incomes, by a massive 50 per cent. In real terms the average farm income fell from £22,530 in 1980 to £10,160 in 1990. The fall steepened towards the end of the decade as the table on the next page [7] illustrates.

All the statistics suggest that it still makes sense to speak of agriculture as 'the backbone of the rural economy'. Undeniably, however, the massive changes that face farming over the next decade have the capacity of breaking that backbone.

Net Income Bracket	% Farms 1989	% farms 1990
Less than £0	9	19
£0 - £10,000	39	39
£10,000 - £20,000	24	18
£20,000 +	28	24

THE COMMON AGRICULTURAL POLICY

Roughly 80 per cent of agricultural land in Wales, much of it above 700 feet, is officially classified as Less Favoured Areas by the European Union, including over 60 per cent of arable land and more than 75 per cent of permanent grazings. The result is that Welsh farming is very heavily subsidised, through the European Union's Common Agricultural Policy (CAP). The annual direct level of support is something like £110m, to which must be added commodity price support for milk, beef, sheepmeat and cereals. In all CAP support to Wales is around £140m a year. A quick, if crude, calculation reveals, therefore, a direct subsidy to Welsh farmers of some £7,000 per holding.

The aim has been to support incomes to maintain the population of the rural areas and to maintain the land itself. However, subsidy dependence means that Welsh agriculture is intensely vulnerable to policy change in Brussels. There are intense pressures to reform the Common Agricultural Policy. These include wasteful over-production; the environmental costs of intensive agriculture; and international free-trade pressure for a substantial reduction in CAP support.

There is bound to be a substantial long-term decline in market support, combined with temporary relief for small farmers and those in the poorer farming regions. Wales will benefit from the latter but to an extent which is difficult to predict. The result is uncertainty.

A study on the *Rural Economy in the Less Favoured Areas of Wales,* published in April 1993 by the Department of Economics at the University of Wales, Aberystwyth, observes:

> We would expect the effects of future policy changes to be much more serious than anything experienced in the 1980s. We anticipate a decline

in full-time agricultural employment and a further polarisation of farm holdings structure between the small and the large. If farm households are to survive, there will be an accelerating need for additional sources of income, other than farming, in the rural areas of Wales. [8]

The Aberystwyth study also concludes that in the 1990s,

> Many Welsh farm businesses will become unviable as a basis for supporting a household. Farm households will only survive if they can find alternative sources of income. These may come from any of three possible sources: from traditional on-farm diversification; from work on other farms; or from jobs off the farm altogether. [9]

DIVERSIFICATION

The logic of this conclusion is already being widely followed across rural Wales. Some 70 per cent of Welsh farmers are already engaged in activities other than pure farming. The most obvious farm-related activities are farm contracting, tourism, and value-added food-processing.

Farm contracting is likely to increase as the number of residential holdings and part-time agriculture creates a class of farmer who will not wish to invest in machinery or will not have the time or skill to use it. Insurance requirements, new technology and the specialised character of environmental work also point in this direction. Tourism, however, appears less promising. Many believe it has already reached saturation point, with a proliferation of farmhouse bed and breakfast establishments and with quality rather than quantity in short supply.

So far as food processing is concerned a daunting statistic is that of the 7 per cent of all UK farmers involved in processing or marketing their own output, only 40 per cent break even, let alone make any profit in return for a significantly increased workload and financial commitment. The proliferation of hypermarkets across rural as well as urban Wales would seem a more accurate signpost to the future. Unless policies change, therefore, it is unlikely to expect that farm-based marketing will become a significant source of additional income on more than a small number of Welsh farms.

A sobering statistic is revealed, too, in a large-scale *British Farm Diversification Study*, involving 10,000 farms (1,620 of them in

Wales) carried out during 1989-90. This found that with full-time farms in Wales the average income from farming activities was £3,581 and from diversification activities £2,109. For England and Wales as a whole, the figures were £22,058 and £3,625. [10]

The contrast reveals two harsh realities. *Proportionately*, diversification was much more important in Wales (37 per cent of the total) than in England and Wales combined (14 per cent). At the same time, however, the income from these activities was relatively much smaller in Wales. Moreover, it was found that the smaller the farm, the less likely it was to be diversified.

In the Aberystwyth study already quoted, 427 farmers were questioned on what ideally they would prefer to be doing. The answer was unqualified: their main motivations were, first, living and working in a rural area; second, being their own boss; and, third, building up a farm to pass on. As the study remarks, 'Though these preferences are not entirely inconsistent with off-farm work, they do at least suggest the possibility that it may not be the preferred option.' [11]

On-farm diversification, therefore, seems to indicate the most appropriate route for change in activity though the 1990s. There are strong indications that this is likely to be closely linked to environmental management, and the production of environmentally-related goods.

OVERGRAZING

Over the last twenty years the numbers of sheep in Wales have almost doubled. For every person in Wales there are now four sheep. The numbers vary through the seasons due to breeding. However, taking the total — that is the number between May and September during the lambing season — the figures increased from 6,551,658 in 1973, to 8,721,209 in 1983, and further increased to 11,371,000 in 1993. [12]

There are a number of interlocking reasons for this rapid growth, some of which directly follow on from the problems facing farmers that have already been discussed:

* Virtually the whole of Welsh farmland comes within the European Union Less Favoured Area (LFA) categorisation for

mountain and hill regions where agriculture is difficult, and so entitled to special subsidies.
* Changing farming policies of the European Union have resulted in the quotas on cattle aimed at decreasing milk production, thereby pushing farmers into sheep production.
* The price of lamb has been rising as a result of the Single Market. The export price for lamb has also been rising disproportionately, pushed by the effective devaluation of the £ coming out of the ERM.
* There has been an increase in small holdings, with a growing number of 'part-time' farmers who tend to keep sheep rather than cattle, because they are easier to look after.
* There has been a sharp fall in the numbers of 'family farms' in Wales which have been steadily merged into large, sheep-ranch holdings.

A direct result of the increasing numbers of sheep, however, has been overgrazing. It is become so widespread and is taking place on such a scale that it is now regarded as one of the most serious Welsh environmental problems. Certainly, many environmentalists and conservationists regard it as the most important issue affecting nature and conservation in Wales.

The impact is subtle and not obvious to the casual onlooker. Hence, overgrazing has not received a great deal of attention. Most people are unaware of it. Nonetheless, over a relatively short period of time overgrazing is bringing about major changes to the landscape and wildlife of rural Wales.

If their concentration is too high sheep progressively change the natural cover of the land. They eat and trample the heather until it disappears, to be replaced by coarse grasses and bare soil. Large areas of Wales, especially in the Brecon Beacons and Berwyn Mountains were once covered by heather which has now disappeared. Heather typically supports wildlife, a wide range of invertebrates and birds which have disappeared. In substantial parts of upland Wales serious soil erosion is also occurring.

Using aerial photography the Countryside Council for Wales estimates that since 1946 there has been a 44 per cent heather loss on the Welsh uplands. All the evidence indicates that the rate of loss has been intensifying since the early 1980s as the numbers of sheep have escalated.

Among the bird species affected by overgrazing are red grouse, dunlin, golden plover, hen harrier, merlin, black grouse, and the short-eared owl. In 1877 six or seven hundred red grouse would be shot on the glorious 12th on the Berwyns. In 1992, an RSPB survey found there were only 900 pairs in the whole of Wales. There are just 45 pairs of dunlin and 80 pairs golden plover left in upland Wales.

Overgrazing is also having a serious impact on river bank fauna and flora. It is difficult to maintain fences along rivers, especially spate rivers which tend to sweep away minor obstacles like fences. The sheep are eating the seedlings and roots of trees and bushes along many Welsh river banks, and especially in Dyfed. The result is that the present generation of vegetation that so marks out the landscape of our valley floors, especially the mature trees, will simply not be replaced.

On the smaller streams this has considerable implications for fish. Small streams are shallow by their nature and many of them provide the natural habitat for brown trout and are also important spawning grounds for salmon. In summer the water heats up and fish escape this by going into deeper pools or hiding underneath overhanging vegetation. On overgrazed upland pastures there is very little of this. Of course, many factors are at work here, including pollution, netting, and acidification. However, the wider impact of sheep overgrazing on these upland streams has so far gone largely unnoticed. On the lower reaches of the rivers the impact of overgrazing on the habitat of otters, is also worrying environmentalists.

There is an awareness of the overgrazing problem amongst specialists, especially those within the Countryside Council for Wales. Policies are being initiated, some not directed at overgrazing as such — but rather at other problems facing agriculture and the rural economy — though they have an effect on overgrazing as well. However, there seems to be little awareness of how policies in one field impact on another across the range of agencies which have responsibility for rural Wales.

ENVIRONMENTAL MANAGEMENT

While 10 per cent of the land area of England and Wales is covered by National Parks, in Wales it is 20 per cent. Add on five Areas of Outstanding Natural beauty and the figure rises to 25 per cent. It does not stop there. Other tracts of land have been designated as Environmentally Sensitive Areas (ESAs) where farmers are assisted in maintaining traditional landscapes. They are Anglesey; the Lleyn Peninsula; the Clwydian Mountain range; the Cambrian Mountains in Ceredigion; and Preseli, that is the whole of Pembrokeshire to the north of Milford Haven.

In addition there are hundreds of smaller Sites of Special Scientific Interest. What this means is that some 50 per cent of the land area of Wales has already been identified in ways where it is possible to both support and control for environmental reasons the activities of farmers and those concerned with housing or economic development.

All of this opens up the prospect for environmental needs being brought into a direct relationship with the economic dilemmas of Welsh farmers through the creation of a market for 'environmental goods'. Increasingly, farmers will be paid to stay on their land and protect it by undertaking an agreed programme of environmental conservation. Indeed, this is part of the thrust of the CAP reforms under which farmers will be rewarded for taking land out of production and allowing it to lie fallow.

In 1993-4 some £4.5m was spent in the Welsh-designated ESAs as a result of environmental planning agreements made with farmers. A more comprehensive pilot scheme, known as Tir Cymen and organised by the Countryside Council for Wales, is presently underway in Meirionnydd, Dinefwr and the Gower. This is comprehensive in the sense that it applies to whole farms, offering farmers annual payments in return for the management of their land to benefit wildlife habitats and the landscape. It is asking the question: is there a market in environmental goods? That is to say, should farmers be rewarded for using their skills and resources to look after the land in the same way they are paid for their agricultural produce?

There is no doubt that rural planners see a role for farmers in environmental conservation as a key way forward. Yet it cannot be a complete answer to Wales's farming dilemma.

There is a fundamental risk in encouraging farmers to rely on environmental payments for a significant part of their living. First and most obviously, the payments may be cut when global Treasury budgets come under pressure. In practice it may prove difficult to link environmental payments to constructive work on any scale. A further, often overlooked, consideration is that the labour to do the designated work may simply not exist on many family farms. More generally, as the Aberystwyth study already referred to comments:

> Environmental conservation will play a bigger role in agricultural policy, and farmers in Wales can expect more opportunities to obtain income in this way. However, its potential should not be exaggerated. For example, if the present Environmentally Sensitive Areas Scheme, currently operating in the Cambrian Mountains and the Lleyn Peninsula, was extended to the whole of Wales, the level of payments to farmers would only be a small percentage of the current value of market support.[13]

THE FUTURE

The Aberystwyth study concludes:

> The time is ripe in the 1990s, as it was in the 1840s and in the 1940s, for a sea-change in agricultural policy. There is every indication that such a change will occur, and that it will take the form of a shift of emphasis away from agriculture as a sector towards the needs of regions (and of rural regions in particular).[14]

This conclusion implies planning. Yet, although Wales has no lack of planning agencies, there is very little debate occurring around the directions in which Welsh agriculture should be heading. In no other policy area is the lack of a democratic forum at the all-Wales level so transparent.

There is a growing understanding that the needs of agriculture will have to be brought into a much closer relationship with the needs of the environment. However, precise policies how this can be achieved in practice and on the scale required to keep Wales's Welsh-speaking community of farmers on the land with a reasonable living, are in short supply.

A glance at the Welsh party manifestos produced for the 1992 general election makes the point. The Welsh Conservative manifesto devoted just four lines to agriculture, together with a passing reference to the work of the Countryside Council for Wales. Labour's manifesto revealed little sense of urgency either, suggesting that it would 'consider the establishment of a Rural Affairs Unit at the Welsh Office.'

The Liberal Democrat and Plaid Cymru manifestos were better, as might be expected from parties with such strong connections with rural Wales. The Liberal Democrats, for example, called for an Agricultural Bank for Wales while Plaid Cymru described some detailed policies to sustain the family farm and help young people make a start in farming.

Nowhere, however, was there a comprehensive vision of how the Welsh countryside could be managed to bring the needs of the environment and the needs of farmers for an economically sustainable future into a relationship one with the other.

Britain is an overwhelmingly urban society and its politics reflect that. The European Union is now the leading player in developing farming and rural policies, but as yet Wales has no effective voice in its deliberations. On the Council of Ministers there is a theoretical right for the Secretary of State for Wales to sit, but he never does. When agriculture is discussed, it is England's Minister of Agriculture who attends, a Minister who has no responsibility for farming in Wales. Equally, when the key issues of the environment come before the Council, again it is England's Secretary of State who fills the United Kingdom seat.

Wales has a pressing need for a coherent and imaginative rural policy to be developed and vigorously implemented. Under present arrangements the dimension of the need has not been recognised let alone the policies debated to address it. Who could doubt that both would be more swiftly and effectively dealt with inside a Welsh Parliamentary chamber?

NOTES

[1] The case is quoted by Cynog Dafis, Lewis Griffith, Peter Midmore, and Alan Thomas, 'The Young Farmer's Predicament' in *Towards a Green Welsh Future*, published by the Ceredigion and Pembroke North Plaid Cymru and Green parties, December 1992, p. 22.

[2] The figures were quoted by Lewis Griffith of the Farmers' Union of Wales at a 1989 conference organised by Plaid Cymru in Lampeter.

[3] *Western Mail*, 3 March 1993.

[4] Welsh Office, *Welsh Agricultural Statistics*, published annually.

[5] *Western Mail*, 11 March 1993.

[6] The statistics and the judgement in this and the following paragraphs

are contained in David Bateman et.al., '*Pluriactivity and the Rural Economy in the Less Favoured Areas of Wales*, Department of Economics and Agricultural Economics, University of Wales Aberystwyth, 1993, p. II-3.

[7] Cynog Dafis et. al., op. cit., p. 21.

[8] David Bateman et. al., op. cit., p. II-10

[9] Ibid.

[10] John McInerney and Martin Turner, *Patterns, Performance and Prospects in Farm Diversification*, Agricultural Economics Unit, University of Exeter, 1991.

[11] David Bateman et. al., op. cit., p. III-18

[12] 'Welsh Agricultural Statistics', op. cit.

[13] David Bateman et. al., op. cit., p. II-9.

[14] Ibid., p. II-19.

CHAPTER 12

THE WALES WE NEED
Sustainable Development and a Welsh Parliament

Margaret Minhinnick

During the last two generations we have had our innate ideas of personal and cultural sustainability corrupted and diminished. This has occurred on a global scale, most clearly by nuclear technology, but also on a local level by environmental and linguistic decline. For some the nuclear bogey has replaced the idea that the world might end apocalyptically, due to an act of God and because of humankind's sin. Now we understand that the world as we know it could end at any time, due to a technical error. One result is greater hedonism, as we confront a world that might incinerate itself because of a banal computer mix up.

'I'm-all-right-Jack' attitudes and unsustainable practices, whether private or corporate, are understandable because our idea of the future, of life continuing endlessly after us, has been besmirched. And following nuclear technology there is now the revolution in genetic engineering, a process that further desanctifies life. Species — even human ones perhaps — may now be the products of laboratories.

Such knowledge influences the concept of sustainable development and subtracts from it. By nature people are conservers, but also developers. In past generations sustainable development has resulted from a balance being achieved between these two opposing influences. Now, however, we have become totally unbalanced in favour of the development side. We have opened a Pandora's Box containing dilemmas such as untrammelled technological development and massive population growth.

A tragedy is that after only a decade of use, the words *sustainable development* have become a meaningless cliché, abused by politicians, industry, the media and also by the special interest groups that mouth it. An urgent need is to rescue the idea from those who deliberately seek to ensure that 'sustainable development' remains a fragment of hollow rhetoric.

INHERITANCE AND THE FUTURE

The Wales we know has been shaped almost entirely by uncontrolled economic developments: from agriculture, coal, quarrying, and the steel industry to the influence of the multinationals, tourism and now a massive growth in consumerism and organised leisure. We cannot pretend that much of this development was or is sustainable. Even so it has shaped the present, and brought us to where we are today.

Now, however, the pace of development threatens within the next fifty years to obliterate much of the cultural and environmental variety that makes Wales the distinctive place and society it is. Much of our industrial experience clouds this reality about our future. Though it is now clear that our major past industry, coal-mining, was unsustainable — in part because of excessive, all-out exploitation — nonetheless it seemed, until the 1960s at least, to create sustainable communities. Scores of those communities still exist and are having to cope with the essential unsustainability of the industry that gave them life.

The coal industry, was full of paradoxes. On the one hand it imposed a cultural and social uniformity on much of south Wales that, with hindsight, was unhealthy. At the same time, however, it created a social strength that acted as a shield for traditions and a seed-bed for political ideas. It created a focus for social beliefs that can protect us from the consequences of unsustainable development that are obvious elsewhere, for example in the 'overheated' southeast of England.

Wales is now threatened with a different type of unsustainable development based around increasing consumerism, burgeoning directed leisure, and a shrinking political consciousness. From being a society with a well-developed work ethic, we are now more controlled by a leisure ethic. These are the background impulses behind the massive, anonymous and homogenising developments of Cardiff Bay and Cardiff Gate, and smaller ones such as the Swansea Marina and the proposed Usk Barrage.

Wales is also influenced by the consequences of Britain's incoherent and market-led energy policy. Opencast coal, oil, gas and other developments directly threaten areas such as Cardigan Bay and parts of the Swansea and Neath Valley which, until now, have never been exploited industrially. These areas would be integral to a future in which environmentally-sensitive tourism became an important Welsh industry.

The recent study by the Institute of Welsh Affairs entitled *Wales 2010: Creating our Future* is one chilling example of a Wales completely subject to unsustainable development, at the mercy of 'free marketeers' and those who are not prepared to take the time to plan for integrated transport and energy policies.

This report advocates an eight-fold growth over the next fifty years in the Welsh economy, explains that this is feasible, and implies that considerations such as cultural and environmental protection will occur inevitably as a result of market forces. The report commits the fundamental error of assuming that the future will have to be created by the same mistakes, misapprehensions and exhausted thinking that are now shaping the present. Central to this is the idea of employment.

EMPLOYMENT AND SUSTAINABLE DEVELOPMENT

Today there are three million people classified as unemployed in the United Kingdom. Yet if we add to these the numbers of the fit and healthy retired, and categories such as housewives and husbands working at home, it will be seen that the number of people without 'paid jobs' is much greater. All of the big political parties in Wales claim the three million figure can be much reduced, although it is noticeable that people such as Neil Kinnock are now admitting that full employment, or unemployment on early 1960s levels, are impossible.

For true sustainable development to occur we must first redefine the concepts of employment, work and jobs. Only the Green Party has done much thinking on this, and has been brave enough to discuss such policies as a basic citizen's allowance that would enable people to choose whether to 'work' or not.

Until we destroy the stigma of unemployment, the social shame supposed to be felt by people on the dole — until we destroy the demeaning concept of the dole — we will always be threatened by unsustainable development in the shape of 'jobs at-any-price'. No matter how culturally or environmentally destructive in the long term, such projects invariably receive support from planning authorities. The chance of creating jobs — no matter how few, or for how brief a period — is seen as the overriding consideration.

An obvious case is the opencasting of coal, for example the go-ahead for British Coal's proposals at Selar Farm, near Glynneath. Communities in this area will now be completely surrounded by opencast workings. It seems we are quite prepared to sacrifice immemorial landscapes and rare habitats, pulverise geological and drainage patterns, threaten human health and create pollution for schemes which often employ fewer than thirty men and continue for less than a decade. To make such proposals more attractive, we fail to incorporate the cost of the destruction, or subsequent landscape 'restoration' in the price of opencast coal. In this way we rig the market by passing on the real bill to future generations. All this is classic unsustainable practice.

The way we have corrupted, misused and deliberately limited the concept of *work* in our culture threatens progress towards a more sustainable Wales. In such a Wales, rather than 'employment' as we know it, cultural, social and environmental health would take first priority on the political agenda. This might appear an irony to those who consider that the mining and quarrying industries created or maintained many of Wales's cultural traditions. Yet the philosophy of jobs at any price — which still appears one of the principles shared by all major parties — is proving the greatest threat to environmental and cultural sustainable development.

It is depressing that only the Green Party now seems willing to discuss the type of work that society requires, and the kind of jobs that might bring dignity, fulfilment and social stability to Welsh people. The American example is enlightening here. Between 1979 and 1989, the USA economy created 32 million jobs — as opposed to the 5 million created in the whole of Western Europe. But the work created mostly involved what Charles Handy has called 'hamburger work for hamburger pay'.[1]

The American novelist Douglas Coupland has gone farther. His book *Generation X* depicts young people who must work at 'McJobs', live a 'McLife', and exist in a 'McCulture'[2]. His world — and ours — is one that increasingly adopts the values and philosophy of companies like McDonald's.

However, we are as much influenced in Wales by Japanese as American work ethics. In 1989, the Chairman of Sony claimed that the average Japanese worked 2,159 hours per year, compared with

1,546 hours clocked by the average German. It seems the 'Gradgrind ethos' outlined by Dickens in *Hard Times* is still with us. So to 'remain competitive', a German worker must make one hour as effective as one hour and twenty minutes laboured by a Japanese person.

As Charles Handy says, work today is about 'profit, performance, pay and productivity'. Whatever happened to 'family, friends, festivals and fun'? Of course, competition in industry can be healthy. Perhaps it is essential. But there has to be more to life than 'winning' or we shall always be losers.

Many of the jobs created today in Wales are 'McJobs', especially those in tourism. According to the Wales Tourist Board, the industry employs almost ten per cent of the Welsh workforce, and brings £1.3 billion into the Welsh economy. Despite recent investment by companies such as Ford, Bosch and Sony along the south Wales M4 corridor, tourism remains the likeliest sector for employment growth. This is borne out by statistics that show that in the UK's 'boom years', 1985-1990, manufacturing output went up by almost 19 per cent, whilst the labour force fell by 5 per cent. All manufacturing investment is aimed in part at reducing costs. Invariably this means reducing jobs and replacing people with machines.

The stigma of unemployment creates huge unhappiness and division. It also breeds crime and is a problem throughout the European Union, from Greece to Ireland. At the same time affluence is as much a cause of crime as poverty — especially when linked to a media system that constantly triumphalises material wealth and consumer purchasing power. This is illustrated by a 1993 government report which showed that over the period 1979-1990, the poorest ten per cent of the British population saw their income fall by 14 per cent in real terms, whilst the income for the average household increased by 36 per cent. [3]

What we need to explore is the concept of the 'steady state economy'. It was encouraging to see that this idea was at the heart of policy platform that was agreed between Plaid Cymru and the Green Party in Ceredigion and Pembroke North in the period leading to the 1992 general election [4].

An example of the antithesis to a 'steady-state economy' is the dependence of much of present modes of employment on long distance commuting. This has the effect of destroying shared experience through communities and 'communality'. Mobility through private cars which is a boon to almost all of us, is now also a curse. It ensures that many workers have little time or energy to consider the health of the communities in which they live. A 'steady-state economy' is the opposite of consumerist triumphalism, in which a permanent, sizeable minority of people have no means of escaping the snares of means-tested social security. Absence of a 'steady-state economy' means not only encouraging social problems, but building inevitable unsustainability into our future.

THE ROLE OF POLITICAL ACTIVITY

Environmentalists, language campaigners, and those working in the voluntary sector plus our politicians, should look much harder at the nature of work, how it is defined at present, and how it might be defined in the future. Mainstream politics simply does not concern itself with such matters and that is why the current use of the term 'sustainable development' by politicians and industrialists is meaningless.

Sustainable development will always be an illusion until we deal properly with the concept of work and economics. Ecologists have to understand this. An example was the publication in 1994 of *Biodiversity Challenge: An Agenda for Conservation in the UK*.[5] This is a unique guide by voluntary bodies to how we might protect and conserve hundreds of threatened species of wildlife in the UK — from whelks to wildcats. The value of this publication is that it is of massive help in defining what sustainable development would mean if its principles were practised.

However, the actions advocated in *Biodiversity Challenge* and their consequential saving of species, will remain pipe dreams if we do not first tackle our economic system, and embed within it the principles of sustainable development.

The Parliament for Wales Campaign itself has a role in this debate. If it fails to address these issues and merely seeks to give London ideas of growth-at-any-cost a Welsh gloss then it will only help to perpetuate exhausted political mythologies. An example of the way the Campaign can engage in the debate came with the drafting and changing of the *Democracy Declaration* approved at the Llandrindod conference in March 1994. The draft *Declaration* stated that a Welsh Parliament would 'build a better future for our people by . . . the provision of jobs'. Yet this was over-simplistic. We are living in a real world where major companies grow in budget but shrink in staffing terms, where the idea of a 'job for life' is all-but dead, where the manufacturing hub is located in South East Asia, and where 'work' will increasingly be defined in terms of personal entrepreneurial skills and initiatives. So it was encouraging to see that in the *Democracy Declaration* that was finally approved, the word 'jobs' was replaced with the wider, more embracing term of 'work'. It may seem a small point but it connects to large issues. There is little point in moving certain political powers to Cardiff just for the sake of it. If we do not seek to use those powers to create a culturally and environmentally sustainable Wales, then a Welsh Parliament could well prove a hollow achievement.

If the Parliament for Wales Campaign can become the tool to win powers to create a sustainable Wales then it could mark the beginning of a new politics. Of course, as Neil Kinnock has always said, before you can exercise power, you must be plausible and clever enough to win it. In order to do that the Campaign must take part in and influence the debate about what kind of Wales we want. We must have ideals and not be ashamed of them merely because they might appear difficult to realise.

What Welsh politics lacks today is idealism and vision. The Campaign must help to restore those vital ingredients . If it does not, we will fail to attract more young people to participate in the democratic process. Thus the Campaign must prove it is interested in greater things than altering the arrangement of deck chairs on the Titanic — or who gets the chance to sit in them.

SUSTAINABLE DEVELOPMENT AND HOW TO ACHIEVE IT

Sustainable development ensures that we learn from the past and that the present is placed in economic and cultural harmony with the future. It means that the quality of our lives is informed by the positive traditions of the past, and that we, as a matter of course, ensure that culture and society, as well as the atmosphere, the landscape, and the water environment, are passed on to future generations in a condition that we would wish to inherit . This, does not mean, however, that progress — positive and beneficial progress — should or can be avoided.

The following are ten practical ways in which we could move towards creating a sustainable society in Wales:

1. We need to press for an integrated energy policy. Wales is now the fulcrum of the opencast, oil and gas exploration, and wind industries. Sustainable development in Wales will be impossible if our energy industries are not properly combined and directed.
2. We must hammer out sustainable policies for transport and tourism.
3. We must create a system whereby the needs of the environment can be calculated and included with the rest of the more usual profit-and-loss accounts for the Welsh economy.
4. We should create a Centre for Sustainability that would demonstrate practical examples of best practice in work creation, including everything from architecture to insulation.
5. We must convince those involved in pressure groups in Wales - the people who campaign on everything from dirty beaches to access for the handicapped — that often the success of their work depends on issues of democracy and the political enlightenment of our elected representatives.
6. It is time to stop knocking our heads against a wall and ask how that wall should be rebuilt. Veterans who for years have campaigned for groups such as Cymdeithas yr Iaith Gymraeg and Friends of the Earth Cymru, should take the next natural step, and move into politics. Only then will they have the opportunity to implement the changes for which they are calling. We should remember that we get the politicians we deserve.
7. We should encourage those who currently work in pressure groups, and especially young people, to join in local government. At present, the sad fact is that local government is largely in the hands of people with very badly dated political ideas and prejudices. The principles of subsidiarity, coming from the European Union, and of sustainable development from the 1992 Earth Summit, are seen as irrelevant or incomprehensible by many such people.
8. We desperately need greater female participation. Welsh politics is ludicrously dominated by middle-aged and retired men. Young people must also be convinced that they should co-operate in Welsh politics. At present our political landscape resembles Jurassic Park with real dinosaurs.

9. We should try and create political alliances across the parties. A good example is that between Plaid Cymru and the Green Party in Ceredigion and Pembroke North. This is an example of political co-operation and, dare I say it sustainable development, that is unique in Britain.

10. We should understand that the election of a Welsh Parliament is a crucial step towards achieving sustainable development — but only if it provides the appropriate means to ensure true democratic decision making at every level, especially at the level of the local community.

The principle of sustainable development should inform every aspect of our politics and the way we organise our economy. It means preventing multi-national companies possessing the power to wipe out whole species of workers at the stroke of a pen.

It also means putting public money where it is needed, such as into decaying mining communities, and not into grandiose, cosmetic schemes such as the Cardiff Barrage which in their gargantuanism are outdated before they are built. The Barrage, of course, has always been an economic issue with environmental consequences, yet the Green movement has persisted in dealing with it the other way round.

Above all, sustainable development can only be achieved by a radical overhaul of our politics, and a much more enlightened attitude to work, employment and unemployment. Creating a Parliament for Wales is an essential part of the overhaul. But the campaign must be continuously informed by the principles of sustainable development . Until our political institutions reflect that, most of us will continue to pursue careers, interests and above all lifestyles that are even now eroding our capacity to offer to future generations the same things that we take for granted.

NOTES

[1] Charles Handy , *The Empty Raincoat* (Hutchinson, 1994).
[2] Douglas Coupland, *Generation X* (Hodder, 1991).
[3] Charles Handy, op cit.
[4] See, for instance, *Towards a Green Welsh Future*, published by the Ceredigion and Pembroke North Plaid Cymru and Green parties in

December 1992. It includes practical papers on small businesses, energy, farm forestry, the predicament facing young farmers, and pollution in Cardigan Bay.

[5] *Biodiversity Challenge: An Agenda for Conservation in the UK* (Royal Society for the Protection of Birds, 1994).

PART IV

SOCIAL POLICY

BUILDING OUR NATIONAL IDENTITY
Education Policy and a Welsh Parliament

David Reynolds

Wales has a distinctive educational experience and particular educational problems. Yet in few ways are they reflected in the policies that have been devised to cope with them. In the early 1980s there emerged a Welsh 'standards' debate about school achievement. Within a few years, however, concern about these issues evaporated. Instead we were incorporated into an England-and-Wales series of inappropriate strategies based upon the utility of a market-based and consumerist approach. There was, of course, one exception due to the addition in Wales of Welsh as a subject in the 'national' curriculum.

What this experience has demonstrated is that without the willpower mobilised by its own democratic institution — a Welsh Parliament — the Welsh education system will remain directionless and will lack momentum. Welsh education policies *have* differed slightly over the last few years with the Welsh Office Education Department allowing some weak, hesitant initiatives. There has been a more 'collegial' style. And there have been some slightly different school curricular arrangements. In general, however, Wales has failed to develop policies suited to the resolution of its education problems, for meeting its different needs, or for coping with the highly unfortunate consequences of the blanket imposition of a range of policies designed for England.

THE STANDARDS DEBATE

It became clear in the early 1980s that, in terms of the examination results of Welsh children as a whole, our education system was seriously under-performing relative to the results being achieved elsewhere in England and Scotland. Previously unpublished failure rates of schools in Wales revealed that a quarter of Welsh children were leaving school without any qualifications. Data from the Assessment of Performance Unit showed Welsh children with the lowest levels of scientific performance at age fifteen of any region or nation within the United Kingdom.

The malaise in the system was easily explicable, even if it was not defensible. The Labour Party had historically concentrated upon the education of the able through the Welsh grammar schools, being concerned to give every pupil with ability the chance of competing against more advantaged middle-class pupils from England. Welsh Nonconformity had been a somewhat instrumental creed, which utilised the County schools established after 1889 in its own interests to further social class mobility.

Welsh language culture had elevated the educated person to a high status and through its various institutions such as the Eisteddfodau and the Urdd was ruthlessly concerned with the importance of cultural excellence and competition. Given all this, and given the status of the old grammar schools of Wales, it was not surprising that the comprehensives of Wales were simply like grammar schools in their ethos, organisation and ultimate educational purposes. That is to say, they were concentrating on elevating the chances of the brighter pupils and neglecting the needs of the less able.

Initially, in the early 1980s, there appeared to be a rapid response to such criticisms. In 1979-80, 25.8 per cent of Welsh children had left school with no qualifications. By 1982-83 this figure had dropped to 17.9 per cent. This improvement was not bought at any cost to the education of the able, since a record 27.2 per cent of children left school with five or more 'O' levels in the latter year. It seemed that the comprehensive schools of Wales were changing their leadership from the original former grammar school personnel, were changing organisation and curriculum to focus more on lower ability pupils, were entering more pupils for public examinations, were eroding their grammar-school ethos and were relating more to their parents and to local communities. There was hope that an authentic Welsh blend of traditional grammar-school concern for excellence would combine with the best of the 'new radicalism' from England.

A Schools Council Committee for Wales 'Disaffection Conference' of 1983 spawned Wales-wide school improvement initiatives, with each Local Education Authority selecting a named 'under-performing' school and encouraging it to review and improve its internal functioning. In a British context, the project was unique because of the openness with which schools were examined.

A wide range of HMI publications were produced. *Response to Under-achievement, Attendance and Achievement in Secondary School, Home/School Links, Homework in the Secondary School,* and *Departmental Organisation in Secondary Schools* were instances of high quality, specifically Welsh material addressed to the remediation of specifically Welsh problems. However, by the mid-1980s the momentum of the school focused policies that had begun a few years before ceased. Symbolically, the Schools Council Committee for Wales was wound up at about this time.

In 1986-87 and 1987-88, around 16 per cent of pupils left school with no qualifications, indicating that the rapid fall from 1978-79 up to l982-83 had ceased. In fact in 1988-89, the figure *increased* to 17 per cent. Since the English systems' failure rate had also 'settled' over these latter two years at around 9.5 per cent, it was obvious that by the late 1980s the Welsh system had found a 'steady state' level of failure considerably above that of the English system.

By the early 1990s the position had not improved. The publication of the 1993 Summer examination results, presented and analysed in the form of individual schools' figures, enabled comparisons to be made with English examination results. At GCSE, 42 per cent of English pupils obtained five or more grades A-C, compared to only 37 per cent in Wales. At 'A' level, the average points score was 16.0 for English pupils, and 14.0 for Wales. The marginal differences in levels of social deprivation between England and Wales cannot explain the contrast in the effectiveness of the two systems.

Variations between LEAs within Wales was also a matter for concern. For example, West Glamorgan in 1993 recorded a 'failure' rate of 6 per cent of pupils achieving no examination passes, which compares to 30 per cent in 1976-77. South Glamorgan recorded a higher rate of l0 per cent in 1993, but had a rate of only 19.6 per cent in 1976-77. Why did one local authority improve considerably and the other to a much lesser extent? At 'A' level, South Glamorgan and West Glamorgan had identical points scores (14 per student), but the social class background of the South Glamorgan pupils is considerably more advantaged than that of the West Glamorgan pupils. Why is South Glamorgan not a better performer? Why does West Glamorgan do so relatively well?

Such evidence of ineffectiveness within the educational system is not, of course, the only problem. In many other respects Wales has 'needs' markedly different from those that occur in England. Among them are:

* A far higher proportion of primary schools in rural Wales are small, having only one, two or three teachers, which imposes demands on teachers in terms of curriculum range and experience;
* There is a bias in the system towards the study of the humanities. In comparison with England and especially Scotland, a higher proportion of students from Wales study arts and social science subjects, rather than science and applied science.
* There are continuing problems of ensuring equal opportunities for women within the Welsh teaching force. The proportion of women head teachers has actually fallen over the last decade, by comparison with substantial rises in other parts of Britain.
* The historical remit for Welsh Higher Education institutions to be broadly-based institutions offering virtually all subjects to their communities has resulted in relatively adverse ratings in research selectivity exercises. Competing Universities in England and Scotland, with more specialist traditions, have been better rated.

THE EMERGING WELSH EDUCATION POLITY

When the Conservative Government began to 'pilot' its ideas on educational reform in the election campaign of 1987, Wales was yoked to England with the distinctive nature of Welsh problems and needs only being recognised by the inclusion of the Welsh language as a core subject in Welsh medium schools.

However, in the years since the passage of the 1988 Education Act, more and more differences have occurred in the policies applied to the two countries, divergences which increased markedly after the Conservative Government's educational changes were severely criticised and interrogated by teachers and parents in the Spring and Summer of 1993. The differences include:

* A distinctive Welsh component to the curriculum in the subject areas of History, Geography, and Music.
* Differing advice to Ministers from the National Curriculum Council in England and from the Curriculum Council for Wales

concerning the nature of English as a subject. The Welsh preference was to introduce 'Standard English' later than proposed in England and to avoid the prescription of specific forms to be learned.

* A different consultation process on the revision of the school curriculum which involves in Wales the obtaining of data through writing to individual schools to ascertain their opinions. This is in marked contrast to the procedures followed in England where there is greater imposition. It is hard to imagine any English Education Minister ever using language such as that used by Sir Wyn Roberts: 'We have always tried in Wales to listen to what teachers have to say. Teachers are the people who know about the curriculum because they know the pupils they have to teach.' [1]

* The absence in Wales of any City Technology Colleges, which are a controversial presence in sixteen areas of England. Informal soundings of the Welsh Education Office by one Cardiff comprehensive that was seeking to change its status to a City Technology College were met by the response that they did not want such an institutions in Wales because it would be troublesome and controversial.

* The omission of Wales from the area of operation of the new Teacher Training Agency.

* The creation of the separate Further and Higher Education Funding Councils for Wales with the potential for pursuing different priorities from those set in England.

* The creation of a separate Curriculum and Examinations Authority for Wales.

* Different 'performance indicators' being used for England and for Wales, with Wales also not publishing any figures on 'truancy' rates.

This is an extensive list and it does not include the Welsh-medium sector, the main area where distinctive Welsh policies have been allowed to evolve to meet distinctive Welsh needs. Support for the Welsh language has proved to be a very successful example of the use of Welsh autonomy.

Currently, 400 of the 1,704 Welsh primary schools and 19 of the 227 secondary schools are designated Welsh-medium. However, the category the Welsh Office is increasingly adopting is described by the term 'Welsh-speaking schools' where more than half the curriculum subjects are taught through the medium of Welsh. When this criteria is applied, the number of 'Welsh-medium' or, more accurately, Welsh-speaking secondary schools climbs to 55. By the year 2001 the figure is likely to have risen to at least 60.

The use of this categorisation reflects the increasingly mixed-language character of 'Welsh-speaking Wales' and also the requirement in the Welsh school curriculum that Welsh must have a presence in all schools. With 'autonomous' boards of School Governors increasingly making the decision on their linguistic status, rather than relying on an imposed local authority policy, more schools are likely to move in this direction to reflect parental demand, both in 'Welsh-speaking' and 'Anglicised' Wales.

The reasons for the increasing demand are well known. Most important is the experience that bilingual schools do more for their children than simply encourage them to speak Welsh. This is measured by the higher academic success of Welsh-medium schools. In 1992, for instance, 50% of their pupils achieved five or more GCSEs at grades A to C. This compared with 33 per cent in Wales as a whole and 38 per cent in England.[2] The strong social identity of the pupils in Welsh-medium schools, and their apparent social and affective qualities, all make the bilingual sector an authentically Welsh *and* extremely effective system. Indeed, it may be that in its bilingual schools system Wales has discovered a blueprint for success that has eluded it since the dissolution of the Welsh grammar schools in the 1960s and 1970s.

The diagram opposite shows the emerging structure of the Welsh education polity. This pattern, which will be fully in place by 1996, reveals a maturing and autonomous Welsh administrative system of education, with its own, separate, institutional framework. A key question is whether a mature and autonomous Welsh education policy will flow from it.

IMPOSITION OF AN ALIEN SYSTEM

Despite the signs listed above that a distinctive Welsh approach is beginning to emerge, it is only as a result of a generally imperceptible drift resulting from a separate administrative system. On the whole Wales remains subject to English education policies that are at best irrelevant to our culture and educational traditions and

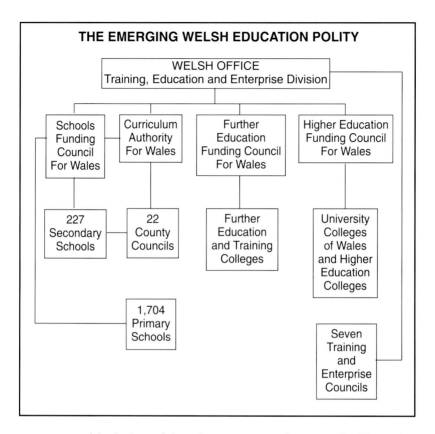

at worst positively harmful to the prospects of our pupils. Examples include:

* Underlying the changes brought in by the 1988 and 1993 Acts has been the notion of competition so that 'good' schools will expand and 'poor' schools contract and ultimately close. In Wales, where perhaps 40 per cent of parents have no realistic choice because of the large geographical distances between schools, 'levelling up' school quality in this way is impossible.
* All schools in Wales have one more subject to be taught to their pupils than schools in England, either Welsh to pupils in Anglicised areas or English to pupils in Welsh speaking areas/schools. Crucially, however, the standards of attainment expected at the various age levels are the same in Wales as in

England, despite the increased Welsh curricular range. How are schools in Wales expected to teach the 'extra' material? Should the standards expected be lower in Wales? How can performance be compared in future between schools in Wales and those in England?

* The Assisted Places Scheme, which is currently taking about one half of one per cent of mostly able pupils out of English comprehensives and helping them to attend schools in the independent sector, was designed to improve standards in State schools by increasing the competitive pressure from the independent sector. In a Welsh setting where historically only a very small proportion of pupils have ever attended the independent sector (2.5 per cent of all pupils as against the English rate of 8.5 per cent), and where there are very few independent schools to attend, this policy is completely irrelevant.

* All pupils in schools in Wales (except a very small number of mostly older pupils in the dozen or so schools exempted by the Secretary of State for Wales) have the experience of learning a second language, whether it be pupils from English speaking homes learning Welsh for the first time or pupils from Welsh speaking homes learning English. Given this clear difference in linguistic experience, one would have expected that distinctive programmes of study for modern foreign languages in Wales would have been developed. Instead, Wales has identical programmes of study for modern foreign languages to those of England.

Nowhere has the imposition of alien policies on the distinctive Welsh education culture been more clearly seen than with the pressure and inducements that have brought to bear to persuade schools to opt out of local authority control and become grant-maintained, that is directly funded by the Welsh Office. By mid-1994 only 16, a handful of Welsh schools, had opted out — eleven secondary schools and five primary. Yet in March 1994 the 15 schools that had then opted out were awarded an astonishing £7.5m capital allocation for the forthcoming financial year, that is an average of £500,000 per school. Comparisons are difficult to make, but in 1991-2, the latest year for which global figures are available, Wales's 52 nursery, 1,704 primary and 227 secondary schools in the local authority sector were awarded a total capital allocation of

£42.15m — that is, an average of just £21,230 per school. A Welsh Office spokesman said, 'The funding that is available to grant-maintained schools is designed to ensure that they are not worse-off than LEA-maintained schools. It is not a bribe.' [3]

However, in July 1994 the Welsh Office announced increased aid for schools in the grant maintained sector and a requirement that governing bodies of all schools in Wales consider grant-maintained status at least once every school year.[4] Whatever culture or country was in the minds of Tory Government policy makers when their education policy was framed, it certainly cannot have been Wales. The irrelevant and, in certain cases, harmful nature of these policies is of course joined by the continued neglect of the distinctive Welsh needs so far as rural schools, equal opportunities and many other areas are concerned.

TOWARDS A DISTINCTIVE EDUCATION POLICY FOR WALES

It is important to realise that Wales has the potential to implement a distinctive and more appropriate education policy. In particular, we have in place the necessary organisational infrastructure. There exists the Training, Enterprise and Education Division in the Welsh Office, experienced in the practice of generating distinctive policies on the Welsh language, and fully capable of generating policies on other topics.

There is the separate Welsh branch of OFSTED, the successor to the Welsh Inspectorate, with its production of separate Welsh reports on educational standards and on numerous other issues. The Research and Statistics Division of the Welsh Office routinely collects specifically Welsh data on schools and education performance. The Welsh Joint Education Committee is still the examination board chosen by almost all schools in Wales. The Higher Education Funding Council for Wales and the Further Education Funding Council for Wales, together with the University of Wales, give an increasingly distinctive orientation to policy and practice for those over the age of sixteen.

If we now turn to examine the precise policies that could be delivered by a Welsh Parliament priming this sophisticated Welsh administrative structure, then it is clear we are entering an already trampled field of debate. In the Summer of 1993, the Institute for Welsh Affairs published its report entitled *Wales 2010: Creating Our Future*, in which specific proposals were made to improve Welsh educational standards to the levels of our industrial competitors, to improve the skills and enterprise base of the Welsh labour force, and to encourage a broader and more vocationally minded 16-19 curriculum . As the report put it:

> Wales should seek to develop its own, distinctive qualification for post-16 education by establishing a 'Welsh Baccalaureate' . . . the Training, Education and Enterprise Division of the Welsh Office should be more willing to determine what is best for Wales, independently of the Department of Education in London.

Later in 1993, the Welsh Office published its consultation document *People and Prosperity: A Challenge to Wales*, in which a further range of educational policies were aired for discussion. Again, the focus was upon the importance of vocational qualifications and enterprise, the encouragement of vocational guidance, the importance of training at all stages of individual lives and the need for teamwork between organisations, statutory and voluntary, to ensure that there was effective action to realise these priorities.

However, the usefulness of these documents is limited because they do not spell out the detailed structure of what the alternative Welsh educational policies and organisational systems might look like. Other recent British reports that have argued for the need for more nursery education and for changes in the curriculum for older children, fail to acknowledge distinctive Welsh needs. Moreover, with the exception of the issue of the Welsh language, even the Curriculum Council for Wales curriculum review links Wales directly to England in its recommendations.

In framing a distinctive education policy a Welsh Parliament would need to examine the following areas:

General Policy Orientation:

• Wales should look beyond England for its educational policies. Countries such as Scotland, Japan, Taiwan, France, Germany and the Netherlands all have lessons to offer. In particular, the Scottish

experience of generating high levels of academic attainment and in the vocationalising of its curriculum is interesting.
• We should ask how there can be a strategic and democratic direction to policy after the dissolution of the eight county education authorities in Wales and their replacement by the 22 'most- purpose' authorities during 1995/96.
• We should consider how effective and democratic oversight can be given by a Welsh Parliament to the present administrative educational structure — the Training, Education and Enterprise Division at the Welsh Office, the Higher Education, Further Education and Schools Funding Councils for Wales, the seven Training and Enterprise Councils, and the new Curriculum and Examination Authority for Wales.

Macro-level Policies:

• We should consider what specifically Welsh policies are appropriate to ensure high quality schools, colleges and universities since market based solutions aimed at closing down low quality provision are unlikely to work in a Welsh context, where consumers cannot exercise their preferences. Such policies for Wales may need to involve a more substantial role for 'non market' systems based upon local authorities performing the evaluative, support and accountability roles that are increasingly organised through the market in the English system.

Curriculum and Assessment:

• We should consider whether the assessment and information provision systems of Standard Assessment Tests and the publication of school examination and attendance rate data that are a necessary part of the English educational system's market oriented policies are necessary in Wales if the educational market is absent.
• We should consider whether the crowding of the curriculum suggests a need for further substantial pruning of subjects and attainment targets within Wales, particularly since we have one more subject in nearly all our schools compared with England. This pruning should be in addition to that recommended by the Curriculum Council for Wales, and should centre on the

rationalisation of foreign language teaching, where children in Wales already have experience of language learning.
• We should consider whether all the curriculum subjects taught within Wales should have a distinctive knowledge base appropriate to our specific history and culture.

Language Policy:

• In contrast to the Curriculum Council for Wales recommendations on Welsh in Key Stage 4 of the curriculum, we should consider how the success of our existing bilingual educational policies can be expanded and built on, since all Welsh children will shortly be bilingual from primary school onwards. Trilingualism, beginning from the introduction of a modern foreign language such as French or German into primary schools from age 7, would give Wales many further competitive advantages in the global economy of the future.

Education for Employment:

• We should consider the nature of the curricular experience appropriate for children in an increasingly information-oriented society, and in a society where breadth of knowledge is increasingly as important as depth. Rather than being tied to the English obsession with the 'gold standard' of 'A' levels, a Welsh Baccalaurcatc involving a broad, but slowly narrowing, range of curriculum subjects being studied from age fourteen to nineteen, should be considered. This would involve compulsory mixing of science, languages, applied science and humanities subjects, and also entail compulsory training in work-related skills.
• We should consider the nature of the preparation for work and wealth generation offered within the educational system. The encouragement of 'vocational' routes as recommended in Sir Ron Dearing's review of the school curriculum may be less fruitful than the encouragement of skills relevant to the work situation across all subjects, humanities, sciences or applied sciences. The ability to access information, to work collaboratively in groups, the capacity for independent thinking and the capacity to link together creatively different bodies of knowledge are all capabilities frequently emphasised as desirable by industrialists.

Further, they can be developed independently of any 'vocationalising' of the late secondary age curriculum as in the Howie model in Scotland, or the Dearing model in England.

The Rural Dimension:

- We should consider how the community education functions of schools in rural Wales can be protected and restored, given that funding now separates funding for schools from funding for adult and community education.
- We should consider how the special needs of small schools can be provided for, both in funding and in terms of curriculum support.

Equal Opportunities:

- We should consider special forms of positive discrimination to enhance the role played by women in Welsh schools and colleges.

EDUCATION AND THE FUTURE OF WALES

Ultimately, the approach to the education policies a Welsh Parliament should pursue are dependent upon the kind of Wales the Parliament will wish to shape and nurture. In a world where increasingly the individual relates more and more directly to the central State, and where the community level is increasingly emasculated and destroyed by central State actions and interventions, Welsh history and culture have always emphasised the importance of community as the third dimension upon which societies must rest. If we truly wish for a three dimensional society in which the individual, the local community and the State (Welsh, British, and European) interact, then this must be planned for consciously.

Our education system must be geared to produce people whose heads and hearts are developed through handling the complex interactions between these three organisational levels. To achieve this our policies must be designed to focus as much attention on the 'middle' community tier and build upon what our local authorities have done historically.

More generally, our attitudes to our Welsh educational policies must be determined by Welsh attitudes to issues of human and social identity. In a world where increasing internationalisation removes cultural barriers and where 'culture' flows freely to make all increasingly similar and homogenised, the recent rediscovery within many countries and settings of the importance of the local, the ethnic, the minority and the specific, all suggest a need for individuals to retain distinctive identities in the face of global homogeneity.

Somehow we need to use the local, the community and the Welsh identity, not to build nationalistic cultural walls to repel outside influences but to create a strong identity on which individuals can draw as they look outwards. Using the Welsh educational system to build that national identity is something that Wales may still have a chance of doing. Many other societies have lost the chance. If we in Wales can balance young peoples' need for identity, alongside their intellectual need for exploration, then we will accomplish something which has great utility and importance for the rest of the world. There is no self respect in continuing to collude in the application within Wales of policies from England. They are policies which are not working in England and which can never be appropriate to Wales.

The young Welsh citizens of the future will need to be locally-rooted with a sense of security in their ideas of Wales. But they will also have to be at ease as citizens of the European Union. These are not alternatives. We need a Parliament for Wales to ensure that the vision of a national identity merging with an international consciousness for our young people becomes a reality.

NOTES

[1] Welsh Office Press Release, 27 April 1993.

[2] See Wynford Bellin, 'Language and Education' in Wynford Bellin, John Osmond and David Reynolds, *Towards an Educational Policy for Wales* (Institute of Welsh Affairs, 1993).

[3] *Western Mail*, 31 March 1994.

[4] Welsh Office Press Release, 14 July 1994. From September 1994, the development grants for schools opting out were increased from £42.50p per pupil to £50; special purposes (premises) grant increased to 50 per cent of actual cost of insurance instead of being limited to a maximum of £6,000;

special purpose grant for staff restructuring extended to include non-teaching staff; schools with less than two years experience running a delegated budget eligible to receive £30,000 plus £30 per pupil; capital grants were increased from £11,000 to £12,000 per school plus £20 for each pupil, with a minimum allocation of £16,000 to any school.

CHAPTER 14

CLOSING THE GAP BETWEEN RHETORIC AND PRACTICE
The Health Service and a Welsh Parliament

Emrys Roberts

The Health Service is the biggest area of Welsh public administration and expenditure. It has 65,000 employees and a total revenue of around £2 billion a year. It operates through 158 hospitals, 1,800 general practitioners, 800 dentists, and a wide range of community care workers. Each year NHS Wales treats nearly half-a-million in-patients and around 140,000 day cases.

Yet, despite making strenuous efforts to take note of the views of its patients, the Welsh health service is accountable only to the Welsh Office and in no way to the people or their communities.

In this respect it differs from the Health Service in England where Regional Health Authorities (RHAs) were created as part of the 1974 reorganisation (although it is now proposed to reduce and eventually abolish them). Despite being appointed rather than elected, the members of the RHAs do represent various professional and community interests.

Some of the work undertaken by the English RHAs was delegated to Area (now District) Health Authorities in Wales. However, their strategic policy-making and resource allocation functions were taken over by career civil servants in the Welsh Office who could not hope to have as balanced a view of the total needs of the people of Wales as a more representative body.

The activities of the NHS in Wales are subject to scrutiny by Parliamentary Select Committees but inevitably they tend to review what has happened after the event, and then usually only in selected specific areas. It is extremely rare for them to become involved in strategic and policy issues which are vital for future development.

Both the structure and the funding of the NHS need urgent consideration. On both counts the consensus of opinion in Wales might well be markedly different from that in England. A democratic society would cater for such differences. Yet without the overall strategic direction a Welsh Parliament would give, the NHS in Wales is likely to remain in its essential features a mirror image of the service developed to meet the needs and values of our English neighbours.

THE SPLIT BETWEEN PURCHASER AND PROVIDER

There are undoubtedly some benefits to be gained from separating the purchaser and provider functions of the NHS. Whereas previously District Health Authorities managed services, and consequently planned development programmes from the perspective of the service provider, they no longer have any point of reference other than to identify and meet the needs of the population they serve.

However, from this point of view, General Practice Fundholders — regarded by the Government as in the vanguard of their reforms — are something of an anomaly since they are both purchasers and providers of services. Their funds are deducted from the total allocation available to Health Authorities. As a result, therefore, the greater the number of GP Fundholders in any area the more resources available to Health Authorities are diminished. The greater the number of GP fundholders, the less a Health Authority is able to influence the delivery of services.

In addition, whilst it is obviously desirable that all health professionals be aware of the level of resources they commit, a system which continually induces them to balance financial and clinical judgements in individual cases may not be appropriate. Purchasing by Health Authorities rather than GP practices, though in full consultation with GPs and community groups, may well be a preferable option for a Welsh Parliament to consider.

Splitting the purchaser and provider functions has its downside too. Health Authorities may identify a need for a particular service, but they can no longer automatically provide it. Instead they have to invite tenders from independent providers. Where there is a multiplicity of potential providers, as in some of the large English conurbations, this might reduce costs (though there is always a danger that costs will be estimated at too low a level in order to win a contract, with the quality or quantity of the service suffering as a result).

In many other parts of Britain, however, including much of Wales, there is often little choice of alternative providers. As a result the providers are placed in a strong position to demand a higher price than the service justifies. Moreover, in some instances it may be difficult to find anyone interested in providing the type of service the Health Authorities wish to purchase.

An 'internal market' certainly produces competition. But it does not necessarily produce a more cost-effective service. Even in the business world, where competition can sometimes reduce prices for customers, there is often a great deal of duplication and waste, for example through the establishment of parallel marketing and distribution systems.

Another problem with the split between purchaser and provider in the NHS is that it has inevitably increased the percentage of expenditure on administration. Specifications and contracts have to be drawn up and negotiated. All activity must be identified and costed. The quantum of service provided must be checked. Administrative tasks escalate. The system inevitably breeds managers and accountants and cannot operate without them. Inevitably, the percentage of total funding spent on direct patient care is reduced. The shortfall can only be made up by an injection of substantially more cash — and that is not happening.

A public debate on these issues would hopefully expose the insecure financial basis of current NHS orthodoxy, which goes something like this: 'Introducing the disciplines of business into the NHS will make the organisation more efficient, unit costs will be reduced, thus enabling us to cope with an ever increasing workload at little or no extra cost'.

The reality is, of course, that the increase in activity (currently a political as well as a moral imperative in the NHS in order to reduce unacceptably long waiting lists) increases the number of units processed. The lower cost per unit has to be multiplied by a larger number of units and overall costs increase. In the business world this extra cost is recouped by increased income from sales. In the NHS, however, the increased resources necessary to sustain increased activity are not being made available. Hence the phenomenon of ward closures and staff time and facilities not used to their full capacity towards the end of each financial year.

Recent investment in better management such as more precise and bespoke information systems is therefore largely wasted. Paradoxically, increased investment in information technology will result in a less effective service unless substantial additional resources are made available. Only then can advantage be taken of the greater efficiency that is offered.

PUBLIC ACCOUNTABILITY

There is a welcome tendency in the Welsh NHS to consult the public far more than in the past on priority issues and ways of tackling priority needs. However, unless more adequate funding is made available the process can often appear to be little more than seeking public approval for cuts in low priority services. The result enables health purchasers and health service providers to remain afloat but any plans for improving services go by the board.

There cannot be a justification for consulting the public on the way in which limited resources should be deployed without first consulting them on the totality of resources to be made available. A Welsh Parliament would be able to institute such a debate, in public. An acute awareness of our social conditions in Wales coupled with our traditional social values provide hope that various social programmes would receive a higher priority under a Welsh Parliament than at present. Though in view of other pressing social needs, whether this would result in significantly increased spend on the NHS is open to question.

A Welsh Parliament would also have the opportunity to take the NHS out of the hands of civil servants and unelected Quangos and bring it under more explicit democratic control. The precise structure that would be appropriate depends on whether it were deemed advisable or not to retain the purchaser/provider split in the NHS and on the structure of local government and other public services.

Undoubtedly, a level of strategic thinking and decision-making is required between the all-Wales level and that of local communities. Locating services requiring a large element of professional advice and expertise at too local a level can restrict horizons, produce inflexible structures and mitigate against the provision of the professional support required by those working in the field. This seems to be recognised even by those in favour of the 22 new most-purpose local authorities — hence the talk of consortia, agency arrangements, and so on, for sectors such as Social Services.

This is not necessarily an argument in favour of retaining the existing County Councils. Rather we need to discuss the precise nature and purpose of elected regional authorities within Wales before considering what their boundaries should be or what areas they should serve. We may well determine that five or even as few as three are appropriate. The whole question of local and regional government in Wales should be debated in a Welsh Parliament before changes are made to current structures. If this is not done we shall once again end up with a structure imposed on us rather than one which grows out of our own needs and wishes.

Whatever pattern is adopted, it is vital that NHS structures match — or, preferably, are integrated with — those of other important public services. Now that we are thinking more in terms of improving the health status of communities rather then merely responding to the ill-health needs of individuals it becomes ever more imperative that we work closely not only with Social Services but with other services such as Housing, Environmental Health, Education, Leisure, Employment, and Community Development .

Whatever structure is eventually deemed appropriate it must consist of democratically elected bodies — both for the NHS and other public services. The argument in the past has been that the NHS is too complex an organisation — containing too many powerful professional interests which need to be balanced against each other — to be the responsibility of local government. If the division between purchasers and providers of health services is maintained, however, that argument loses most of its weight — certainly with regard to purchasing authorities, which are now quite small and compact. The provision of services could well remain with independent contractors (both family practitioners and NHS Trusts) which need not necessarily be under direct democratic control.

It is more and more being recognised that the NHS should be about locally identified needs rather than balancing competing professional interests. Viewed in this light there is no need why the task of identifying need should not be the responsibility of a democratic body. The main strategic issues could be dealt with by authorities working at a regional level within Wales, leaving more local authorities — possibly the new most-purpose authorities — undertaking most of the detailed planning and purchasing of services to meet local needs.

Overall strategic direction would remain at the Welsh level with the Welsh Parliament. One thing the Parliament would certainly do, as a matter of urgency, would be to address how the following two fundamental principles of good medical practice can be applied to Health Service Management:

(i) No new procedures or interventions should be sanctioned for widespread use until they have been thoroughly tested.
(ii) Apart from a few very exceptional cases no intervention should be undertaken without the patient's informed consent.

Unfortunately all too often these have often not been applied to the way in which health services are provided. Wholesale reorganisations have been introduced time and again without any pilot schemes to assess their strengths and weaknesses and with little, if any, attempt to secure general public approval. A full evaluation of recent NHS reforms is needed to establish their effectiveness and their acceptability to the people of Wales. Such a review would undoubtedly be instituted by a Welsh Parliament.

There is a great deal of doubt and uncertainty throughout all levels of the NHS at present, yet it is vital to maintain and improve staff morale. As things are there is a significant gap between NHS rhetoric and NHS practice. Turning the NHS into a health gain, resource effective, and people-centred service — which is the stated aim — is unlikely to become a reality without a thorough review of the way the service is structured and financed. A Welsh Parliament is needed to ensure that Wales, as well as inspiring the creation of the NHS fifty years ago, will breathe new life into it today.

CHAPTER 15

A POLICY FOR WALES, NOT ENGLAND
Housing and a Welsh Parliament

Gareth Hughes

It is undeniably clear to those of us living in Wales that we have a major housing problem. Some of us would go further and describe it not as a problem but as a crisis. All too often, however, housing as an issue is portrayed as an English, or perhaps only as an inner-London concern. This perception has more to do with the centralism of our mass media than with reality. In any objective analysis it would be clear that Wales has some of the worst problems in Britain.

What are the characteristics of Wales's housing need? Put simply, it is a lack of affordable and appropriate housing for many of our people. The latest census indicates a rising population in Wales and a change in many aspects of our social structure, all leading to increased housing demands. In 1992, according to the Welsh Office, 10,270 households were accepted as homeless by the local authorities. This was an increase of four per cent over the previous year and a staggering 83 per cent increase over a ten-year period. Bad though these figures are, they are dwarfed by Shelter Cymru's estimate that the true homeless numbers are 60,000. In the same ten-year period in Wales, there has been an absolute decline in the homes available for rent of 48,000.

We are currently adding to the social housing stock by about 3,000 homes a year. Yet Wales requires between 7,500 to 10,000 houses each year to meet the real housing needs of its population. All would agree that behind these statistics lies a homelessness problem that needs addressing. The supply of housing has not been available to meet the demand at the prices that many Welsh people can afford. Moreover, our existing housing stock is older than elsewhere in the United Kingdom and as a consequence the levels of unfitness are much higher.

That Wales requires a different approach to its housing provision has been recognised by successive governments since the early sixties. Within the Welsh Office there is a Housing Division and one of the Welsh Office ministers has a housing portfolio. This recognition by government of the need for a different approach went further with the passing of the 1988 Housing Act and the establishment of Tai Cymru-Housing for Wales — a new Quango created to finance, support and supervise housing associations.

With the creation of such a formidable administrative structure, one might have presumed that the tackling of the Welsh housing problem would follow a Welsh agenda and would reflect the needs of Wales. Unfortunately, this is far from being the case. Whilst there has been a nod to the different needs of Wales in the administrative structure, the reality has been that the government has been following its own very English housing agenda.

THE ATTACK ON THE HOMELESS

Apart from the establishing of Tai Cymru-Housing for Wales there has been no piece of housing legislation that has not been framed for an English purpose and then applied to Wales, whether relevant or not. In the main, differences made by the Welsh Office in housing policy have been presentational only. This is perhaps best illustrated by an early 1994 consultation paper produced by the Welsh Office entitled *Access to Local Authority and Housing Association Tenancies*. It proposes that:

- The duties of local councils towards homeless households will be separated from the allocation of rented social housing.
- The duties of local councils towards those in housing need (including the homeless) will be reduced and amended in a number of ways.
- Social housing allocations will only be made from the waiting list, and the Government are minded to issue regulations on the way those waiting lists are operated.

What the paper argues is that a household's immediate need for shelter should be dealt with separately from any decision to offer it permanent re-housing. Households for whom the councils find temporary housing will then have to wait. Not only that, the Government are proposing significant limitations to the duties local authorities have toward homeless households:

(i) Currently a person qualifies for assistance if they have no interest in a property (that is, ownership or tenancy). This will change in a move to prevent households who leave parental or friends' homes from being accepted as homeless unless a court order has been obtained, they are severely overcrowded, or at risk from violence.

(ii) The household should have no access to alternative accommodation (for example, in the private rented sector). The local authority would have powers to determine that such accommodation was available, for example by being aware of the local housing market. Crucially, the household could be expected to use accommodation outside the local authorities area, which in effect allows the local authority to export its residents' housing needs.

(iii) The duty to a household by the council would be after the council had determined that household's circumstances. It would be 'expected' (not 'required') to provide immediate assistance in an emergency.

(iv) The authority could discharge its duty by securing temporary housing in its own, a housing association's or a private sector dwelling. The authority might provide rent deposits or guarantees which would secure access into a private sector tenancy which the household could not secure with its own resources.

(v) This temporary accommodation would be available until the household has had sufficient time (as determined by the council) to find alternative housing. If the household was genuinely unable to do this, the duty to secure temporary housing would recur, leading the household through a series of revolving doors, generating instability and disruption for them.

(vi) There would be no duties to those entering the country on the understanding that they do not resort to public funds. Neither will there be a duty to those who have accommodation at their disposal in their country of origin, or who are asylum seekers.

The underlying principle is that local authorities' duties should provide a safety net against rooflessness and not automatically extend — as at present — to provision of a permanent home. We are being asked to address this principle. All of us who are concerned about the need for decent housing for all should reject the principle and assert that it is the responsibility of the state to provide a decent shelter for all its citizens.

The justification for the proposals given by the English Housing Minister, Sir George Young, is that the move was necessary because people on the waiting lists were losing out. He said homeless people were getting council homes on average within seven months, compared with between one and two years for those on waiting lists.

Sir George Young may have some slight evidence to justify his proposition if he was simply looking at London. To apply it to England as a whole is difficult to understand on the basis of the evidence available. However, what is certain is that there is no evidence that there is a problem that needs addressing in Wales.

In Wales in 1992-3 only 22 percent of new council tenants were homeless (2,676 people), while 71 percent were from the local councils' waiting lists. Welsh local councils are entitled to nominate to at least half of the new houses built by housing associations in Wales, yet only one in four Welsh council nominations to housing associations were for homelessness.

The number of Housing Association lets to homeless people increased from 436 in 1991 to 1,270 in 1993, but the proportion has remained roughly the same at around 26 per cent. The number of Housing Association lets going to the priority homeless in Wales has been rising gradually, increasing from nine per cent in 1991 to twelve per cent in 1993. Far from indicating that the homeless were queue jumping, the evidence is that in Wales quite the opposite is happening: the homeless seem to be getting a much smaller proportion of Housing Association and Local Authority lettings than would be expected.

TRAILING THE COAT-TAILS OF ENGLAND

What this consultation illustrates is that the Welsh Office, far from addressing the housing needs of Wales, yet again proposed to embrace legislation aimed at solving England's, or more accurately London's, housing problems. Despite the Welsh Office having been given a massive thumbs down to these proposals by all who submitted evidence, Sir George announced his intention to proceed, and surprise, surprise, the legislation will cover Wales.

As a consequence, homeless people in Wales are likely to be

unnecessarily disadvantaged. Unfortunately, this and similar situations are likely to recur unless there is a radical rethink as to how housing policy, its legislation and administration, are handled in Wales.

Currently, there is little opportunity for a clear housing policy to emerge that meets the needs of Wales. Welsh Office Ministers cover a number of different portfolios which allow them little time to develop a comprehensive understanding of housing issues. Even if there was such an understanding it is difficult to see that the parliamentary time would be available at Westminster to embark on legislation that might stem from a policy initiative.

What is true for major policy initiatives is also true in terms of assessing how existing policy is working. The opportunities to question housing priorities, policies and practice are limited to the short time available in the House of Commons to ask questions to the Minister. Occasionally valuable work has been done by the Select Committee on Welsh Affairs. However, as this Committee can only cope with looking at one area of the Welsh Office's responsibilities in depth in any one parliamentary year it is clear that major areas of policy concern are unlikely to be often scrutinised.

Another factor that inhibits Parliamentary scrutiny is that all too often, the Welsh Housing Minister is able to claim that he has delegated his concern to a Quango such as Tai Cymru-Housing for Wales — the body charged with distributing grants and supervising the work of the 102 registered Housing Associations. Immediately that puts him beyond the direct scrutiny of Parliament. This is a serious matter when it is considered that Housing Associations now have the lead role in developing new social rented housing policies which involves a substantial area of provision.

When it is also considered that Tai Cymru-Housing for Wales has responsibility for the distribution of significant public moneys each year — £185m in 1994-5 — democratic accountability for its priorities is minimal. The provision of housing for the various groups in our society is complex and needs prioritising. These priorities should be set by the community as a whole. In Wales this is not the case. We have a democratic deficit. It needs rectifying.

THE DEMOCRATIC AGENDA

The case for a Welsh Parliament so far as housing is concerned is overwhelming. There is a need for policies to be developed which answer a housing situation that is specific to Wales. Policies should be developed through discussions and debate at both the local and the all-Wales levels. We must involve the people of Wales in developing their own priorities. Further still, the people of Wales need the ability to vote resources to meet those priorities.

Currently, what is presented as a tailor-made Welsh housing policy is determined either by a small elite in the Welsh Office or by the smaller but even more unrepresentative group who run the Quango, Tai Cymru-Housing for Wales. It is by having such unrepresentative groups that policies are devised that are inappropriate for Wales.

A Welsh Parliament would set up its own housing committee and, together with the appropriate Welsh government departments, this would develop and sustain a consistent approach to housing policy and legislate accordingly. This Welsh Housing Department and Parliamentary committee would lay claim to the required resources. More appropriately they would be answerable to the electorate of Wales for their actions.

Housing is a basic human need and as such everyone should be able to have influence over the type of provision best fitted to their requirements. It is important that housing policy should be developed upwards from the people within their own communities, through local government to a national Welsh Parliament. The Parliament would have funds to allocate towards housing. The policy it developed would be based on the knowledge and experience of members from all parts of Wales. It is only through such a democratic system that all the needs of Welsh communities can be balanced fairly and priorities set.

The Government see their housing policy through English eyes to meet the needs of England. Wales's needs are an afterthought. Wales, with probably the worst housing problems in the United Kingdom, urgently requires to set its own housing agenda. The only acceptable solution is to establish a national Parliament for Wales with powers to legislate and raise revenue so that a housing policy appropriate to Welsh needs can emerge.

PART V

CULTURAL QUESTIONS

CHAPTER 16

STRANGERS IN OUR OWN LAND?
Our languages and cultures and a Welsh Parliament

Hywel Francis

I hope I understood the essence of Professor Hywel Teifi Edwards's remarkable inaugural lecture *Arwr Glew Erwau'r Glo* which was delivered at University College Swansea in 1994. In it he reflects on the lack of any real intellectual flowering of the Welsh language in the mining valleys of south Wales during the century from 1850 to 1950. Somehow the vast economic, social and political changes of the region just did not fit the Welsh Establishment's image of what a *parchus* Welsh collier should be.

'Tonypandymonium' was not sober, liberal, deferential, pious, Welsh speaking. This 'American' Wales was not legitimate and so the experience was not allowed — could not be allowed? — to find expression through the Welsh language. Although it did of course through English, the other language of the valleys which ultimately eclipsed Welsh as the majority language of the majority experience of Wales in the twentieth century. It is not clear whether the rich and varied Welsh language dialects of the valleys at the turn of the century could have coped with a popular secular culture which was global in its trajectory, but the creation of the 'Mabon' role model ensured that it never had a chance.

For Hywel Teifi Edwards — and for most of us who care about the languages and cultures of Wales today — this was and is a double tragedy which needs to be addressed. In our desire for a Parliament for Wales we must start from a mutual recognition that we have a diversity of languages and cultures in Wales: otherwise, we will all be strangers in our own land. The lesson of the Welsh language in the valleys in the period 1850-1950 is now ironically and paradoxically paralleled by those who feel that English is not a legitimate form of cultural expression within Wales.

It is not clear what Saunders Lewis would have made of Hywel Teifi Edwards's revisionist and refreshing thoughts nor the sight of Nigel Walker hurtling towards the French line. But what we do have is his eccentric letter in 1931 to Kate Roberts which goes to the heart of the matter, albeit unintentionally:

> Mi roddais innau dair darlith yn ddiweddar ar y nofel Gymraeg ym Mlaen Dulais (dan y coleg) . . . os drwg yw Aber Dar, beth am leoedd fel Blaen Dulais a'r cymoedd eraill oll . . . oblegid ei pellter o bob cyfannedd gwareiddiad o unrhyw fath . . : un felly yw Blaen Dulais. Ni welais erioed y fath gynulleidfa o anwaraidd syml. Petawn yno ddiwrnod mi'm lladdwn fi hun, rwy'n siwr bron.

> [I gave three lectures recently on the Welsh novel in Seven Sisters (under the College) . . . if you think Aberdare is bad, then what of such places as Seven Sisters and all the other valleys . . . because they are so far from any kind of civilisation . . . one such place is Seven Sisters. I have never seen such an audience of simple barbarians. If I were compelled to spend a whole day there, I would surely kill myself.]

For 'barbarism' one presumably should read 'proletarian' for that is exactly how Sir Alfred Zimmern whose generosity of spirit and erudition a decade earlier perceived matters. He however revealed a different and finer definition of civilisation:

> The Wales of today is not a unity. There is not one Wales; there are three . . . There is Welsh Wales; there is industrial or, as I sometimes think of it, American Wales, and there is upper class or English Wales. These three represent different types and different traditions. They are moving in different directions and if they all three survive they are not likely to re-unite.

> Of American Wales, the Wales of the coalfield and the industrial working class . . . let me only say . . . for the benefit of those who are apt to sneer at South Wales as a 'storm centre' what a joy it has been to pass a too fleeting and infrequent weekend among men and women who really care for ideas and love the search for truth . . .

> It is more than material light and heat that Wales may yet win from her coalfield.

(Quoted by Dai Smith in *Aneurin Bevan and the World of South Wales*, University of Wales Press, 1993)

That generosity of spirit, free from class prejudice and snobbery, is truly at the heart of the recognition that Wales, then as now, is a multi-cultural and multi-lingual society which requires a pluralist democracy rooted in citizenship and universal values, not language or ethnicity.

A NEW POLITICS, AGAIN ?

In his *Towards 2000*, Raymond Williams wrote of the vitality and energy of ideas provided by the newer social movements of our time, involving peace, the environment and women. Such movements, because of their essentially non-patriarchal and non-hierarchical structures (unlike the labour movement), had much to offer the new century. And so it is with Wales. The most encouraging feature of the Miners' Strike of 1984-85 — in Wales and only in Wales — was the way in which (albeit fleetingly) extra-parliamentary and non-parliamentary organisations aligned themselves in broad coalition with the miners' cause — notably Cymdeithas yr Iaith Gymraeg, the Welsh Council of Churches and the Gays and Lesbians support the Miners Group. Such pluralism, briefly harnessed by the Wales Congress in Support of Mining Communities, did raise some fundamental questions about democracy and accountability which go far beyond a Parliament for Wales.

After all, Wales today is in many ways a great deal less democratic than in 1945. With the rise of the Quangos and the sharp decline in the democratic powers of local government, a Parliament for Wales needs to be more than a glorified County Council. It will need to have legislative and tax raising powers in order to have any real meaning for *all our people* who will naturally and rightly demand much from their citizenship in the new Wales.

Much is currently written in Europe today about 'social exclusion', that a fundamental part of citizenship throughout Europe is the right of access to education as a means of cultural integration in the fullest sense. Without such rights, for minorities of all kinds, mass unemployment allied to racism and lack of educational opportunity will de-stabilise the whole of society.

It is only in this wider context, of universal values, can we prepare for a Europe of the Regions in which rights of citizenship are guaranteed to all, irrespective of language, ethnic or cultural background. With that accepted, a Parliament for Wales based upon respect for cultural diversity and a pluralist democracy, can be achieved, in which Welsh Somalis in Bute Town, Welsh Spaniards in Abercrâf and Welsh speakers in Gwynedd all know that they will not be strangers in their own land. To paraphrase Gwyn Thomas, our Wales will be a cross between Somerset, Pontllanfraith and Zanzibar.

CHAPTER 17

THE CULTURAL HEALTH OF THE NATION
The Arts and a Welsh Parliament

Gilly Adams

The arts in Wales are in danger of coming a poor second to the bureaucracy which surrounds them, so a few definitions of what is meant by 'artistic' and 'cultural' should serve as a necessary reminder of what the arts are really about.

The (British) National Campaign for the Arts, followed by the Arts Council of Wales, have successfully argued the economic case for the arts — jobs, tourism, exports, urban re-generation. Even so a Welsh Parliament should begin by reminding itself that money isn't everything and that the true value of the arts is, dare we say it, spiritual rather than financial. The arts are about self-fulfilment through creativity. They are about opportunities for participation and sharing and celebration. They are about value and enlightenment and civilisation in the profound sense of that word.

Some pursue the arts for love on a part-time basis and some practice them daily for money as well as love and that's the main difference between the professional and the amateur. Professional artists have more opportunity to experiment, push boundaries and set standards, so that risks can be taken and progress made. Yet everyone needs access to the skills which empower people to take active control of their lives, rather than succumbing to the passivity of the television and VCR culture.

Communal arts activity helps to create a sense of community and occasion and puts people in touch with their own passion and joy. All of which sounds far distant from the world of political and parliamentary debate, but in a society which can never again expect full employment, issues to do with quality of life are of the essence. Reminding ourselves of the fundamental importance of the arts is a good place from which to launch any assessment of the state of the arts in Wales.

DEVELOPMENT OF THE ARTS

In any historical account, the professional arts would feature as a footnote at the end of the twentieth century in Wales. Our tradition has been that of the honourable and accomplished amateur — amateur music making, particularly choral; amateur dramatics and operatics; amateur writing and painting, all supported by the amateur culture of the Eisteddfod. Not until the establishment of the Welsh Arts Council (WAC) in 1967 was there any real attempt to professionalise the arts or create an arts industry, and in comparison with the arts in Scotland and Ireland, much artistic work is still in its infancy.

Constitutionally the WAC was a committee of the Arts Council of Great Britain (ACGB), established to develop and support the arts at 'arms length' from government and politics, although funded by central government. In practice the WAC was autonomous and able to dispose of its 7-plus per cent share of the ACGB's grant in its own way. Funds were distributed as the members of the Council (selected by the ACGB in consultation with the Secretary of State for Wales) saw fit; and with the advice of specialist sub-committees. In the early 1970s this system was reinforced by the establishment of three regional arts associations (RAAs) which operated at a more local level.

In the almost 30 years since the WAC and the RAAs came into being there has been an enormous growth in the arts in both languages. As a result of the ACGB's Housing the Arts fund the WAC was able to respond to initiatives in the 1970s to build theatres and arts centres all over Wales. The Welsh National Opera Company has professionalised its chorus and gained an international reputation, as has the National Orchestra of Wales, funded by BBC Wales in conjunction with the Arts Council.

There are a significant number of drama and dance companies operating all over Wales. A theatre in education and community dance service has existed for every county in Wales. Professional artists of all disciplines have worked in communities and institutions of many different kinds. Partnership funding for all these activities has grown commensurably so that in the financial year 1994-95 the Arts Council's own funding of some £14 million was being matched by between £10-12 million pounds from the local authorities.

ROLE OF THE WELSH ARTS COUNCIL

How much of a success story is this? There is, of course, much of which to be proud, and much which has made a promising start. Yet it is difficult to claim either that the arts have been made accessible to every inhabitant of Wales or that much has been created which demonstrates a distinct Welsh identity in either language. There is a lack of confidence and a lack of real coherence in what has developed.

How would we assess the role of the WAC in this? To begin with, the Council has never been a consistently pro-active body. Generally speaking it has tended to react to initiatives. One result is that there has never been a central vision or overview which could link different activities or make connections across art forms in an inspirational way. A good example was the proliferation of arts buildings in the 1970s. The WAC made an attempt to provide a post-hoc rationalisation for the theatres and arts centres which were built in unlikely places by referring to them as a 'touring circuit'. It would have been much better, however, if there had been a strategic plan which related the locations of the buildings more accurately to the demography and topography of Wales and perhaps to the cultural habits of the population.

In the main the purpose-built theatres and the arts centres have remained pale imitations of their English counterparts and it is interesting to speculate what would have happened had a theatre circuit been planned which utilised some of the many chapels in Wales. An example of the potential in such an approach was provided by the WAC itself when, as part of the Valleys Initiative in the late 1980s, it participated with the Welsh Office and district councils in establishing nine new Valleys arts venues, mainly in refurbished working men's halls. Unfortunately, however, it was unable to go on to provide significant assistance with the running costs of these new venues.

The WAC is, of course, one of the many Welsh Quangos, even if it has had a less controversial history than some. Consequently the membership of the Council is not democratically elected but part of the fiefdom of the Secretary of State for Wales. In several senses, therefore, it represents 'jobs for the boys'. Add to this the Welsh passion for being seen to be fair, which makes it difficult for arts practitioners to be accommodated on the advisory committees — for fear of bias — and the result is a very establishment situation.

In the main, the members of the Arts Council and its committees are white, male, middle class and middle aged — in other words, the great, the good and the stuffy. Few of them will want to rock the boat because they are either members of the crew or related to them. Certainly this is not a recipe for radical considerations, real vision or informed artistic debate. Given the fact that the larger the arts organisation the better the establishment connections, it seems that at least some of the Council's decisions must be politically rather than artistically influenced.

Perhaps the WAC's greatest failure has been its lack of advocacy. Taking its cue from the ACGB the WAC failed to stand up to the central government against the cuts imposed on the arts during the Thatcher years and by subsequent Tory governments. Consequently much work that was potentially flourishing has been nipped in the bud and many younger artists have found it almost impossible to get started. Indeed far from fighting to maintain the already inadequate sums of money made available for the arts, the WAC has sought to maintain its own staffing levels while being complicit in the cutting and paring which the reductions in central government subsidy have necessitated for its clients.

Another trend has been the emphasis on commercial sponsorship, which is automatically a kind of censorship, and in any case only available substantially to the larger organisations like the Opera Company. The result has been less and less experimentation and less opportunity for work of quality to emerge. Art and safety should not be synonymous.

Whilst artists are used to producing work with a mix of adrenaline and mind over matter, the circumstances of recent years have been such that on occasion artists have found themselves shot in both feet before they start. This is because of traditional under-funding. There is little point in producing the Great English Bard for the National Curriculum if the production is so dull that it induces catatonia in the audience.

THE UNDERMINING OF LOCAL GOVERNMENT FUNDING

However it would be unfair to blame all the problems of arts funding on the Arts Council. Recent difficulties have come also from the reduction in spending power at the box office and very significantly from the changes in the education structure which threaten artists in schools, the theatre in education service, peripatetic music, dance and drama training, and which prevent young people from going to see live performances. The disappearance of discretionary grants also deprives those with the necessary talent of assistance to undertake the appropriate vocational training.

The most recent cloud on the horizon comes with re-organisation of local government and establishment of the 22 new most-purpose authorities from 1995-6. Although there is no statutory requirement for local authorities to support the arts, the present 37 districts and eight counties in Wales have been spending nearly as much as the WAC and the RAAs, mainly on the direct management of theatres and galleries, the promotion of arts events and in grant aid to independent professional and amateur arts organisations. The major spenders have varied from one part of Wales to another, with Clwyd County Council, Swansea City Council and the Valleys district authorities being in the forefront.

The creation of 22 new authorities, most of them small in population and resources compared with the existing eight counties, has enormous potential for dislocation and confusion and directly threatens existing arts provision. It is difficult to imagine that the smaller most-purpose authorities will want to take on responsibility for organisations which have a national or regional significance and provide a service which extends beyond their borders. A good example is the uncertain future now facing Theatr Clwyd which represents a huge investment by Clwyd County Council. There is also a risk that the new smaller authorities will be less sympathetic to creating a national pattern for the arts, but will be more inclined to pursue their own, more parochial ambitions.

MOTH OR BUTTERFLY?

We are assured, however, all is not lost, because at midnight on 31st March 1994, like Cinderella's pumpkin, the Welsh Arts Council (WAC) became the Arts Council of Wales (ACW).

Even for those of us with a vested interest in understanding the form and organisation of this 'new' funding body, it is difficult to see much difference between the old organisation and its reincarnation, although the Arts Council of Wales has been at pains to convince us otherwise. In fact the changes are about as significant as the reshuffling of the words which form its title.

A rather spurious consultation process and the inevitable and no doubt expensive feasibility study has led to a new body which is hardly at all different from that which existed previously. The Regional Arts Associations have lost their autonomy and become regional out-posts of the Arts Council, and despite the rhetoric, of which there has been a great deal, that is about all. There have been few redundancies. Rather, some new posts have been created. Certainly there has no perceptible lessening of the convoluted bureaucracy by which the arts in Wales have been run.

The change in nomenclature has come about because the Scottish and Welsh Arts Councils have ceased to be committees of the Arts Council of Great Britain, funded by the Department of Heritage, and become autonomous organisations responsible to the Scottish and Welsh Offices respectively. This might have been an opportunity for a radical re-organisation. However, the newly appointed council of the Arts Council of Wales, even more strongly in the fiefdom of the Secretary of State, is chaired by Sir Richard Lloyd Jones, former Permanent Secretary of the Welsh Office, and reflects the same mixture of largely Establishment figures.

As for the subject committees, any real knowledge of, or track record in the arts of more than an amateur nature remains a disincentive to appointment, for fear of bias. So discussions will continue to be impartial but not necessarily informed. Predictably, women, who represent more than fifty per cent of the audience for arts events, continue to be under-represented, both on Council and in the senior management.

It will be interesting to see whether the new structure will make it easier for the Arts Council to acknowledge that the accountability which it demands from its clients is a two way process and that it, too, needs to be accountable, not just to the Welsh Office, but also to its clients, its funding partners, and to the general public. Openness about decision making, about the process by which clients are assessed, and about the people who make the assessments, should be part of the process of living in a democracy. It should not be a secret process in which information is dragged out through Welsh whispers, insinuation and implication. Respect needs to be mutual and mutually earned. The WAC thrived on secrecy. Will the ACW be any different?

MISSION STATEMENT OR STRATEGY?

It is difficult not to think that the Arts Council has missed the opportunity for taking on some of the major issues of Welsh society and therefore, of the artist at the end of the twentieth century . They include the role of the arts in education, multi-culturalism, and the community arts. Indignant voices will exclaim that the new Arts Council does indeed have policies and a team capable of coping with such concerns, and there has been evidence of a lot of paper-work . Behind the rhetoric, however, there is little sign of meaningful action. And, indeed, how could it be otherwise when the Council itself is unrepresentative, and when its officers are paid comparatively so much more than artists in their peer group? This last means they are protected from knowing what the realities of life are like for the artist on a day to day basis. It is much easier to make plans on paper than to establish a practical means for the implementation of real strategies.

In the 'accessible' literature which the Arts Council produced to celebrate its new persona there is no longer mention of aims and objectives. However, the blurb does include a list which tells us that the ACW's task is to work with all its partners to:

(i) Improve standards of creativity in the arts.
(ii) Increase the number and range of people who attend arts events and participate in the arts in Wales.
(iii) Increase the funds going into the arts.

Speaking for the arts is a conspicuous omission from that list and reinforces the anxiety that the Arts Council is not going to prioritise advocacy amongst its functions.

In order to accommodate its new responsibility for the Arts Council, the Welsh Office has reorganised itself and established a Culture and Recreation Division. In addition to the arts, this deals with the National Library and the National Museum, the Welsh Language Board including 'European minority language matters', the Sports Council, planning for the Cardiff Bay Opera House, and 'broadcasting matters', however they are defined.

Much to everyone's surprise the Welsh Office began its relationship with the Arts Council by providing a 4 per cent increase in its budget, in contrast to the minus 1.7 per cent received by the English Arts Council. This presumably came as recognition of the importance of the arts for the Welsh economy since half of it was tied to priorities involving education, marketing the arts and international initiatives. What are known as the cultural industries employ 5,000 people in Wales and generate an income of around £90 million.

On the face of it, it seems as though the Welsh Office is shaping up to push forward a more integrated arts policy with an emphasis on the image of Wales abroad, with trade missions being regularly supported by cultural initiatives. A particular opportunity for this kind of thing is the economic agreement which Wales has entered into with the four leading European motor regions — Baden-Württemberg, Lombardy, Rhone-Alps and Catalunya.

Certainly, this is a way in which we could develop a more distinctive artistic policy and identity. Wales in Europe is a much more exciting proposition for the arts than Wales as a pale acolyte of England. Many of the Welsh companies already have international and European contacts and links which could be developed. However, such a policy for the arts needs to be pushed forward with vision. The danger is that the Welsh Office will view it as a promotional and cash exercise only.

A DEMOCRATIC AGENDA

And that's the rub really. The Welsh Office is unable to develop a creative policy for the arts without real knowledge of the subject. The evidence so far is that in the absence of knowledge the Culture and Recreation Division is busy asking the wrong questions and demanding much unnecessary information. The result has been yet another increase in the amount of paper work required from arts organisations. It is understandable that the Welsh Office should be nervous about accountability given the disgraceful record of the more notorious Quangos. Yet the arts are about flexibility, quality, imagination and creativity, not about performance indices and endless paper schemes.

The urgent need for the arts in Wales remains a cogent policy which unites the different existing activities, promotes Welsh culture to the world and makes arts opportunities available to the whole population through attendance and participation. The Welsh Office cannot fulfil this role adequately because economic interests are paramount and its staff have no specialist arts knowledge.

Meanwhile, the ACW has much of the knowledge but doesn't have a coherent overview or the power to enforce such a view, nor is it remotely democratic. The Welsh Parliament could provide both the democracy and the coherent policy through a parliamentary committee with responsibility for the arts and culture. This committee would mainly comprise democratically elected members, but it would also have powers of co-option so that arts practitioners of both sexes and all ages could be involved in creating an informed policy. Such a committee would monitor the work of an Arts and Culture Department of the Welsh Government which would take over the work of the Arts Council of Wales. In addition to the existing subject areas such as drama, music and literature there would also be created administrative units with responsibility for broadcasting, the Eisteddfod, Welsh-language initiatives, the Museum, Housing the Arts and so on. The Department would, of course, through its Ministerial head be directly responsible to the Welsh Parliament. Undoubtedly, priority would be given to ensure proper co-ordination between the various subject areas and the emergence of a coherent strategy for the arts.

The first step in this process would be to place the arts firmly on the political agenda alongside health and social services and education and then to look at the ways the arts can contribute to those very services. In particular the Welsh Parliament would need to address the damage done to the arts in education through the recent re-organisation of educational structures.

The Parliament would also need to implement a statutory requirement for local authorities to support the arts and to look at the changing needs of our society, so that community arts and multiculturalism are given their proper place and the contribution of the living artist is valued more than that of the dead.

The arts make a vital contribution to the cultural, social, economic and educational life of Wales. Over half the population engages in arts activity every year either by attending events or by taking part. The Welsh Parliament, in the interests of the 'health of the nation', should aim to provide the opportunity for everyone to benefit from the arts as a matter of priority.

CHAPTER 18

ARE WE BEING SERVED?
The Press, Broadcasting and a Welsh Parliament

Kevin Williams

The media landscape has gone through profound change since the failure of devolutionists to convince the people of Wales of their case in 1979 referendum. There has been a considerable growth in the media industries in Wales. With the introduction of Sianel Pedwar Cymru (S4C), the increase in the number of English language television programmes screened by BBC Wales and HTV, the growth of *papurau bro* and freesheets and the establishment of a new Sunday newspaper, the people of Wales appear to be better served by their media than ever before.

The mushrooming of the media in Wales, however, has been accompanied by a fundamental shift in the whole media ecology. Changes in the economic structure of both the print and broadcast media have initiated a radical change in the nature and quality of the product served up to the people of Wales. Market forces, in particular, are having a growing influence on what we see, hear and read. New media technology is changing the relationship between the media and its audience. These changes are having a considerable impact on the coverage of political, social and economic life in Wales today — making as much if not more impact than fifteen years of Tory rule.

One important consequence has been the shift in the balance of power between the press and broadcasting. Television is a far more important political and cultural force in contemporary Wales than the press. The *Western Mail* can be seen as an increasingly marginal force. In 1979 it played a crucial role in the referendum debate; today it struggles with the idea of becoming a tabloid in order to keep itself above water. However, as television has become the dominant force, the medium has seen a shift from information toward more entertainment programming which has contributed to a devaluation of cultural and democratic debate in Wales.

It is against this background that a Parliament for Wales will have to campaign for a new agenda for Wales. If the Parliament is to act as a forum for the expression of 'our unity, national identity and cultural diversity' — as the Llandrindod *Democracy Declaration* requires — then it will have to develop a media and communications policy which allows the people of Wales to fully participate in the debate.

In comparison with Wales, Scotland has a relatively strong and cohesive sense of national identity. This is in no small part due to the platform provided by the Scottish media system which is distinct, both in press and broadcasting terms. Over two thirds of Scots read newspapers published, printed and edited in Scotland. The *Daily Record* is the country's best selling newspaper with a circulation of over 700,000. The *Glasgow Herald* and the *Scotsman* sell six times as many copies as the Fleet Street quality papers.

BBC Scotland was set up as a 'national region' as long ago as 1930 and since the last ITV franchise allocation in 1990 most of Scotland is served by two financially strong companies in Scottish Television (STV) and Grampian. Scotland has also a range of independent radio stations led by Radio Clyde in Glasgow. Sociologist Jeremy Tunstall estimated that in 1983 more than 40 per cent of all radio listening in Scotland was to Scottish radio stations.[1] A Gaelic broadcasting service has recently started with a budget of £10 million and now produces over 200 hours of television every year. Thus Scots are served by a highly developed media system which is separate and apart from the London media. In turn this has helped the development of national consciousness in Scotland.

WELSH MEDIA HISTORY

In contrast with Scotland, the history of the Welsh media is that of an industry highly dependent on London. There has never been a national newspaper of Wales despite the claims of the *Western Mail*. Daily newspapers are centred on the highly populated urban centres in the south — Swansea, Cardiff and Newport. North Wales is served by the Liverpool *Daily Post* which through its Welsh edition claims to be 'speaking up for Wales'. By and large the content of these newspapers has been highly localised. According to Ian Hume from his study of the content of the media in Wales in the early 1980s, 'there is little in the English language press — particularly the weeklies — which offers any support to the idea that Wales is a distinct nation'.² The best read newspapers in Wales are the *Sun*, *Mirror* and the *Daily Express*.

The fight to establish a separate broadcasting service for Wales was long and arduous. It was not until 1937 that a separate Welsh Home Service of BBC radio was set up. This was the product of a campaign led by Saunders Lewis against *Bradwr Budr Cymru* (BBC) — 'dirty betrayer of Wales' — which in his opinion administered Wales as a 'conquered region'. Ironically the crucial pressure which led the BBC to set up a separate service for Wales came from the West of England which complained of having to share a wavelength with Wales. The *Bristol Evening World* in 1931 aired the grievances of many West Country people about having to listen to 'services from obscure Welsh chapels'. The paper called for the divorce of the two areas by stating that the 'West wants wireless home rule'.³

Commercial television also had a difficult time in establishing itself in Wales. Wales West and North (WWN) which began broadcasting in September 1962 failed because of a number of technical, cultural and financial reasons. The main reason, however, was that the audience was already receiving ITV programmes from Cardiff and Manchester. It was Granada that produced the first Welsh language programmes while south Wales was served by Television West and Wales (TWW) which produced programmes for the west of England, south Wales and Welsh speakers in Wales. This situation reflected the view of those in charge of ITV that the population of Wales was too small to sustain a commercial channel through advertising. The poverty and low purchasing power of Wales has been the major factor in the resistance to setting up an independent television channel for Wales.

However the arrival of Harlech Television (HTV) which took over the franchise for Wales and the West region in 1968 did see a greater commitment to Wales — at least on paper with the names of many of Wales's greatest cultural patriots supporting the company. In commercial broadcasting terms, however, Wales has never been treated as a national entity. Thus, as the sociologist Jeremy Tunstall has observed , the 'Welsh media are much less Welsh than the Scottish media are Scottish'.⁴

WINDS OF CHANGE IN THE 1980s

Since 1979 there has been a rapid growth in the media industries in Wales. It can be argued that this is leading to the emergence for the first time of a distinct media system in Wales. The first development was the decision in 1977 to split BBC radio in Wales into two channels broadcasting in Welsh and English. Radio Cymru broadcasts 110 hours per week while BBC Radio Wales 113 hours. The division of radio set the pattern for broadcasting in the 1980s. The most significant step forward, however, was the setting up of S4C in 1982. Both Radio Cymru and S4C treat Wales as a distinct nation. Ian Hume, in his study of content of the broadcast media in Wales in 1984-5, judged that the 'broadcast media in the Welsh language appear to have a relatively clear identity, linked to a perception of Wales as a spatially defined political, social and cultural entity'.[5]

This is achieved by providing Welsh speakers with a Welsh perspective on international affairs through current affairs programmes such as *Y Byd Ar Bedwar* as well as features programmes and dramas which represent popular culture in Wales. Of course, it should not be a surprise since the Welsh language media have always been more conscious of Wales as a nation than their English counterparts. A recent report from the Institute for Welsh Affairs found that Welsh speakers are more supportive of an English language television channel for Wales than English speakers.[6]

The presence of S4C provided the impetus for the growth of English language television in Wales. Following the advent of S4C both HTV and BBC Wales have appeared to give more time to issues of Welsh national significance. The fact that both BBC and HTV are making programmes for S4C has, it can be argued, resulted in a more Wales oriented approach in production values throughout the whole of Welsh broadcasting. Moreover, the success of S4C in serving the needs of Welsh speakers has led to calls for an English language television service for Wales. While such a service has not materialised it is certainly true that BBC Wales and HTV have produced a 'new deal' for English language television in Wales. Both channels have devoted more attention to Wales in the 1980s with an increase its English language output to about ten hours each a week.

There have also been significant changes in the print media. *Wales on Sunday*, a new English language Sunday newspaper, was launched in 1989 in recognition of Wales's 'over-dependence on the London press'.[7] After a shaky start the newspaper has established itself as one of the fastest growing papers in Britain with a circulation of around 62,000. In contrast the *Western Mail* has seen a steady decline in circulation since 1979. From the heady days of the early 1960s when over 104,000 people bought the paper, today circulation has sunk to 68,456 and falling. Similar declines in circulation are seen with the rest of the major newspapers printed in Wales.

The most striking change since 1979, however, has been the emergence of community newspapers, especially the Welsh language *papurau bro*. These monthly newspapers began in the mid 1970s and there are now 52 of them with a circulation of around 72,000.[8] Free newspapers have also proliferated. It is now estimated that there are 50 of these with considerable circulations — the *Cardiff Independent* for example boasts a weekly circulation of 110,000.[9]

Since 1979 there has been an increase in the quantity of media in Wales, that is media made in Wales, by Welsh people and for the Welsh and English speakers of Wales. The growth in the Welsh media is another example of the growth of government and non government organisations in Wales which give the nation an identity beyond that of language. However what does this media system produce? What sort of national agenda does it promote? Does it assist in the development of a national consciousness? What sort of Wales does it represent?

DECLINE OF THE WELSH PRESS

Aled Jones has pointed out that the newspaper industry in Wales in the 19th century was highly localised.[10] It has only been in the 20th century that efforts have been made to appeal beyond the locality to the Welsh nation as a whole. The conservative *Western Mail* throughout its history has made the most concerted effort to achieve a national readership. By the early 1960s it had established itself in most parts of Wales. The exception was north Wales. At the same time readership of the *Western Mail* was high amongst both the Welsh and English speaking people of Wales. Despite being critical of its editorial line and its news coverage people read the paper because of the range of its reporting of Welsh affairs.

The *Western Mail*'s commitment to news about Wales, however, has declined in recent years. This is the result of two factors: first the decision of newspaper since the late 1970s to place equal emphasis on reporting news from Britain, Wales and abroad. The aim was to produce a newspaper which would cater for all the reader's interests. He or she would not have to buy another newspaper to obtain news about something not covered in the *Western Mail*. The second factor was the increased financial difficulties of the newspaper. Falling circulation and advertising revenue led to cutbacks, fewer pages and reporters. As a result there was less coverage of national events.

The trend towards less all-Wales news is also apparent in other newspapers. The *Daily Post* has made a great effort in recent years to be 'The Paper for Wales'. It has expanded its news gathering operation in Wales and appointed a Welsh Affairs correspondent based in Cardiff. In the run up to the recent twenty-fifth anniversary of the investiture of Prince Charles in 1994, the newspaper emphasised its commitment to Wales. In a commentary piece to accompany a special 12 page supplement assessing the role of Prince Charles in Wales, the *Post*'s editor highlighted the newspaper's coverage of Welsh issues compared to the London dailies. While all the Fleet Street newspapers together carried only 19 stories about Wales on June 23rd, his newspaper had more than 60 news, business and sports stories from Wales. Such coverage, according to the *Post*'s editor, shows how the newspaper puts the readers and advertisers of Wales first. However, many of these stories are still not national Welsh stories but highly localised, emanating from traditional institutional sources such as the courts and councils around the country.

Wales on Sunday has perhaps made a greater effort to provide an all Wales coverage. Welsh stories are important as the then editor spelled out in 1993: ' I'll give them [the readers] a choice with a good Welsh story. What I do is make us a good second buy'.[11] The newspaper has also placed emphasis on crusading journalism, calling itself the 'campaigning voice of Wales'. However, the newspaper struggled at the outset with its overt commitment to serving Wales. *Wales on Sunday* was first launched as a quality broadsheet in 1989. After selling its first edition to 97,000 people, circulation declined rapidly. It was only after its reincarnation as a tabloid newspaper positioned somewhere between the *Mail on Sunday* and the *Sunday Mirror* that it began to achieve some circulation success.

One casualty of the change, however, was the serious attention given by the newspaper to the cultural, political and social life of Wales. The tabloid paper concentrates more on lifestyles and entertainment features; personalities, gossip and fashion. Welsh news is there but the focus is primarily on human interest stories and serious Welsh news is lost amongst the welter of lifestyle features and commentaries. The claim to be a campaigning newspaper is also far from convincing. As one former Welsh newspaperman says: 'The paper's investigative stories have no substance. They are superficial. You think you are in for a good read but the story simply runs out of steam'. This is not a surprise as good investigative journalism requires staff, money and time — all of which are in decline with *Wales on Sunday*, as with other daily newspapers in Wales.

Since 1979, therefore, there is less Welsh news in the contemporary Welsh press and what does exist is more concerned with entertainment and lifestyle than information. This is a reflection of the changing relationship between the newspapers and their audience. All the newspapers in Wales have been losing circulation in the 1980s. This is most pronounced amongst young people. In a recent British newspaper readership survey only 59 per cent of young people between the ages of 16 and 24 said they read a newspaper. Younger people say that they do not find reading a newspaper a pleasurable activity. Hence newspapers are now resorting to colour, eye catching graphics as well as more lifestyle and entertainment stories to make reading a newspaper appealing to the younger audience who are vital to their long term survival.

It is also the case that the Welsh audience is as firmly attached to their locality as to the nation as a whole, if not more so. This was demonstrated by the success of community and local weekly papers in Wales in the 1980s — in both the Welsh and English language — as well as newspapers such as the *South Wales Argus* and *South Wales Evening Post*. By looking inwards and placing more emphasis on news about their locality they have been better able to arrest the more general decline in newspaper circulation elsewhere.

The press in Wales is increasingly marginal to Welsh life. In 1979 John Osmond could write that 'television in Wales is strongly influenced by newspapers; the way that television deals with the news, issues and personalities is more often than not a consequence of the way in which the same items have been dealt with by the newspapers'.[12] Today it is more plausible to argue that television 'sets the agenda' for debate and discussion in Wales. Newspapers have fewer resources and less inclination to gather news around and about Wales. It is more likely that Wales's leading papers are taking their cue from television news and current affairs in Wales. Even so, there is still a tendency amongst Welsh intellectuals and political activists to attribute great influence to the press. The 19th century myth of the newspaper as a 'great engine of thought' is still firmly entrenched amongst the political and intellectual elite of Wales. However, for most Welsh people what Wales is and what it wants to be is something that comes from television.

VOICE OF THE NATION

Most people in Wales identify television as their main source of information about what is happening in the world. In recent years both BBC Wales and HTV have reiterated that the role of television is not only to provide information and entertainment but also to play a significant role in the development of Welsh identity. The Controller of BBC Wales has recently made the firm commitment that 'BBC Wales' s programme agenda should be dominated by that which is significant to the lives of the people of Wales'.[13] Similarly HTV in its struggle to retain the ITV franchise emphasised that its mission was 'to unify Wales'. Or, in the words of Huw Davies, the then Director of Television for HTV, the *raison d'être* of the company was 'the reinforcement of our identity; to present the Welsh to the Welsh and to be proud, in so far as it is justifiable, of who we are'. Broadcasting in Wales then has a cultural mission.

For Welsh speakers this is clear. Despite criticism about the size of its viewing figures and the cost of the service, S4C is popular with its audience. Nearly a quarter of all Welsh speakers claim to watch the channel more often than they watch network television. The channel offers a range of programmes from news and current affairs, documentaries and dramas, to soaps and farming programmes and comedies and quiz shows, all of which achieve a high penetration of their potential audience.[14]

The status of the language has been enhanced as a result of S4C's existence and the channel has played a significant part in the development of other cultural industries in Wales. Over the years there has been criticism from some parts of the Welsh-speaking audience that their needs have not been fully met. One example is

Welsh youth. There have also been criticisms about the kind of product served up by the channel. The emphasis on the language has sometimes meant that insufficient attention has been paid to programme content. Overall, however, the channel has 'solid support' from the Welsh speaking community.

For English speaking Welsh people the position is not as clear. In theory the setting up of S4C allowed BBC Wales and HTV Wales to devote more attention to providing programmes for the non Welsh-speaking community. However the expansion of the English language output of Welsh television was slow. BBC Wales and HTV Wales were more concerned with supplying programmes for S4C than meeting the needs of the English-speaking Welsh. BBC Wales's Controller, Geraint Talfan Davies, has pointed out that behind the development of BBC 'regional' broadcasting in Wales 'there is no doubt that the driving force was the demand for the proper provision of the Welsh language'. For as Davies says: 'Despite the urgent need to develop our English language television service and to allow a credible career path for non Welsh-speaking talent, the Welsh language remains the most obvious and important expression of our difference and the ultimate bulwark for both Welsh and non Welsh speakers against the dilution of our national remit'.[15] HTV was only forced to take more seriously the demands of English speakers by having to bid to retain its ITV franchise in 1990. Throughout most of the 1980s the company was more concerned with its lucrative contract to provide programmes for S4C.

The bulk of the output of BBC and HTV Wales in English is news and current affairs. BBC Wales produces just over six and-half-hours each week and HTV nearly six hours. BBC has devoted more time, money and attention to news and current affairs, appointing specialist correspondents to more fully and expertly cover Wales on a regular basis for both radio and television. HTV has recently revamped its evening news programme. In addition BBC Wales has started to invest in the production of drama, music, documentaries and the arts. HTV has also produced more entertainment, children's and family programming for Wales.

However the quality the programmes produced has been subject to criticism. For critics such as Clive Betts and Mario Basini of the *Western Mail* 'much of the quality of the increased output from both BBC Wales and HTV Wales has been poor bordering on the downright bad'.[16] One does not have to agree with the special pleading of the spokespersons of an ailing newspaper thrashing out at its rivals to have doubts about the 'quality' of the recent output of BBC and HTV.

The cultural mission of S4C, HTV and BBC Wales controllers is anchored in the economic realities of the day. There is less money and resources in Welsh broadcasting today to make programmes. HTV has to pay the Treasury £20.5 million per annum for the privilege of operating its franchise. The result has been cost cutting and restructuring. Staff levels at the beginning of the 1990s were reduced to below the figure the company itself stated was necessary to provide a quality service to the TV audience in Wales and the West. The news operation in north Wales was affected by a cutback in reporters and the closure of the HTV's studio at Mold. Recently news and current affairs in HTV Wales have been able to claw back some of the lost resources but, still, the whole operation is subject to financial restrictions. Spending is carefully scrutinised by accountants who often appear the main arbiters of what is transmitted.

At BBC Wales the recent commitment to increase the money for programmes from £11 to £20 million a year indicates a healthy financial situation on the surface. However in the last couple of years the BBC has been subject to vast restructuring. The 'Birt revolution' is about 'downsizing, delayering and outsourcing' — in other words lay-offs, close-downs and cutbacks. It remains to be seen, despite London's greater commitment to programme making in the BBC's 'national regions' (Wales, Scotland and Northern Ireland), how long BBC Wales can maintain its rate of expansion.

Yet it is not simply a case of a financial squeeze in the broadcast world. In Wales as elsewhere in Europe there has been a shift from the concept of public service to market forces as the basis for running broadcasting. Deregulation has meant that broadcasting is driven more and more by the market. This is most apparent in the ITV sector since the changes brought about by the Thatcher government in 1990. Broadcasters must now produce the kinds of programmes that maximise the audience that can be delivered to advertisers. The BBC financial base is supposedly protected by the licence fee. But, in order to justify the fee, the BBC is also having to show it can gather large audiences for its programmes.

Hence the pressure throughout British and Welsh broadcasting is towards more entertainment programmes such as soaps and quiz programmes which bring in viewers in large numbers. HTV Wales since 1991 has brought us cheap magazine programmes such as *Get Going* which dealt with 'leisure activities' including 'flower arranging, cookery and water colour painting', and quiz shows such as *Ready Money* . Local programmes on the ITV network are more often aired in the late night or early afternoon ghetto slots although HTV Wales is unique amongst ITV contractors in maintaining its commitment to local current affairs and moving its flag ship programme *Wales This Week* to an early evening slot. The trend, however, is towards more 'pap television': more programmes but less choice.

BBC Wales is also concerned with entertainment. It produces five hours of sports coverage including highly choreographed, pompous trailers for sports events aimed at uniting the people of Wales around a 'national' sporting occasion. But besides such Boys Own material, much of the increased investment by BBC Wales has been in worthy, 'auntie knows best' programmes such as *The Slate*, a smug, self-satisfied arts programme whose appeal is narrow and limited. Thus the Welsh viewer is caught between 'pap' and 'patrician' broadcasting, with the space to represent daily life in Wales shrinking.

THE WELSH TELEVISION AUDIENCE

The changes in the output of Welsh television cannot be discussed separately from the changes in the Welsh audience since 1979. Today fewer people are watching television. As more television has become available with the development of satellite, cable and video, so the demand has slumped. People would rather do other things with their leisure time. It is also clear that many people in Wales still do not watch Welsh television. The removal of Welsh language programmes from BBC and HTV has not led to people turning back their aerials to Wales. Many viewers in south Wales, particularly in South Glamorgan, still boycott Welsh television by pointing their aerials to the Mendip transmitter. It has been estimated that as many as 55% of the households in the Vale of Glamorgan tune their aerials to HTV West than HTV Wales. In Cardiff the figure is 37% and Newport 46%.[17]

In north Wales HTV Wales is challenged by Granada; certain reception areas including much of Wrexham and Deeside are not even able to pick up HTV Wales. Despite this situation there has been little effort by either BBC Wales or HTV Wales to mount a campaign to persuade viewers to tune into Wales.

Part of the difficulty is that very little is known about the television audience in Wales. Audience research is limited to the broadcasting institutions which jealously guard their ratings. The only piece of recent qualitative research into the Welsh television audience indicates that people in Wales still regard their local programmes as being of 'poor quality' in relation to network production. The study completed for the Institute for Welsh Affairs in 1990 also found that people throughout Wales wanted more 'serious' programming about Wales such as news and current affairs, documentaries and natural history programmes.

However, the most interesting finding concerned attitudes to an English language channel for Wales. The idea for such a channel came out of the scramble for the ITV franchise and in February 1990 the *Western Mail* found that 73 per cent of people in Wales would be 'in favour of Wales having its own television channel to serve the English speakers in the same way that S4C serves Welsh speakers'. The Institute for Welsh Affairs survey found a similar number of people supporting the idea of such a channel (65 per cent) but of these only 63 per cent said they would watch the channel very much. Support for such a channel was also much stronger amongst Welsh speakers, the younger age groups, the C1's and C2's and people in Gwent and Mid Glamorgan. The desirability of such a channel varied considerably throughout Wales reflecting what the report referred to as 'the general disunity of Wales — geographically and culturally'.[18]

Thus in terms of providing a voice for Wales broadcasting agencies are today confronted by a number of problems. There is a commitment from Welsh broadcasting organisations to developing national consciousness and reporting the national agenda. This is reflected in the increase in programmes. However, the changing economic foundations of broadcasting are making it more difficult to produce programmes of quality which can cater for the diversity of Welshness.

The focus on entertainment at the expense of information can also been seen as undermining democracy in Wales. There are fewer resources to scrutinise those institutions responsible for running people's lives. The huge growth of the Quangos has not been matched by a corresponding growth in the resources and effort devoted by the media to the investigation of these institutions. If a healthy democracy is measured by the extent of informed debate then Wales is less democratic today than twenty years ago. The quality of information flowing into the public domain has declined as journalism and broadcasting have become increasingly under-nourished.

A WELSH PARLIAMENT AND MEDIA POLICY

The media have an important part to play, not only in mobilising opinion around the campaign for the establishment of a Welsh Parliament, but also in the renewal of cultural, political and economic life in Wales. If the Parliament is to succeed it must, while recognising the diversity of Welsh life, build national consciousness throughout Wales. People will have to be mobilised to see themselves as citizens of Wales if they are to be active in the political life of Wales.

It is primarily through the media that national consciousness and citizenship can be developed. However, to play this role fully and effectively the media must be responsive and accountable to the people of Wales. Structures must be developed so that people can be involved in the media. One of the great ironies of the development of the public service broadcasting system is that it has excluded the public. One example is the National Broadcasting Council for Wales. Few have even heard of it. Yet it is one of Wales's most long-established Quangos. It is responsible for the policy and programme content of BBC Wales and is supposed to represent the views of the Welsh public. But the body does not have any public profile in Wales and most people do not know who the Council's members are. There are also few opportunities for the Council to keep in touch with the people of Wales. Similarly the Independent Television Commission's Viewers Consultative Committee in Wales is another body that operates in anonymity. The contempt this body has for the views of the public was highlighted during the run up to the renewal of the ITV franchise in 1991 when the ITC Representative in Wales refused to attend any public meeting.

Both of these so-called public bodies are unrepresentative. The average age of members of the National Broadcasting Council, for example, is over 35 and there is no one from the ethic minorities, nor a disabled person.[19] A Parliament for Wales should encourage the establishment of representative and accountable bodies to oversee broadcasting in Wales.

There should be some effort to encourage greater public access to the airwaves in Wales. Feedback programmes could be established during which programme makers and their superiors should give an account of their work. All the broadcasting organisations in Wales have been loathe to provide such a forum. S4C's experiments in this area were short lived: *Ar y Bocs* and *Sbectrwm* came and went very quickly. Even with a Parliament, the struggle to obtain such a space on Welsh television screens may be considerable given the approach of one senior HTV manager who argued that quiz shows are the best way of getting viewers on screen.

There should also be access for local communities throughout Wales. Too much of the output of Welsh television revolves around official Wales. There should be some effort to ensure the provision of a range of programmes that reflect the diversity of Welsh life. A Parliament should encourage the 'public service ethic' in broadcasting because it is only in such an environment that the creative talents of programme-makers can be released to produce a range of programmes of high quality. A Parliament could also campaign for the establishment of an English language television channel for Wales, persuading people to turn their aerials to Wales. Crucial to all this is the provision of structures that involve people.

The Parliament must commit itself to the provision of a high quality of information to the public. Too much information about life in Wales is locked behind the doors of the Welsh Office or hidden away in the closed sessions of Quangos or council meetings. A Parliament for Wales must ensure that there is a free flow of information to assist the debate over the best way to build a better future for the Welsh people. The Parliament should itself set an example. Its workings must be open and accountable. Reporting arrangements for a Welsh Parliament must not replicate the closed world of the lobby which dictates the reporting of the Westminster Parliament. Representatives should be made accountable and responsive to the public by media arrangements which underpin open government.

If a Parliament is to bring about a renewal of Welsh political and cultural life then it is essential that there is an integrated media system which is critical, accountable and committed in more than words and pictures to the development of Welsh identity in all its forms.

NOTES

[1] Jeremy Tunstall, *The Media in Britain* (Constable, 1983), p. 228.//
[2] Ian Hume, 'Mass Media and Society in the 1980s' in I. Hume and W.T.R. Pryce (Eds.), *The Welsh and their Country* (Gomer Press, 1983), p. 331.//
[3] Rowland Lucas, *The Voice of a Nation?* (Gomer Press, 1981), p. 53.//
[4] Jeremy Tunstall, op cit., p. 228.//
[5] Ian Hume, op cit., p. 338.//
[6] Martin Evans, *Television in Wales - Opinion Survey: an exploratory research programme*, Institute for Welsh Affairs, 1992.//
[7] Aled Jones, *Press, Politics and Society: A History of Journalism in Wales* (University of Wales Press, 1993), p. 227.//
[8] Emyr Williams, *Y Papurau Bro a'r Farchnad Hysbyebu* (Canolfan Gydweithredol Cymru, 1992).//
[9] David Skilton, 'More Words and Pictures in the Air', in David Cole (Ed.) *The New Wales* (University of Wales Press, 1990).//
[10] Aled Jones, op cit.//
[11] *UK Press Gazette,* 2 August 1993.//
[12] John Osmond, 'The Referendum and the English language press' in David Foulkes, J. Barry Jones and R.A. Wilford (Eds.) *The Welsh Veto: the Wales Act 1978 and the Referendum* (University of Wales Press, 1983), p. 155.//
[13] *Western Mail*, 22 July 1993.//
[14] Dennis Balsom, 'Solid Support for S4C Survey', *Western Mail* , 27 February 1991.//
[15] Geraint Talfan Davies, 'Broadcasting and the Nation', *Planet* No 92, April-May 1992, p. 16-25.//
[16] Clive Betts, and Mario Basini, 'Give English-speakers more TV of quality', *Western Mail* , 14 July 1994.//
[17] John Osmond, 'Broadcasting TV figures', *Wales on Sunday* , 4 March 1990.//
[18] Martin Evans, op cit.//
[19] Wales Campaign for Quality Television, *Power to Choose: the future of the BBC in Wales*, 1993.

PART VI

THE POSITION OF THE PARTIES

CHAPTER 19

HARNESSING OUR LATENT ENTREPRENEURIALISM
A Liberal Democrat View

Alex Carlile MP

Sir Wyn Roberts, the Conservative Member of Parliament for Conwy, has dismissed the notion of a Welsh Parliament with the argument: 'They had their chance in 1979 and they rejected it'. Perhaps Sir Wyn is unaware of the feelings of most Welsh people, for if a week is a long time in politics then for many of us fifteen years under the Conservatives has been like eternity in the pits of Hades.

So much has happened in the last fifteen years without our democratic consent that few people remember what Wales was like in 1979 and before. Sir Wyn and the rest of the dinosaur tendency have failed to grasp that a whole new generation has grown up and it has not been given the chance to determine whether it wants devolution of power for Wales or not.

Sir Wyn and his friends should go out and ask young people in Wales what their view is. I am sure they are overwhelmingly in favour of a devolved Parliament. Indeed, it goes further than that. Young people throughout the United Kingdom, not just in Wales and Scotland, are dissatisfied with what passes for our constitution. A new constitutional settlement for the whole of the United Kingdom including a Parliament for Wales is now a priority on the political agenda. Those young people have watched the government make a hash of things from Westminster, and they want to decide the future of Wales themselves.

This is not a linguistic matter. We should be very careful not to divide Wales on linguistic lines. English-speaking Welsh people and Welsh-speaking Welsh people want a Parliament for Wales. They want Wales to rule itself as far as is compatible with its role in the United Kingdom and in Europe.

Many who voted against the Assembly in 1979 now fervently desire devolution to Wales. Among those who have changed their minds I remember a particularly vocal Neil Kinnock who campaigned strongly with Leo Abse and others against devolution. Neil Kinnock is now prepared to campaign with at least equal fervour in favour of a Welsh Parliament. That should be welcomed. We should not be suspicious of our friends in the Labour party who have changed their minds. The road to Damascus, from Wales at least, is a long one, and many people have found their own junctions upon it. Neil Kinnock is a welcome example.

I sometimes listen to the Government's proposals for Wales and wonder how on earth they think they're going to get away with them. Do they think that we are stupid? Consider as an example the Local Government (Wales) Act which will abolish the ancient county of Montgomeryshire and replace it with the Powys pudding as it has come to be known. This is a measure which has no support among people in Montgomeryshire. It is totally insensitive to their views. Opinion polls show that getting on for 80 per cent of the people of Montgomeryshire are in favour of a unitary authority for their county. Welsh Office ministers have received shoals of letters opposed to their proposals. Even the Montgomeryshire Conservative Association realise that having one unitary authority a quarter of the whole land area of Wales is an absurdity if there is to be local government in any meaningful sense. Such a proposal would never come out of a Welsh Parliament sensitive to the views of the people of Wales.

Of course, there have been many different discussions about the ways in which a Welsh Parliament could operate, but we should not allow ourselves to be bogged down in arguments about how many committees it should have, precisely what powers it should have or, least of all, semantic arguments about its name. I can live with the word 'Parliament', the word 'Senedd', the word 'Assembly' so long as we get it.

There are many reasons, quite apart from local issues such as the case for Montgomeryshire, why we need it. A London-based government will not grant Welsh equal status with English as a language. A London-based government will continue to set up Quangos to augment the 111 which already govern Wales — and will continue to present them with a huge budget amounting to 40 per cent of Welsh Office expenditure. They are in truth, barely accountable to the Westminster Parliament. Of course, everything that Quangos do is theoretically accountable in that once every few weeks Welsh Office Ministers face a Monday afternoon Question

Time on the floor of the House of Commons. However, that is not a real form of accountability.

When Lord Hailsham wrote of government in this country being an 'elective dictatorship' he was right, and that is what we want to change. Unlike some, most of us don't want to change Wales into an socialist republic. We don't want to turn Wales into some kind of autonomous third-world country on the fringe of Europe. Yet if we are to take the advantages of being part of the European Union, and to take Wales into that Union with the ability to govern itself, while remaining part of the United Kingdom, then a democratic Parliament for Wales is the right approach. It is necessary not just for the social cohesion of Wales, and not just to give us a more respectable constitutional position in the world, but fundamentally to ensure the economic regeneration of Wales.

As things are Wales is not creating the kind of indigenous economic growth that we would like to see. With a government for Wales as a country we would be able to give the political and policy impetus to enable our economy not just to welcome companies from abroad, and of course we welcome the jobs they bring, but also to create real Welsh entrepreneurialism and enterprise. There is an entrepreneurial spirit which has long been latent in Wales. We need our own democratic political institutions to give us the confidence and élan to tap into it.

It is the Liberal Democrat position that a Welsh Parliament must have real powers. It must not be a talking shop. It should have powers to raise and to spend revenue. We should consider establishing a system within Wales of hypothecated taxation. This would present taxpayers with a receipt at the end of the year detailing exactly how their money was spent. Indeed, if that was applied to Britain as a whole it might dissuade governments from, for example, spending vast amounts of overseas aid on projects which are tied to an arms link.

The Welsh Parliament should have legislative powers to determine transport policy, health policy, housing and education. Thereby we would avoid having policies forced upon us which we resoundingly rejected at the ballot box. The Welsh people did not vote for opted-out schools, nor for privatisation of the railways, yet they are having to put up with them all the same. If we were able to determine our own policies things would be very different.

But let us not shirk an essential question. If you give the Welsh

Parliament the power to raise taxes, taxes might be lower in Wales and they might be higher in Wales. That would be for the Welsh Parliament to determine. We should not run away from that as if it were *unrespectable* to say that a Parliament raising taxes might have higher or lower taxes. After all we're used to a government that tells us that it is giving us lower taxes and then does the opposite.

Though no one will be surprised at my stating it, I believe that it is actually for the good of a new democratic institution that it should have proportional representation in its elections. At the same time it is important to contain as strong a constituency link for members of the Welsh Parliament as it is for those sitting in the Parliament at Westminster.

To ensure the future of Wales we must create a strong and distinctive voice for our people, a voice that is heard not only within the United Kingdom but within Europe as well. A Welsh Parliament will give us a chance to raise that voice and to propel Wales to a prosperous national and international future.

CHAPTER 20

A WELSH GOVERNMENT THAT EVOLVES
A Plaid Cymru View

Cynog Dafis MP

Plaid Cymru was founded as a result of the failure to achieve progress on a Parliament for Wales through the major British parties early in the twentieth century. The need was felt, in the wake of this failure, and inspired by the struggle for Irish self-government, for an independent political party dedicated specifically to the task of ensuring the establishment of a Welsh Parliament.

Plaid Cymru's habitual use of the term 'self-government' to describe its constitutional aims, in preference to 'independence' deserves mention. Merely a matter of semantics, it might be said, for Plaid Cymru's aim is pretty well indistinguishable from that of the Scottish National Party, which demands independence loud and clear. However, Plaid Cymru's preference for self-government tells us something, perhaps, of the party's emphasis on the reality of independence in the modern world. We have never found any conflict between our kind of nationalism and an avowedly internationalist outlook.

When we talk about Wales achieving full national status within the European Union, we are not talking about separatism. The concept of Britain has undoubted legitimacy. The peoples of Wales and Scotland share the same islands and there will always be a need for shared institutions and arrangements. The Nordic Union provides a comparable example. Norway's withdrawal from union with Sweden in 1905 did not prevent the evolution of close co-operation with the other Nordic countries.

In 1971 Plaid Cymru defined its constitutional aim as an establishment of a British confederation, so the notion of federalism, the subject of so much controversy in the current debate about Europe, has been prominent in the party's thinking all along. That confederation would have involved the establishment of parliaments for Wales, England and Scotland, with various mechanisms for ensuring close collaboration between them.

The party's willingness to consider and examine objectives short of its full constitutional aim is illustrated by the fact that we co-operated in — some people would say, led — the Parliament for Wales campaign in the 1950s, whose outcome was a significant advance. This was the establishment of the Welsh Office. Similarly, we co-operated in the campaign which ended in the 1979 referendum debacle.

Our willingness to compromise was illustrated when in 1987 we adopted as an interim objective the creation of a Welsh Senate — it was we in Plaid Cymru who gave the term currency at that time. We proposed a Senate that would take over the powers of the Welsh Office and be able to legislate through statutory instruments. It would also have the power to issue circulars to local authorities, initiate policy and participate in the legislative process alongside Westminster.

Since 1987 the development of the European Community, now the European Union, has come to dominate Plaid Cymru's perception of the situation. We see this as a process of immense historic importance, as the key context within which political advance for Wales can occur. It is a pioneering experiment in transnational integration based on the principle of subsidiarity.

This last we regard as an absolutely crucial political concept. It means, of course, not that regional seats of government should be allowed to carry out certain subsidiary functions, but that the centre —the European and member-state levels of government — should be subsidiary to the national / regional and local levels.

The process of the European Union's evolution entails a major erosion of the sovereignty and powers of the British Parliament. Concurrently the historic regions and small nations of Europe are gaining in significance, making direct contact with each other, and, by-passing member states governments, dealing directly with the European Union itself.

The Maastricht Treaty made only limited progress in the democratisation of Europe, leaving real power by and large with the Commission and the Council of Ministers. Even so the role of the Parliament has been strengthened and the Committee of the Regions established. Democratisation and Enlargement to include the Nordic countries and Austria are important priorities. We advocate a framework in which a bi-cameral parliament would initiate legislation, with the Committee of the Regions becoming the second chamber of the European Parliament, representing the regions and the non-state nations.

By the early 1990s Plaid Cymru was recognising the need to clarify the means whereby we envisage the establishment of a Welsh Parliament and the process of moving towards our ultimate constitutional aim, however defined. Increasingly in Plaid Cymru people are saying that we are not in the business of creating a new nation-state on the familiar, Nineteenth century, model. We have in mind a new pattern of government in which decisions are taken within the European Union at the most appropriate level.

The policy proposals set out at our 1993 Conference are broadly as follows. We see the Welsh state in the first stage of its development as having three components: the Crown, a House of Representatives and a Congress. The House of Representatives, elected by proportional representation, would correspond to the existing House of Commons while the second chamber, the Congress, would consist of representatives from local authorities. The pattern within Wales would therefore directly parallel that at the European Union level.

The Parliament of Wales would have the power to legislate in all areas of competence except those reserved for Westminster. The reserved matters would be: defence and international affairs, monetary policy including banking, control of the currency and exchange rates, and social security. However, the Welsh Parliament would have certain competencies in relation to Europe. It would be represented by its ministers in meetings of the Council of Ministers where matters of importance to Wales were being discussed. The 1980s saw a series of significant failures in relation to the representation of Welsh interests, specifically as regards agricultural and regional policy. The Welsh Parliament would also be able to establish its own working relations with other European Regions for political, cultural and economic purposes.

The Crown would be represented in Wales by a Representative Officer. In both the House of Representatives and the Congress there would be equal representation of men and women and the Welsh and English languages would have legal and effective equal status.

Representation from Wales in the House of Commons would remain unchanged. However, Welsh members in the House of Commons would only vote on the reserved powers listed above.

The Parliament of Wales would have the sole right to raise taxes and a contribution would then be made to the British government to finance the reserved matters. The amount of the contribution would be determined by a Joint Exchequer Board having two representatives each from Wales, England and Scotland. It would be chaired by a member of the European Monetary Institute.

Plaid Cymru envisages that after five years the Welsh Parliament would have the power to call down the reserved functions so that Wales would then become a fully-fledged self-governing state. The decision as to whether to proceed along that path would be a matter for the people of Wales to decide through the ballot box. I see no substance at all in the slippery slope theory whereby one is inexorably driven on to a further stage. In any case, we live in an evolving and difficult-to-predict European situation so that the relationship between our Welsh government and those of other levels within the European Union would undoubtedly require periodic review.

A STEP ON THE ROAD TO INDEPENDENCE
A Conservative View

Jonathan Evans MP

Some say that one reason for the resurgence in support for a Welsh Assembly or Parliament is because there have been four successive victories by the Conservative party in the United Kingdom. These elections have led to fifteen years of Conservative government in Wales. Yet, as we know, in Wales there is only minority support for the Conservative party, albeit support that is consistently around 25 to 30 per cent of the vote at general elections

Another explanation for the increase in support for a Welsh Parliament is said to be widespread concern over the existence of the Welsh public bodies, the Quangos. In some cases concern about the Quangos has been compounded by their performance. Negative headlines have led to a widespread perception that the Quangos are not democratically accountable.

In essence these are the reasons that supporters of a Parliament for Wales say their campaign is once again starting to catch the imagination within Wales. The thrust of these arguments is this: that a government which does not have the majority vote in Wales has no legitimate basis for legislating in Wales.

Yet what is the real aim of those who believe that these issues can be addressed by the creation of a Welsh Parliament ? An opinion poll undertaken by BBC Wales in March 1994 indicated 45 per cent support for the establishment of a Welsh Parliament (with 22 per cent Against and 33 per cent Don't Knows). What I find to be of real interest, however, is that 37 per cent of those participating in the poll favoured independence for Wales within the European Union. There were 36 per cent Against , and 27 per cent Don't Knows. I calculate from these responses that 82 per cent of those who favour the establishment of an elected Assembly or Parliament for Wales see it as a step on the road to an independent Wales.

That is welcome news, no doubt, for Plaid Cymru. If the poll was anywhere near accurate there must also have been a majority of

Labour party supporters who shared the view that there should be an independent Wales within the European Union. One wonders the extent to which the Labour leadership feel comfortable with that position.

Let me make my own position absolutely clear. I believe that Wales benefits from its status as an integral part of the United Kingdom. At the time that I joined the Conservative party it was known as the Conservative and Unionist party. I am a Unionist first and a Conservative second.

However, I welcome the renewal of the debate over a Parliament for Wales. There has been far too much complacency amongst Unionists in Wales since the referendum result of 1979. It was, after all, Nicholas Edwards, now Lord Crickhowell, who said immediately after the result of the referendum was declared, that he did not anticipate that it would be the last word on the subject of devolution.

The key issue for Unionists is the one that I have already outlined: we believe that the setting up of a separate Welsh Parliament would be an irrevocable step on the road to separatism. There are three main reasons. The first is because, as the opinion poll I have already quoted demonstrated, that is what the supporters of a Parliament for Wales actually want.

The second is what has become known as the West Lothian Question, named after the Scottish Labour MP, Tam Dalyell, who persistently raised it during the debates in the 1970s. This is the problem of English MPs being put at a disadvantage if Welsh and Scottish Parliaments were established. In that eventuality English MPs would be prevented from voting on devolved matters in Wales and Scotland, while Welsh and Scottish MPs would continue to vote on such matters for England at Westminster.

This would not be tolerated for long. The fact of the matter is that there has hardly ever been a time when there has been a majority of Labour MPs elected in England. I am certain that English MPs would wish to remove the right of Welsh members of parliament to participate in any of the devolved subject areas in the Westminster Parliament. Those who support a Welsh Parliament that ultimately does lead to separatism would treat this issue with equanimity and relaxation.

The third reason why a Parliament for Wales would be a step on the road to independence for Wales concerns finance. In the short term, at least, any devolved Parliament would be financially reliant for its expenditure on a block grant from the Treasury in Whitehall. That is bound to be a focus for discontent between a Welsh Parliament and the Westminster Parliament. We already see conflict between the Welsh Office and the local authorities, and recently a conflict between the Home Office and the South Wales Police Authority. These demonstrate issues of clouded accountability with disputes arising between central government and authorities within Wales over their respective accountability in these areas. A Welsh Parliament would be bound to increase and exacerbate such disputes leading to discontent and more pressure for an independent solution.

There are those who say that the proposal for a Parliament for Wales is quite normal seen in the context of the European Union, that countries like Germany, France and Spain all have decentralised, regional forms of government. Why, they ask, should Britain be any different? That might be a plausible view if there was any appetite for regional government in England. I know the Liberal Democrats have campaigned for many years for a federal system for the whole of Britain and now the Labour Party is advocating Assemblies for the English regions as well as Parliaments for Scotland and Wales. But even if such an all-round policy was sustainable, in practice the change would come first in Wales and Scotland and inevitably, as a result, lead to the kind of frictions I have described.

But if there is to be constitutional change then those advocating it should be prepared to put it to the test in a vote of the Welsh people in a referendum. The argument for this is especially strong because only a relatively short time ago, in the 1970s, the whole matter was debated extensively and substantially rejected in a referendum.

There are those who argue that the Single European Act and the subsequent Maastricht Treaty entailed significant constitutional changes and that these were not put to a referendum. However, the substantive issue, of Britain's membership of the European Community, now the European Union, was settled in a referendum, in 1975. The changes we negotiated at Maastricht did not fundamentally alter the direction of that decision. However, I believe the establishment of a Parliament for Wales which, as I have argued, would inevitably be a step on the road to independence, would be a fundamental constitutional change. For that reason it should be decided in a referendum.

CHAPTER 22

EMPOWERING THE PEOPLE
A Labour View

Peter Hain MP

During the 1990s and especially since the 1992 general election I have noticed a sea-change in favour of a Welsh Parliament within my constituency in Neath and, indeed, across Wales. There are three main reasons. The democratic case becomes ever stronger as the Tories ride roughshod over our democratic rights in Wales. There is the growing importance of the European dimension in our affairs. And there is a growing realisation that it is economically more successful to devolve power.

We are seeing fragmentation of government in Wales and across the rest of Britain that is very dangerous for democracy. It is not just a question of the Quangos, though they are bad enough. Alongside them is the new structure of 22 relatively powerless unitary local authorities. They won't have the powers or the resources to deal with strategic issues such as education, social services, let alone economic regeneration. The position is compounded by the Conservative obsessions of opting out, contracting out, privatisation, and market testing.

The only way of coherently tackling our fragmenting democracy in Wales is to make an uncompromising demand for an all-Wales level of government capable of dealing with strategic Wales-wide issues. Even the Conservatives have recognised the absence of a strategic dimension by creating a new Quango, the Economic Council. This is a forum mainly for the Chairs of the leading Quangos such as the Welsh Development Agency and the Education Funding Councils.

The promise of this latest Quango was made by the Conservatives at the 1992 election where they stated its purpose rather well. The aim, their Welsh Manifesto said, was to 'ensure greater cohesion and a more united effort on the part of the Principality's major employers' and employees' organisations.' While recognising the need for a strategic, all-Wales approach that was a recipe for corporatism not democracy. And that is what we have. Where are the people in all of this?

At the same time we are seeing a European evolution in which economic decisions are increasingly channelled through the Regions. For instance, the European Union's structural funds operate at a regional level. The system of government at the Brussels and Strasbourg level is increasingly focusing on the regions through the new Committee of the Regions. Admittedly this not much more than a talking shop at present. But it is evolving towards something more powerful. I would like to see, not only the European Parliament given much more power over the unelected bureaucrats in Brussels, but also a bicameral Parliament in which there is a second chamber in which the Regions and the nation-state Parliaments can have direct representation. That is another argument for a Welsh Parliament.

The third reason is that it's economically more successful to devolve power. In the European Union those countries which have more successful economies than ours have a more decentralised political system. This is the way modern capitalism is working. Economic management throughout Europe is focusing increasingly on the regional level. To be successful we have to the have political structures to work with the grain of this process.

Political structures have always evolved as economic systems have evolved, often lagging behind as is the case in Wales now. But if we don't catch up soon then we are going to lose out. Unless we have our own political voice capable of mobilising the political will to ensure economic regeneration, we will find Wales reduced to a peripheral region of Europe and to a sink economy.

My view of government and how it should be organised in Wales springs from a socialist analysis — a libertarian socialist analysis, not a statist one — in which power comes from the bottom upwards. We need structures of government which empower people rather than oppress, constrain and shackle them.

We need a Welsh Parliament as part of a far-reaching programme of radical reform. The House of Lords should be abolished and replaced with an elected second chamber. Local government should be empowered instead of being relegated to an administrative outpost of Whitehall. There should be a Freedom of Information Act, giving new powers and rights to workers and trade unionists, and to women. We need a new constitutional settlement which entrenches civil rights such as an equal age of consent.

It is important to place the demand for a Welsh Parliament within the wider context of democratic reform and constitutional change for Britain; otherwise it can easily become a surrogate for separatism. My own vision is to position the future government of Wales within both the United Kingdom and the European Union as part of a federal structure. I'm not afraid to describe myself in that sense as a 'federalist', because federalism means that structures of government should be designed to enable effective power to be operated as closely as possible to the people. As we see the European project going forward, it is very important to place the demand for a Welsh Parliament within that overall philosophy and context. It has nothing to do with separatism, but with federalism within the European Union.

The one mildly sectarian point I have to make is that the only way we are going to achieve a Welsh Parliament or Assembly is through a Labour government legislating for it at Westminster. Nobody else can form a government capable of delivering it. So what will Labour do? We have made it clear that we will bring in legislation to establish a Parliament or Assembly for Wales within the first year of a Labour government.

I'm not really interested in a referendum, but I am not afraid of one either. Through their votes at the election the people of Wales will overwhelmingly indicate that they want a Welsh Parliament. At the last election 70 per cent of the people of Wales voted for parties which were in favour of an elected Parliament or Assembly. I think the proportion will be higher next time. The idea of a referendum is being used by those opposed to a Welsh Parliament as a delaying device.

The Wales Labour Party has established a commission to look into the range of detailed questions concerned with the creation of a Parliament or Assembly. For instance, do we want the National Health Service to be brought under its control? I would certainly favour this because the kind of opted-out, privatised health service that is presently being constructed does not accord with the views of the large majority of our people.

An example of another, very different question, is whether proportional representation of some kind should be used in the elections to the Parliament. I personally favour the alternative vote system, whereby you vote 1, 2, 3 within two member seats. I think this is the only system which creates local accountability. It means that every person elected has to achieve at least 50 per cent of the vote at the same time as being clearly identified with a specific locality in a two-member constituency.

I also support, as does the Labour party generally, the question of equal representation for women, which means that there must be a minimum of one woman elected per two member seat. That is, a minimum not a maximum. It could be up to each party to stand two women candidates — and what's wrong with that? I hope the Labour Party will lead the way in that respect as well.

Another, difficult issue is the question of tax-raising powers for the Parliament. Here we have to bear in mind that Wales is one of the poorest parts of the United Kingdom, and it is important to retain the ability at a UK level to redistribute income and wealth. We have had profits over the decades, over the centuries, repatriated from Wales to England and the City of London and we do not want to lose the power to recover some of those resources back to Wales. We are not going to allow ourselves to be placed in a position where the Conservatives will be able criticise us for wanting to increase the level of taxation to the point, for instance, where they can claim there could be a double tax in Wales compared with other parts of Britain.

In my view, too, we have to keep the Secretary of State for Wales, at least until we have a fully federal structure in the United Kingdom. Of course, that remains our medium-term aim as a party. We want devolution throughout Britain: regional authorities for England as well as Parliaments for Wales and Scotland.

I hope that a Welsh Parliament will operate in a different fashion from the English-style of government that dominates British politics. It should be a participatory body, reflecting a participatory democracy. That means it should work with and alongside organisations such as women's groups, trade unions, the voluntary sector, and business as well as local authorities. That would be a refreshing change from the top-down version of government which all too often we see practised not just by the Welsh Office but by local authorities throughout Wales as well. We need an empowering participatory-style democracy at a Welsh Parliamentary level to make this happen.

History teaches us that the English Establishment always responds in a reactionary fashion to any demands for reform. That was true of the demand for the vote for working-class people. It was especially true of the demand for women to have the vote. It has been true of the demands for racial equality. Now we're seeing the familiar pattern played out before us with the demand for a Welsh Parliament. The first thing they do is rubbish the case. After that they resist it, sometimes uncompromisingly, as we're seeing at the moment.

Then we slide over into the third phase, which is when they start to co-opt the argument. That is why we're having to go through this nonsense of an Economic Council and the other nonsense of an all-Wales forum, a so-called reporting back mechanism for the appointed Welsh representatives on the European Committee of the Regions.

The final stage of this familiar pattern is that they cave in. When that happens I can guarantee that nobody will be found to admit that they ever opposed a Welsh Parliament in the first place.

LLANDRINDOD DEMOCRACY DECLARATION

The following Declaration was Agreed by the Llandrindod Democracy Conference, March 1994; approved by the Annual General Meeting of the Parliament for Wales campaign, Llanbadarn Fawr, June 1994; and presented as a petition to the European Parliament.

1. A Welsh Parliament will ensure that policies favoured by a majority of the people of Wales are followed. It will build a better future for our people by placing emphasis on economic regeneration and the provision of work. It will give us the freedom and responsibility to renew our culture and express our unity, national identity, and cultural diversity.

2. A Welsh Parliament will ensure, from the start, that there is a gender balance in its elected representatives, and will ensure that its procedures will enable women, men and minority groups to participate to the fullest extent.

3. The Parliament will be directly elected by a system of proportional representation.

4. The written and verbal proceedings of the Parliament will be conducted through the two main languages of Wales, Welsh and English.

5. The Parliament will take over all the powers and functions currently exercised by the Welsh Office and its Quangos (appointed bodies) and bring them under democratic control.

6. The Parliament will be able to make laws and determine taxes.

7. Amongst its responsibilities the Parliament will directly control job creation and the Welsh economy, the health service, housing, education, the environment, roads and transport, agriculture, the arts and culture, and local government. As things are decisions on all these are made by the Welsh Office and the people the Secretary of State for Wales appoints to run the Quangos — the 80 unelected bodies like the Welsh Development Agency, Health Authorities, Education Funding Councils, Countryside Council, and Housing for Wales. This is a bureaucratic, undemocratic tier of Welsh government.

8. The Parliament will ensure that local authorities, and especially the Community Councils which are closest to the people, are strengthened. The powers and duties of each level of government will derive from the people and will be defined by the Welsh Parliament. These powers and duties will be in conformity with the general principle of subsidiarity.

9. Public and civil servants working for all tiers of government in Wales will belong to an integrated Welsh Public Service responsible to the Welsh Parliament.

10. The larger continental members of the European Union — including Germany, France, Spain, Italy and Belgium — all have elected Regional Governments. Their average size and population is 8,000 square miles and three million, very similar to the size and population of Wales. A Parliament will enable us to participate fully with the rest of the European Union and be properly represented on the Committee of the Regions set up by the Maastricht Treaty.

A NOTE ON CONTRIBUTORS

Gilly **ADAMS** Artistic director of the Made in Wales Stage Company since 1984. This produces original plays and encourages new writing. Drama Director of the Welsh Arts Council 1976- 1982. Chairperson of the Magdalena Project, the International Festival of Women in Contemporary Theatre, based at Chapter, Cardiff; and also Welfare State International, based at Ulverston, Cumbria, which organises celebratory arts events.

Neil **CALDWELL** Director of the Prince of Wales Committee, an organisation that promotes local, environmentally sustainable projects throughout Wales. Director of the Campaign for the Protection of Rural Wales, 1988-1994. Born and brought up in England he studied Earth Sciences at the University College of Wales, Aberystwyth, and the Polytechnic of Wales, Pontypridd. Member of the Welsh Language Board.

Alex **CARLILE** Liberal Democrat Member of Parliament for Montgomery. Former Liberal candidate in Flintshire East in the 1974 and 1979 general elections. He gained the Montgomery seat from the Conservatives in the 1983 general election, with a majority of 668. His majority in 1992 was 5,209. Former chairman of the Welsh Liberal Party, he is now the Leader of the Liberal Democrats in Wales. At Westminster he is the party's spokesman on Wales and on Employment, formerly spokesman for Trade and Industry, 1990-2, Home and Legal Affairs, 1984-88, and Foreign and European Affairs, 1988-89. He became a QC in 1984, and has been a Recorder of the Crown Court since 1985.

Martin **CATON** Political Assistant and Researcher for David Morris MEP. In 1988, he won the West Cross seat on Swansea City Council for Labour after more than 30 years Tory representation. He was re-elected to the City Council in 1992. Has lived in Wales for 22 years, first in Aberystwyth where he worked at the Welsh Plant Breeding Station and since 1984 in Swansea. Secretary of the South Wales-West European Constituency Labour Party and past Secretary of the West Glamorgan Region of the Parliament for Wales Campaign.

***Cynog* DAFIS** Plaid Cymru MP for Ceredigion and Pembroke North which he won at the 1992 general election, standing in an alliance with the Green Party. He previously contested the seat at the 1983 and 1987 elections. Patron of the Parliamentary Environment Group at Westminster and promoter of the Energy Conservation Bill, 1993. Formerly Research Officer with the Department of Adult Continuing Education at the University of Wales, Swansea, and Head of English at Dyffryn Teifi Comprehensive School. Campaigned for Welsh-medium education in Dyfed from the 1960s to the 1980s. Author of *Maniffesto Cymdeithas yr Iaith Gymraeg* (first published in 1972 and translated by Harri Webb in *Planet* 26/27, Winter issue, 1974-75). Past editor of *Y Ddraig Goch* and member over many years of Plaid Cymru's National Executive.

***Siân* EDWARDS** Freelance translater, researcher and scriptwriter. Member of Plaid Cymru's National Executive, 1987-1993. Plaid Cymru Chairperson, 1992-93. Contested Cardiff South and Penarth for Plaid Cymru at the 1983 and 1987 general elections. Member of the Editorial Board of *Radical Wales*, 1983-90

***Tom* ELLIS** Vice-President of the Welsh Liberal Democrats. Vice-President of the Electoral Reform Society. Editorial Board member of *Representation - the Journal of Electoral Record and Comment*. MP for Wrexham, 1970 - 1983, initially representing Labour, but from 1981 as a founder member of the Social Democratic Party. Founder member, Welsh Liberal Democrats, 1987. Member of the European Parliament, 1975 to 1979. Formerly chairman (1974-81) of the Labour Campaign for Electoral Reform. Chairman of Clwyd Committee of the Parliament for Wales Campaign and also a member of the Campaign's National Council. Among his many articles is 'From Labour to Social Democrat' in *The National Question Again: Welsh Political Identity in the 1980s* (Gomer, 1985).

***Jonathan* EVANS** Conservative MP for Brecon and Radnor since 1992. Born in Tredegar he is a solicitor and formerly a managing partner with Leo Abse and Cohen. Contested Ebbw Vale twice in 1974, Wolverhampton NE in 1979, and narrowly failed to win Brecon and Radnor in 1987. Formerly Deputy Chairman of Tai Cymru/Housing for Wales. Involved, as a defending solicitor, in the Cardiff Explosives 'Conspiracy' Trial, 1981-3. Member of the Select

Committee on Welsh Affairs. In 1994 resigned as PPS to the Minister of State for Northern Ireland over the Local Government (Wales) Act which entailed merging Brecon and Radnor with Montgomery to create a new Powys most-purpose authority.

Paul **FLYNN** Labour MP for Newport West since 1987. Opposition front-bench spokesman on Welsh Affairs. Contested Denbigh in 1974. Member of Newport Borough Council, 1972-83, and Gwent County Council, 1974-83. Formerly an industrial chemist at the Llanwern steelworks. Research officer for Llew Smith, MEP for South East Wales, 1984-87. A leader of the Wales for the Assembly Campaign in the 1979 referendum. Founder member of the Welsh Anti-Nuclear Alliance, 1980. Resigned as Chairman of the Broadcasting Council for Wales, 1981, in protest at the Government's decision at that time not to establish a Welsh language fourth channel.

Hywel **FRANCIS** Professor of Adult Continuing Education at the University of Wales, Swansea, since 1992. Adult education projects include the setting up of the South Wales Miners' Library, the Valleys Initiative for Adult Education, and latterly the Community University of the Valleys. In 1979 he was active in the Wales for the Assembly Campaign in West Glamorgan. In 1984-5 he chaired the Wales Congress in Support of Mining Communities. He is the co-author with David Smith of *The Fed: A History of the South Wales Miners in the Twentieth Century* (1980), *Miners Against Fascism* (1984), and *Adult Education in Changing Industrial Regions*, co-edited with Peter Alheit.

Peter **HAIN** Labour MP for Neath which he won at a by-election in 1991. Previously candidate in Putney, 1983 and 1987. He is chair of the Tribune newspaper and was elected Campaign Officer for the Welsh Labour MPs in 1993. Formerly head of research with the Union of Communication Workers. Chairman of the Young Liberals between 1971-73. Joined the Labour Party in 1977. Brought up in South Africa he was forced to leave for London with his family in 1966 following his parents' active opposition to apartheid. He became prominent in 1969-70 as Chairman of the Stop the Seventy Tour Committee which organised demonstrations against South African sports tours to Britain. He is the author of a number of books on socialism, civil rights and democracy including *Community Politics* (1976), *The Crisis and Future of the Left* (1980) and *Political Trials in Britain* (1984).

Stephen HILL Director of the Welsh Economy Research Unit at the Cardiff Business School. Editor of the *Welsh Economic Review*. He has researched widely on the Welsh Economy and its changing structure especially regarding inward investment. Recent books include *Wales in the 1990s*, with Jon Morris (Economist Intelligence Unit, 1991) and *The Regional Distribution of Inward Investment in the UK*, with Max Munday (Macmillan, 1994) .

Gareth HUGHES Director, Welsh Federation of Housing Associations, since it was formed in 1989. Began his working life as a printer. Later read Psychology at the London School of Economics and then lectured at Nottingham University for two years. Joined the National Council of Social Service as Head of Research, for five years. Subsequently became Deputy Director of the National Federation of Housing Associations before returning to Wales to become Director of the Welsh Housing Associations Council, precursor to the independent Welsh Federation of Housing Associations. A member of the Executive of the Welsh Labour Party 1987-1993, and since 1992 a member of the party's Policy Commission on the Constitution.

Mari JAMES Public Affairs Consultant working with the Centre for Advanced Social Studies (CASS) in the University of Wales, Cardiff and with Francis Balsom Associates, Aberystwyth. Returned to Wales in 1993 after working in senior management roles in urban regeneration in London's docklands and in government lobbying. Researched Welsh politics at the University College of Wales, Aberystwyth, in the early 1970s. During 1977-79 worked for the Liberal Party in the House of Commons as part of the party's devolution team during the Lib-Lab Pact and the passage of the Wales Act 1978. During the early 1980s was a member of the joint Liberal/SDP Commission on Constitutional Reform. Published widely on Welsh politics and local government. Co-ordinator of the Parliament for Wales Campaign.

***J. Barry* JONES** Director of Political Studies, University of Wales College of Cardiff. Publications include (with Michael Keating) *Labour and the British State* (1985); *Parliament and Territoriality: The Committee on Welsh Affairs, 1978-1983*; Editor (with David Foulkes and R.A. Wilford) *The Welsh Veto: The Wales Act 1978 and the Referendum* (1983); Editor (with Michael Keating) *Regions in the European Community* (1985) and *Regions in the European Union* (1994). Secretary of the Wales For the Assembly Campaign during the 1979 Referendum.

***Jon Owen* JONES** Labour MP for Cardiff Central since 1992. Previously contested the constituency in 1987. A former teacher at Caerphilly Comprehensive School and Mid Glamorgan NUT President in 1984. Member of Cardiff City Council and chair of its Economic Development Committee, 1987-91. Chair of Campaign for a Welsh Assembly 1987-91, and now a member of the National Council of the Parliament for Wales Campaign. Welsh whip in the House of Commons.

***Margaret* MINHINNICK** Director of Sustainable Wales which — working with schools, community groups, industry and local authorities — seeks to integrate environmental with social and cultural concerns and promote sustainable development. Founder and Co-ordinator of Friends of the Earth Cymru, 1984 - 1994. Founder of Wales Against Opencast, a network of community groups united in their opposition to the expansion of opencast coal mining. Member of the National Council of the Parliament for Wales Campaign.

***Kevin* MORGAN** Professor of European Regional Development in the Department of City and Regional Planning, University of Wales, Cardiff. Brought up in Rhigos in the Cynon Valley he studied at Universities in Leicester, McMaster and Sussex. Author, with Ellis Roberts, of *The Democratic Deficit: A Guide to Quangoland,* 1993; and, with Adam Price, *Re-Building Our Communities: A New Agenda for the Valleys*, 1992. Special adviser to the Valleys Forum and a consultant to a range of organisations including the Welsh Development Agency, European Commission, and the Department of Trade and Industry.

David **MORRIS** Since June 1994 he has been Labour Member of the European Parliament representing the new South Wales West Constituency. MEP for Mid and West Wales, 1984-1994. Member of the European Parliament's Social Affairs Committee. Previously Labour candidate for Brecon and Radnor at the 1983 general election and a former Newport Borough councillor. Born in Llanelli, he worked as a labourer in Waddles Foundry before winning a Scholarship to Ruskin College, Oxford and then attended Swansea and Aberystwyth Universities. A Presbyterian Minister and a County Education Advisor before becoming a full time politician. He is a Vice-Chair of the Parliament for Wales Campaign.

John **OSMOND** Freelance journalist and television producer since 1990. Welsh Affairs Correspondent, *Western Mail*, 1972-1980. Editor *Arcade - Wales Fortnightly*, 1980-1982. Producer with HTV Wales, 1982- 1988. Assistant Editor, *Wales on Sunday*, 1988-1990. Publications include *The Centralist Enemy* (1974); *Creative Conflict: The Politics of Welsh devolution* (1978); *The National Question Again: Welsh political identity in the 1980s* (Ed. 1985); *The Divided Kingdom* (1988); and *The Democratic Challenge* (1992). Member of the organising committee of the Wales For the Assembly Campaign in the 1979 referendum. Chair of the Parliament for Wales Campaign since 1991. Founder signatory and Council Member of Charter 88.

David **REYNOLDS** Professor of Education at the University of Newcastle upon Tyne. Formerly Senior Lecturer in Education at the University of Wales College of Cardiff. Has researched and written widely on educational problems related to to school effectiveness and the Welsh education system. In December 1981, with Stephen Murgatroyd he published 'Schooled For Failure' in the *Times Educational Supplement*, which released data on the relatively poor performance of Welsh schools compared with England, and which provoked a wide-ranging debate. Currently involved in looking at how certain countries generate high levels of learning (in the International School Effectiveness Project). His latest book is *Advances in School Effectiveness* (Pergamon Press, 1994).

Ioan Bowen **REES** Chief Executive of Gwynedd County Council for eleven years until his retirement in 1991. President of the Wales Association of Community and Town Councils. In 1968 the Royal

Institute of Public Administration awarded him the Haldane Medal for a study of Swiss local government. In 1979 he spent a further period of study in Switzerland, mainly in Kanton St. Gallen. In 1988, his visit to Zimbabwe pioneered a scheme for Chief Executive exchanges with the Third World. In April 1994 he was a European Union observer at the South African General Election. Member of the Parliament for Wales Campaign's National Council. His publications include *Government by Community* (1971), *Cymuned a Chenedl*, a collection of essays on autonomy (1993), and an edited anthology of verse and prose *The Mountains of Wales* (1992)

***Emrys* ROBERTS** District Health Manager in Torfaen with the Gwent Health Commission where he is helping lead an initiative in Neighbourhood Health Commissioning, described as 'the new NHS revolution'. Previously Public Relations Officer with the Welsh Hospital Board (disbanded in 1974) and later chief officer with the South Gwent Community Health Council and secretary of the Association of Welsh Community Health Councils. President of Cardiff University Union (1954-55) and subsequently General Secretary (1960 - 64) and Vice-President (1978 - 81) of Plaid Cymru. Fought the Merthyr Tudful by-election for Plaid Cymru in 1972 and in 1976 became leader of the town's Borough Council when Plaid Cymru won control in the district elections of that year.

***Kevin* WILLIAMS** Senior Lecturer in Cultural Studies at Sheffield Hallam University. Lecturer in Media Studies in the Centre for Journalism Studies at the University of Wales College of Cardiff, 1990-1994. Senior Research Fellow in the Mass Media Unit at Glasgow University during the 1980s. He has written widely on the media including a number of books and articles on war reporting, the latest of which appeared in A. Belsey and R. Chadwick (Eds.) *Ethical Issues in Journalism and the Media* (Routledge, 1992). Presently writing a book on the historical development of the mass media in the United Kingdom. He writes a regular column in *Planet - the Welsh Internationalist* on the media in Wales.

***Kenyon* WRIGHT** Priest of the Scottish Episcopal Church, a Canon Emeritus of Coventry Cathedral, and a Methodist Minister. Executive Chair of the Scottish Constitutional Convention since its inauguration in 1989. Director of KAIROS, the Centre for a

Sustainable Society. Vice-chair of the Scottish Environmental Forum. Formerly General Secretary of the Scottish Churches Council. Served in India for 15 years as Director of an Urban-Industrial Institute and the Calcutta Urban Service working in the slum areas of the city. Later was for 11 years Director of the International Ministry of Coventry Cathedral.